W9-CDI-819

SUPERCARS

JOHN LAMM, PATRICK PATERNIE, JOHN HEILIG, AND MATT STONE

BARNES & NOBLE
NEW YORK

This edition published by Barnes & Noble, Inc., by arrangement with MBI Publishing Company

2006 Barnes & Noble Books

M 10 9 8 7 6 5 4 3 2 1

ISBN-13: 978-0-7607-8172-2
ISBN-10: 0-7607-8172-9

The Supercars © John Lamm, 2002
Porsche 911 © Patrick Paternie, 2001
Jaguar © John Heilig, 1997
Viper © Matt Stone, 2004

The information in this book is true and complete to the best of our knowledge. All recommendations are made without any guarantee on the part of the author or Publisher, who also disclaim any liability incurred in connection with the use of this data or specific details.

We recognize that some words, model names and designations, for example, mentioned herein are the property of the trademark holder. We use them for identification purposes only. This is not an official publication.

Printed in China

On the cover: It would be hard to imagine a face any more menacing than this: Dodge's Viper GTS-R concept stole the show at Detroit in 2000 – and at the same time gave us a sneak peak at what the next Viper would look like. Daimler Chrysler.

On the frontispiece: The 1999 Carrera 4 brought all-wheel drive to the 996 model line-up, in coupe or cabriolet body styles. Externally, the only way to spot the 1999 Carrera 4 is by its unique 17-inch wheels and the titanium color of the name badges and brake calipers. Porsche AG.

On the title page: Jaguars are supposed to look sleek, and the XJ220 does just that. The acceleration from the 3.5-liter turbo V-6 gets the 3,234-pound supercar to 60 miles per hour in 3.8 seconds.

On the back cover: The 959 combined all-wheel drive, ride height adjustment, and turbocharging to become a super 911 that was built not so much for off-road superiority as an FIA Group B rally car, but for what Porsche had hoped would become a sports car road racing series based on Group B regulations.

Contents

The Supercars

Jaguar

Porsche 911

Viper

THE SUPERCARS

JOHN LAMM

ACKNOWLEDGMENTS

It would take almost another book to acknowledge all those who have helped—knowingly or otherwise—with this book, so I can only skim the cream off the top. Thanks to people such as Harry Calton at Aston Martin, Michael Schimpke at Porsche, and Ferrari's Antonio Ghini. Reeves Callaway, Steve Saleen, and Louis Ruf, who assisted with the cars that bear their name. Nissan's Miki Kurosu, Mercedes-Benz's Craig Morningstar, probably a half dozen staffers with the Dodge public relations crew, and an equal number at Lamborghini. Bill Donnelly, who was then with Jaguar. Horacio Pagani and Mike Perry at Pagani.

Thanks also to Tom Bryant, Editor-in-Chief of *Road & Track*, for sending me on the assignments that led to the photography and stories included here. To the magazine's art director, Richard Baron, who has always made my photography look better than it really is. And my old friend, Alan Rosenberg, who did the photos of the Ruf CTR-2 and takes perhaps the most delicious food photos in the world.

I cannot forget the patience of MBI Publishing Company editors Zack Miller, Sara Perfetti, and, above all, Paul Johnson, as well as the understanding of my dear wife, Scheri, and our sweet daughter, Holly, for those hours when I disappeared to work on this book.

And to all the exotic car fans whose enthusiasm for these great automobiles never slackens.

—*John Lamm*

INTRODUCTION

He did not have to ask twice.

When Giuseppe Grecco, managing director of Lamborghini, asked, "Are you going to drive now?" I laid down my camera and slipped into the seat of the 6.0-liter Diablo VT. We were at a small track just south of Milan, Italy, with a Ferrari Formula 1 car screaming through a test in the background. Down with the Diablo's door, into first gear, and off we go with all the speed and discretion one can muster in someone else's quarter-million-dollar automobile.

A tough business, but someone has to do it.

When heading out in a new exotic car, I often recall the first one I had the chance to drive. It was a red Ferrari Daytona and we were on one of the well-known canyon roads north of Los Angeles. In the 30 years since then, recessions, fuel shortages, and ever-tightening emissions and safety regulations all threatened to do away with supercars, but never succeeded . . . and for the best of reasons.

Whether called exotic cars, supercars, or wondercars, they all have that same effect. Owners and drivers treat them like honored guests, and car fans go weak in the knees when a Lamborghini Diablo, a Callaway Corvette, a Ruf Porsche, or just about any Ferrari cruises by—it's a natural reaction from anyone who loves automobiles because these are the most exciting, blood-stirring machines in the world.

What makes an exotic car? There are no hard-and-fast rules, but they must be fast: quick to 60 miles per hour, a top speed of 150 miles per hour or more, and able to make tracks along a twisty road at an impressive rate. As a result of all that speed, excellent brakes are also required.

Exotic automobiles must look as fast as they go. To some eyes that beauty means the body must be clean and aero sleek. Others prefer their supercars festooned with wings and spoilers. Either can be correct as long as the car tickles your heartstrings.

It doesn't hurt if a supercar is made in an exotic-sounding place such as Maranello, Italy; Zuffenhausen, Germany; or Newport Pagnell, England; though Bowling Green, Kentucky, and Irvine, California, also qualify if the car is good enough.

Whether Italian, German, British, Japanese, or American, these wondercars tend to be low, so you must step over and down to get in. The seats are usually firm and supportive, so you easily settle in, hook up the seat belts, and adjust the cockpit to your size. The instruments are legible and not far off your down-the-road sight lines. Controls like the steering wheel, shifter, and pedals are logically laid out and have a firm, positive feel to them.

Whether you start the car with the key or a button, it is instantly obvious there's big stuff powering the car, be it the throaty, almost-threatening rumble of a V-8 or the smooth strength of a V-12. Into the first of its many gears, bury the throttle, and the ride begins . . . and it's like no other on earth, whether you are rocketing down a strip of empty German autobahn, knocking down hot laps on an Italian test track, or snaking along a California mountainside highway.

We dare you to not smile.

Exotic cars are not perfect automobiles. Many have only limited visibility to the rear. Some are difficult to clamber into and even tougher to exit. Parallel parking can be a chore. There was a time when they were mechanically fussy, earning exotic machines the label "weekend cars" because they were not dependable, but modern electronics have done away with that down side.

Besides, the exterior styling will steal your practical heart, whether you are an owner, someone by the side of the road, or a photographer caressing the car's shapes and details with a camera as the sun melts into that sweet sunset light.

I can also attest to the fact exotic cars make a wonderful ride: topping 212 miles per hour in a Ruf while riding with 1961 World Drivers' Champion Phil Hill as he deftly catches a sidewind-induced slip; wondering if the legendary Maserati test driver Guerino Bertocchi has noticed how quickly we are closing in on the car ahead during a high-speed early morning Autostrada test run; admiring the steering wheel movements and footwork of rally champion Sandro Munari as he kicks a Lamborghini Countach sideways on a tight Italian mountain road.

The ride of your life in the most exciting cars of our lifetime.

chapter 1

GERMANY

Mention the words "exotic cars" and "Germany" and the words that tend to follow are "Porsche" and "turbo." Few automobiles have captured the imagination of performance-car lovers around the world like the many forms of turbocharged Porsches. Just saying "959" is enough.

Recently, other German automakers have ventured into the supercar business. Mercedes is prepping the SLR. BMW has opened the door with its Z8 sports car. Volkswagen is even getting into the exotic car biz via ownership of Lamborghini and Bugatti.

For years, however, there has been an exotic automotive subculture in Germany built around tuners. Take a walk through the annual Geneva Auto Show and you'll see them; companies with such names as Brabus, Renntech, Gemballa, and Alpina will create any outrageous one-off German hot rod you could dream up. Want a Mercedes V-12 stuffed into your E-Class? A BMW V-12 in that 3-Series? They'll do it . . . for a healthy price.

Germany has created a few purpose-built supercars, such as the Isdera Imperator and the Dauer 962, but the long-term

success of German high-performance cars has been with the tuners who start with stock Mercedes, BMW, Porsche, Opel, or Audi parts and, well, hot rod them.

That's how AMG—provider of Mercedes' high-performance engines—got started, working a backdoor relationship with the automaker for years before it bought the nearby speed shop. BMW had a similar relationship with Alpina, though the two have never grown as close as Mercedes and AMG. Louis Ruf's tuning of Porsches is so extreme his cars are no longer Porsches, but registered as Rufs. And now Porsche has expanded its custom program, willing to build special versions of its cars for customers.

If there is one thing that stands out among the top-line German tuners—as with the country's automakers—it is the superb quality of their work. Between German pride in workmanship, certain laws, and the fact that the cars can be exercised at high, unforgiving speeds on the autobahn, German supercars tend to be among the best made in the world.

RUF CTR-2

Bury the throttle of a silver Ruf CTR-2 and the car leaps forward. Turbochargers instantly spool up, and you can almost feel the horsepower and torque curves go to near vertical. Snatch second gear. Wham, you're on a run that's going to get you to 100 miles per hour in just 7.9 seconds, and on this highly crowned back road in rural Germany you find yourself adding small steering corrections to keep the car pointed straight ahead. And yet for all this speed and fury, the CTR-2 is as well behaved as it is quick.

That's Louis Ruf's way.

In the small village of Pfaffenhausen, Germany, about an hour's drive west of Munich, Louis Ruf creates his own, special breed of automobiles. At first look, you would be justified

in thinking he makes highly tuned Porsches. His cars certainly appear to be just that, but if you search the car you won't find any Porsche nameplates or chassis tags. Ruf and his highly trained crew so completely rework the cars that they replace the Porsche chassis numbers with their own, because officially Ruf is a German automaker . . . the country's smallest, perhaps, but an automaker nonetheless.

Road & Track discovered Ruf's potential many years ago, and invited him to bring a car to its first World's Fastest Cars roundup. It was 1987 and Louis Ruf showed up at Volkswagen's impressive Erha-Lessien test track near Wolfsburg, Germany, with a car nicknamed Yellow Bird. The "sleeper" appeared deceptively simple compared to the other super

They may look like Porsches, but according to the German government, the cars built by Louis Ruf are called "Ruf" right on their serial number plates. Although they may begin as 911s, by the time Ruf has finished, the cars—such as this CTR-2—are so highly modified that they are reclassified. *Allan Rosenberg*

Opposite: Yes, those are the basic design lines of the 911, but the front and rear bumpers and the engine cover are all new, made to Ruf's exacting standards. Louis Ruf also adds 19-inch forged magnesium road wheels of his own design. *Allan Rosenberg*

A chunk of the development time goes into the chassis, with the springs, shock absorbers, and anti-roll bars all being firmed up to match the higher performance of the car. Inside those huge alloy wheels are brakes commensurate with the CTR-2's high performance. *Allan Rosenberg*

Porsches. For one thing, Ruf prefers to start his rebuild process with non-Turbo-fender-flare Porsches because they are narrower, with less frontal area. Since top speed was the issue, the car was wingless. And it was very fast, winning the competition at 211 miles per hour.

From the beginning, Ruf's specialty has been engines. He starts by disassembling the latest Porsche flat-six and meticulously rebuilding it like a race-prepped engine. In the case of the CTR-2 (based on the last-generation 911) he adds larger KKK turbochargers and ups the boost from 13.1 to 16.0 psi. Engine-control electronics are remapped for performance, though the engine will pass all necessary national antipollution laws. Helping on the low-emission front are twin steel catalytic converters plumbed into a Ruf-developed exhaust system. The result? Some 520 horsepower and 505 lb-ft of torque.

Ruf has been known to design gearboxes for his own cars, usually adding a gear, although these days he stays with the Porsche six-speed manual. He also offers the option of either rear- or four-wheel drive, the latter a good idea when you're pasting 520 horsepower to the pavement.

While the need for ultimate velocity has kept many Ruf bodies quite simple for top speed, he will also go after downforce with specially created, beautifully finished bodywork for models like the CTR-2. Front and rear spoilers are calculated to increase downforce, while internal ducting vents intercooler heat away from the car.

To match the car's higher performance, a Ruf chassis receives the same detail attention as the engine and body. Shock absorbers, springs, struts, and anti–roll bars are all firmed and reworked to balance the chassis with the mega-horsepower. Add

The real genius in Louis Ruf's cars is in the engine. Ruf's engine builders start with the Porsche flat-six and, among other things, bump up the turbo pressure to 16.0 psi, remap the electronics, add high-speed catalytic converters, and come away with 520 horsepower and 505 lb-ft of torque. *Allan Rosenberg*

a set of Ruf's unique forged magnesium 19-inch wheels fitted with very low, wide Z-rated tires and you have a platform firm enough to handle the power without being overly rough or rumbly in ride.

The keep-it-simple approach continues inside the car. You will never mistake a Ruf interior for a monk's cell, but it will not be overdone or gaudy. You'll find the air conditioning and sound system needed to cope with warm days and long distances, but you might also find special lightweight door panels with pull-strap door openers in place of the heavy handle mechanism. Ruf-designed seats have less weight than Porsche's and added lateral support. As custom-made cars, Rufs can be ordered with just about any option from a sunroof to, heck, a beverage cooler, though that would be missing the point of the Pfaffenhausen cars.

The point is speed—both terminal velocity and getting there as quickly and as safely as possible.

That's Louis Ruf's way.

RUF CTR-2

Base price:	$280,000

Specifications

General

Layout	rear engine, rear drive
Wheelbase (in.)	89.4
Overall length (in.)	168.9
Overall width (in.)	68.3
Overall height (in.)	51.2
Curb weight (lbs.)	3,045

Drivetrain

Engine	twin-turbocharged sohc 12-valve flat-six
Bore x stroke (mm)	100.0x76.4
Displacement (cc)	3,600
Horsepower	520 bhp @ 5,800 rpm
Torque	505 lb-ft @ 4,800 rpm
Transmission	six-speed manual

Body & Chassis

Front suspension	MacPherson struts, lower A-arms, coil springs, tube shocks, anti-roll bar
Rear suspension	twin lateral links, lower A-arms, toe links, coil springs, tube shocks, anti-roll bar
Steering	rack and pinion, variable power assist
Brakes	14.0-inch carbon-fiber discs
Wheels	19x8-1/2 front, 19x10 rear
Tires	245/35ZR-19 front, 285/30ZR-19 rear

Performance

0 to 60 mph	3.6 seconds
Top speed	217 mph (estimated)

PORSCHE 959

It seemed to take forever for the traffic to clear. We were headed north from Porsche's factory in Zuffenhausen, Germany—a suburb of Stuttgart—on the autobahn in a Porsche 959, and for the first time I had the controls. But when would the line of cars thin and fade to the right so I could safely open up Porsche's supercar?

At this point all we were opening up were eyeballs that stared at the 959. The super Porsche stood out in autobahn traffic like a super hero among everyday wimps: ultra aggressive with its swoopy tail spoiler, a broad stance resting on squat tires, wide cooling slots traced across its nose, and, in our case, bright red paint.

The immediate impression you get when sitting in the driver's seat of a 959 is that you aren't driving a car so much as piloting a system. Perhaps the impression stems from the way the cockpit's tall center tunnel makes you feel compartmentalized behind the wheel, or maybe it's from the added levers and controls of the four-wheel-drive system, or maybe it's because you know you have control over so many variables . . . a great sense of command.

Based on a show car called the Gruppe B, the 959 caused a sensation when it was unveiled in 1987. Many of the car's styling cues, such as the front air inlets, were used on production Porsches for several generations after the 959.

There is something slightly space age about the 959 cockpit, such as the many controls that allow you to command systems including the four-wheel drive. The basics of the design, however, come from the stock 911 and can be seen in the dashboard layout and the seats.

It all began when the 911 Turbo was reworked to adhere to international Group B racing rules. Porsche unveiled a show-car version at the 1983 Frankfurt Auto Show with the name Gruppe B.

Group B racing rules dictated engine displacement-to-car weight scales that restricted the 959's flat-six powerplant to 2.9 liters. The engine was fitted with water-cooled, four-valve-per-cylinder heads and a pair of KKK turbochargers. To aid low-speed torque and response, the exhaust is first routed to one turbo, then to the second as rpm increases. This means a secondary, rushing kick-in-the-back around 4,200 rpm in each of the six gears as the engine winds to 450 horsepower at 6,500 rpm.

Great as the 959's engine might be, however, its main attraction is how that power gets to the ground: all-wheel drive. A steering column stalk allows the driver to choose one of four settings:

Dry, Wet, Snow, or Traction. Normally you'd use the first two, which vary the amount of power going to the front and rear wheels from the normal 40 front/60 rear to 20/80 under hard acceleration. The Snow setting holds the split at 40/60, while Traction then locks the rear and center differentials for maximum grip.

But there's more.

A normal-production 959 has amenities such as air conditioning and electric window lifts, plus an adjustable suspension. Normal ride height is 4.7 inches, but there are also settings of 5.9 and 7.1 inches. While drivers can choose the level via a cockpit switch, should they drive away at the top height, the car will automatically settle down to 5.9 at 50 miles per hour and 4.7 at 100 miles per hour . . . and back up again as the car slows. The shock absorbers are also under driver control, either automatically adjusting according to speed or

Here's what causes the drooling: a 2.9-liter version of Porsche's famous flat-six with a pair of KKK sequential turbochargers and 450 horsepower. Climbing through the 959's six gears, you get a second, substantial turbo rush as the tach needle winds past 4,200 rpm.

being set on the soft setting. Features of the 959 also include specific upper and lower A-arm suspensions at both ends, ABS brakes, and a Bosch system that warns of a tire deflating.

While several of these features were common in 2000, they were quite new and impressive on the production 959 in 1986 . . . all part of an imposing system created by Porsche—and a very potent one.

With a 0-to-60 time of 3.9 seconds and a top speed just over 200 miles per hour, the 959 was a flat-out world beater in its day. It proved its worth in the off-road world of the Paris-Dakar rally, where it was a two-time winner, and on the track in the 24 Hours of Le Mans, winning its class and finishing seventh overall in 1986 (as a Porsche 961).

The granddaddy of the recent crops of four-wheel-drive Porsche Turbos, the 959 was a wondercar in its day, though on my drive day I was just wondering when traffic would clear. When it finally did, the gas pedal went to the floor. Whoosh, we whistled up through third gear, the second turbo kicking in dramatically to pick up the pace. Up a gear, hard on the gas, but, oh no, way up ahead cars are beginning to reappear in the fast lanes. The needle creeps up to 280 kilometers per hour . . . 290 . . . 300 . . . just a needle width over the 300—some 185 miles per hour—then back out of the gas.

Rats. But, you can't take a 959 home to Porsche in Zuffenhausen bent or bruised.

PORSCHE 959

Base price: $280,00

Specifications

General

Layout	rear engine, all-wheel drive
Wheelbase (in.)	89.5
Overall length (in.)	167.7
Overall width (in.)	72.4
Overall height (in.)	50.4
Curb weight (lbs.)	3,190

Drivetrain

Engine	twin-turbo dohc 24-valve flat-six
Bore x stroke (mm)	95.0x67.0
Displacement (cc)	2,849
Horsepower	450 bhp @ 6,500 rpm
Torque	370 lb-ft @ 5,500 rpm
Transmission	six-speed manual

Body & Chassis

Front suspension	upper and lower A-arms, coil springs, dual tube shocks, anti-roll bar
Rear suspension	upper and lower A-arms, coil springs, dual tube shocks, anti-roll bar
Steering	rack and pinion, power assist
Brakes	12.7-inch front, 11.9-inch rear, ABS
Wheels	8x17 front, 9x17 rear
Tires	235/45VR-17 front, 255/40VR-17 rear

Performance

0 to 60 mph	3.9 seconds
Top speed	205 mph

When automobile designers talk about a car's "shoulders," this is what they mean. Those substantial fender flares blend out from the original 911 body, as Porsche bases all its special editions—even many of its race cars—on the well-proven 911 body structure.

PORSCHE 911 GT1

For decades, Porsche has been messing around with its famous 911. While keeping the basic rear-engine body shape, it has blown out the fenders like balloons to cover ever-wider tires, fixed all manner of huge wings to the famous shape, altered the engine displacement up and down, and bolted on great turbochargers. It has looked a bit meaner and nastier each year.

From all this fiddling around we got the famous 935 Turbos, the 959, even a version called "Moby Dick." How much farther could Porsche go with the same basic car?

How about the GT1?

Here's what happened. In the mid-1990s, new endurance racing rules for Grand Touring cars set up an interesting proposition. To enter a car in the GT1 series, the automaker

To meet the GT1 racing rules of the mid-1990s, an automaker couldn't race in that category unless it built a road-going version of the car with which it wanted to compete. The company didn't have to build many of the cars, but it had to meet safety and emissions rules, which is why we have this photo of a Porsche GT1 on the road in Germany. *Ulli Upietz*

Okay, it looks a little busy, but this is the cockpit of the full-race Porsche GT1. The *Strasseversion* was more accommodating to driver and passenger, though you would never mistake it for an overstuffed luxury car.
Ulli Upietz

had to have a street version of that machine. They didn't have to build a lot of that model, but they did need to produce machines that met all the applicable laws—such as emissions regs—that make a car street legal.

The series started out to be a Porsche 911 playground. With its many years of experience and a huge bin of proven speed parts, the Stuttgart company could easily build street-legal versions of the 911 to suit about any racing and government rules in the world. It did, and 911s won that first year.

Then along came the McLaren F1. With its 6.1-liter BMW V-12 and the genius of Gordon Murray behind it, the British car became dominant, even winning the 24 Hours of

Le Mans . . . and sending Porsche engineers back to the drawing boards at the company's Weissach, Germany, engineering center.

What they created was the GT1. First seen in March 1996, the car was built as both a race car and road going *Strasseversion*. In fact, in a turnabout from the usual way things happen, the street GT1 was developed from the race car.

Both versions retained much of the standard 911 structure from the front back through the passenger compartment, albeit suitably beefed up and stiffened. To the back they bolted a tubular frame that had the classic flat-six engine, but turned around, making this the first mid-engine 911.

Typical of a Porsche factory effort, the GT1 did just what it was designed to do, win the 1998 24 Hours of Le Mans. Even tuned for the street the super Porsche covered the time from 0 to 60 miles per hour in just 3.4 seconds. *Ulli Upietz*

Down over this Porsche seemed to droop one of the most outrageous bodies ever designed for a road-going automobile. It was obviously a 911, but the fender flares of the carbon-fiber bodywork appeared to stretch into the next county. There was a roof-mounted scoop for air to the engine. The flat tail and its tall spoiler were pure race car.

Inside it was also obviously a 911, because the dashboard came straight off the production line. But the car's racing purpose was evident in the typical high-sided driving seats. Inner door panels that looked to be sculptures in carbon fiber added to the racer image.

Fixed behind this passenger compartment was the latest in the long line of variations on the flat-six engine. Racing regs kept the displacement at 3.2 liters, but Porsche was allowed turbos and took full advantage with a pair that work in unison (not sequentially like the 959) to stuff as much as 14.7 psi of charge into the water-cooled six.

For the street GT1, this combination takes the 3.2 to 544 horsepower at 7,000 rpm, with 442 lb-ft of torque at 4,250 rpm. Tuned for racing, the six really howls, with 600 horsepower at 7,200 rpm and 480 lb-ft of torque at 3,950 rpm. That last engine in its most successful racing form was matched to

The "civilian" version of the GT1 had 544 horsepower and 442 lb-ft of torque from the highly pressurized 3.2-liter turbo flat-six. Tuned for racing, the engine screamed up to 600 horsepower and 480 lb-ft of torque. *Ulli Upeitz*

a six-speed sequential gearbox, while the *strasse* machine had a standard Porsche six-speed.

There were other variations from street to race GT1s. While both versions had power assisted steering, the road machines had steel brake discs while the latter used carbon discs. The cars meant for the vagaries of common roads were given a bit more ride height and a *slightly* softer suspension, but Porsche did not dial the *Strasseversion* a long way back from those meant for such tracks as Le Mans.

With acceleration that could get it to 60 miles per hour in 3.4 seconds, skidpad numbers over 1.0, and the legendary Porsche reliability, the GT1 did precisely what it was designed to do. In 1996, GT1s finished 2 3 at Le Mans, winning their class. And then in 1998, a Porsche GT1 "Evo" not only won the 24 Hours of Le Mans, but was laps and laps ahead of the McLaren F1.

PORSCHE 911 GT1

Base price:	$1,000,000

Specifications

General

Layout	mid-engine, rear drive
Wheelbase (in.)	113.0
Overall length (in.)	185.4
Overall width (in.)	78.0
Overall height (in.)	46.2
Curb weight (lbs.)	2,480

Drivetrain

Engine	twin-turbo dohc 24-valve flat-six
Bore x stroke (mm)	95.0x74.4
Displacement (cc)	3,164
Horsepower	544 bhp @ 7,000 rpm
Torque	442 lb-ft @ 4,250 rpm
Transmission	six-speed manual

Body & Chassis

Front suspension	upper and lower A-arms, coil springs, tube shocks, anti-sway bar
Rear suspension	upper and lower A-arms, coil springs, tube shocks, anti-sway bar
Steering	rack and pinion, power assist
Brakes	15.0-inch vented discs front, 15.9-inch vented discs rear, ABS
Wheels	11x18 front, 13x18 rear
Tires	295/35ZR-18 front, 335/30ZR-18 rear

Performance

0 to 60 mph	3.4 seconds
Top speed	193 mph

MERCEDES-BENZ VISION SLR

For the past decade, Mercedes-Benz has been blending its heritage with modern times and producing some exciting performance cars. The 600SL is high speed with a luxury touch, the E55 sedan a four-door rocket. And now the Vision SLR show car—unveiled at the 1999 Detroit Auto Show—is evidence that the company is ready to soar into the supercar stratosphere. Scheduled to go into production in 2003, the car will cost around $300,000 and only 600 will be made each year.

The SLR's dramatic exterior design is heavily influenced by the 1998 Formula 1 constructors' championship-winning 1998 McLaren-Mercedes. This is particularly true in the nose, which is meant to resemble the front wings of the Grand Prix car.

McLaren's mid-engine F1 car did not influence the SLR's profile, which has the exaggerated long hood/compact cabin/short rear deck proportions seen in treasured prewar performance Mercedes. The SLR's is a very lithe, athletic shape

Mercedes-Benz takes a giant step into the supercar ranks with the Vision SLR, which is expected to cost around $300,000. Front-end styling hints at cues from the championship McLaren-Mercedes Formula 1 cars. For safety reasons, Mercedes opted for Lamborghini-like swing-up doors instead of the gullwing doors of its famous 300SL.

The interior detailing of the Vision SLR includes these oval metal pedals.

And wouldn't this be a wonderful place to spend the day. Mercedes designers continued the Formula 1 theme inside the Vision SLR and then finished the cockpit in aluminum and leather. The slim carbon-fiber seats ride on little shock absorbers to add to driver and passenger comfort.

Engine specialist AMG got the nod to do the SLR's engine. They begin with the 5.5-liter V-8 used in Mercedes' performance cars and top it with a mechanically-driven supercharger and intercooler. Dynamometers put horsepower at 557, with 530 lb-ft of torque for a 0-to-60 time of 4.0 seconds.

that ends in a rather high tail and has an airy greenhouse. The car's drag coefficient is 0.29, and the nose, combined with the high trunk lid, are said to lessen aerodynamic lift at speed.

Mercedes carried the F1 theme up the hood, into the interior and down a prominent center console. The feeling inside is simple, light, and open thanks to the greenhouse and the silver paint and beige suede finish. The seats are two-piece carbon-fiber shells that sit atop spring absorbers for added comfort. Behind each seat is a removable matching suede backpack.

Simplicity was also key to the instrument design, with all readouts fitting in a pair of round gauges ahead of the driver. The majority of functions such as climate control, lights, and the driving mode of the automatic transmission are on four large round switches on the center console. There is also a navigation/TV display and a CD player.

Drivers enter the cockpit via swing-up doors. For safety reasons, Mercedes has replaced the gullwings of the 1950s with doors that are attached to the A-pillar and swing up 75 degrees for entry.

Mercedes chose a combination of aluminum and carbon fiber for the body. There is aluminum in the front and rear sections where it will deform in the case of an accident. The carbon fiber is a major component in the central cabin, providing an extra strong safety capsule. Mercedes figures the use of aluminum and carbon fiber trims weight by 40 percent over a steel structure.

Aluminum is also a major component in the SLR's suspension, which is a four-link design at the front and uses five links at the rear. Naturally, the supercar's suspension will have all the latest gee-whiz technology such as Electronic Stability Program, though this time ESP is also tied into the braking system. In addition to the ABS signals, a computer takes in such data as steering angle and lateral acccleration so it can individually brake each wheel as needed. The electro-hydraulic brakes have fiber-reinforced ceramic discs that weigh 67 percent less and can handle twice the heat of cast-iron brakes.

The wheel-tire combination for the SLR has Bridgestones, 245/35ZR-19s front and 285/30ZR-20s rear, mounted on aluminum wheels.

The SLR's powerplant is based on Mercedes' 5.5-liter, 24-valve V-8 and is built by AMG, the small specialist firm that Mercedes bought to be its sports department. In hand-building the SLR's V-8s, AMG will add a compact mechanical blower and intercooler between the cylinder banks. AMG expects the V-8 to produce 557 horsepower at 6,500 rpm and 530 lb-ft of torque peaking at 4,000 rpm. The transmission is a five-speed automatic that can be manually shifted via a steering wheel–mounted lever.

Mercedes figures the SLR will get to 60 miles per hour in around 4 seconds and to 125 miles per hour in a tick over 11 seconds on its way up to 200 miles per hour.

While the SLR's design is from Mercedes, the production car will be a joint effort of the automaker and McLaren. Gordon Murray, who designed the McLaren F1, will be the SLR's technical director. The English firm—in which Mercedes has an equity interest—will produce the car in a purpose-built factory. Mercedes' side of the equation is to supply the engine, gearbox, brakes, safety systems, and the structure for front and rear crash protection.

Best of all, there will be variations on the SLR theme beginning with a convertible. Makes you wonder what else they might have up their corporate sleeve.

Previous pages: **Like the automaker's Formula 1 team, the SLR combines the talents of Mercedes-Benz and McLaren, the latter's famed engineering genius Gordon Murray acting as technical director. The long-hood, short-deck SLR will be built as both a coupe and convertible.**

MERCEDES-BENZ VISION SLR

Base price:	$300,000 (estimated)

Specifications

General

Layout	front engine, rear drive
Wheelbase (in.)	104.7
Overall length (in.)	179.7
Overall width (in.)	73.9
Overall height (in.)	49.1
Curb weight (lbs.)	3,086

Drivetrain

Engine	supercharged dohc 24-valve 5.5-liter V-8
Bore x stroke (mm)	97.0x92.0
Displacement (cc)	5,439
Horsepower	557 bhp @ 6,500 rpm
Torque	530 lb-ft @ 4,000 rpm
Transmission	five-speed automatic

Body & Chassis

Front suspension	na*
Rear suspension	na*
Steering	rack and pinion, power assist
Brakes	electro-hydraulic, fiber-reinforced ceramic discs
Wheels	8.5x19 front, 10x20 rear
Tires	245/35ZR-19 front, 285/30ZR-20 rear

Performance

0 to 60 mph	4.0 seconds (estimated)
Top speed	200 mph (estimated)

*na=not available

chapter 2

ITALY

If there is a true home of exotic cars, it is Italy. Is it the fine wines and pasta? No, but Italy does have a tradition of engineering excellence, thanks to such companies as Alfa Romeo, Lancia, and Fiat. Many Americans find this difficult to understand because the United States never got or appreciated in their day the fine products of these automakers. Names such as Lancia Lambda or Aurelia; Alfa Romeo P2, P3, or Alfetta; Fiat 805 or Topolino mean little in North America.

Also unappreciated are the engineers behind those great cars. Although Americans know the names of such great automotive leaders as Enzo Ferrari and Ferruccio Lamborghini, few have heard of renowned engineers Vittorio Jano, Dante Giacosa, Carlo Chiti, Gioachino Colombo, Giotto Bizzarrini, Mauro Forghieri, or Aurelio Lampredi . . . to name just a few.

Italy is also home to the world's greatest automotive design houses. While exotic automotive design became much more international during the last decade of the twentieth cen-

tury, up to that point northern Italy—particularly Torino—was its spiritual center. Pininfarina, Bertone, and Italdesign are the modern giants, but the country's history also contains respected names such as Zagato, Vignale, Boano, and Michelotti. Add a wealth of craftsmen and artisans who can weld a chassis, form exquisite aluminum (and now carbon fiber) panels, and cast and machine almost any metal.

Never discount the passion of the Italian people for great automobiles. You can see it publicly in the enthusiasm of the crowds at the Monza or Imola Grand Prix races or along the route of the historic Mille Miglia rally. Those of us who have had the pleasure of driving a Ferrari, Maserati, or Lamborghini on public roads, into huge cities, or through small villages can attest to the depth of this fundamental feeling and excitement for great automobiles in Italy—all of which conspire to make Italy the birthplace of many of the world's most exotic cars.

FERRARI F50

Here's why you might want to consider becoming an automotive journalist: It's late in the day in Maranello, Italy, home to Ferrari. You've been at the automaker's famous Fiorano test track for most of the afternoon with a crew from *Road & Track* testing all the Ferrari models. That part is finished and the photography is wrapped up. And sitting there is the Ferrari F50. The track is still open and we can't have an F50 feeling neglected, can we?

Walk over and open the lightweight carbon-fiber driver's door. Step over the wide sill and drop into red-and-black upholstered seats. Carbon fiber is all around, dashboard, door panels, and center console. Ahead is a small instrument pod with a speedo that cranks up to 360 kilometers per hour—just shy of 225 miles per hour—how daunting . . . rather like the car's $480,000 price tag.

But you solider on, pushing the button that fires up the 513-horsepower 5.0-liter V 12 behind you. According to *R&T*'s computers, that engine will get this 2,710-pound car to 60 miles per hour in 3.6 seconds. Let's try it.

Grabbing the carbon-fiber shift knob, you're into first and with surprisingly light clutch pressure the F50 pulls away. No fuss, no embarrassing two or three tries to match revs and pedal.

With those sticky P335/30ZR-18 Goodyear Eagles, you get well into the throttle, rocketing away from the pits with no fear of wheelspin. The redline is 8,500, but we're shifting at

Despite its exotic nature, the F50 is not a beast to drive, with reasonably light efforts for steering, brakes, and clutch. The Ferrari can be a semi-race car in the right hands, like those of Grand Prix champion, Phil Hill, here giving famous journalist Peter Egan a high-speed ride.

Opposite: **Ferrari's F50 was debuted in 1996, the second supercar offering from Maranello, succeeding the famous F40. Compared to the earlier model, Pininfarina softened the exterior styling of the carbon-fiber bodywork for the F50, which was an open roadster with a detachable hardtop.**

Having a more civilized cockpit than the F40, the F50 nicely mixes race and road car images in the supercar, with beautifully finished carbon-fiber surfaces. The chassis is based on a central carbon-fiber structure that, like a Formula 1 car, has the suspension attached to it.

8,000, captivated by the howling Ferrari noises behind us. Then onto brakes so powerful it's immediately obvious you're well short of the ultimate braking area.

You quickly come to realize that while an expert like Michael Schumacher can get this thing around Fiorano at lightning speed, it is such a civilized, well-balanced, smoothed-out motorcar that even you can safely get up a good head of steam.

But then, trying to take a Ferrari F50 to the limit is not the point of this drive. It's that glorious sound, the acceleration that flattens you in your seat, the sound of the wind rushing into the cockpit . . . and the idea of driving quickly in a limited-production Ferrari on Fiorano. Wow.

The F50 was, of course, the second small-series supercar from Ferrari. The F40 arrived in the summer of 1987 at a dramatic unveiling in Maranello, which was the last time many of us saw Enzo Ferrari. Delicious pandemonium, the "old man" looking on as the wraps came off the F40, the press going nuts . . .

That one only cost $250,000, with its winged, sharp-edged Pininfarina styling and 478-horsepower turbocharged 3.0-liter V-8. Carbon fiber and Kevlar were used for both the bodywork and as reinforcement for the steel tube frame. The car was a wonderful mix of road and track, race-bred upper and lower A-arm suspensions, and fat tires giving it track manners, but with the option of any of three types of racing or road seats.

For the F50 engine, Ferrari opted for a non-supercharged V-12. With 513 horsepower and 347 lb-ft of torque, the delightfully noisy engine will fire the F50 like a speeding bullet to 60 miles per hour in 3.6 seconds, not pausing until the car is around 202 miles per hour.

Air conditioning was on the option list for the enclosed F40, but you could only get sliding plastic side windows.

Performance testing put the F40's 0-to-60 time at 3.8 seconds, with the top speed around 195 miles per hour. And very quickly the F40 became a worldwide automotive icon.

For 1996, Ferrari came back with the F50, trying to give its customers the feeling of driving a Formula 1 car on the street. Again Pininfarina did the exterior design, but this time the car was sexier, rounder, more liquid.

Like an F1 car, the central carbon-fiber structure had the steering and front suspension connected to it. As in a race car, the V-12, six-speed transaxle, and rear suspension were one unit, the upper and lower A-arm suspensions using pushrods and rockers for spring and shock actuation. The engine was an F1 development, taken out to 4,699 cc and 513 horsepower, yet tuned to meet emissions laws—and all lovingly developed into one of the most exciting road cars of the twentieth century.

The F50 is also a more civilized machine than the F40, not so hard-edged . . . and it even has roll-up windows.

While pushing the F50 to your personal limit around Fiorano, all that fades a bit. What matters are the Ferrari sounds behind you, the power under your right foot, and the joy of being right here, right now, doing just this.

FERRARI F50

Base price:	$480,000

Specifications

General

Layout	mid-engine, rear drive
Wheelbase (in.)	101.6
Overall length (in.)	176.4
Overall width (in.)	78.2
Overall height (in.)	44.1
Curb weight (lbs.)	2,710

Drivetrain

Engine	dohc 60-valve V-12
Bore x stroke (mm)	85.0x69.0
Displacement (cc)	4,699
Horsepower	513 bhp @ 8,500 rpm
Torque	347 lb-ft @ 6,500 rpm
Transmission	six-speed manual

Body & Chassis

Front suspension	upper and lower A-arms, pushrods, rockers, coil springs, tube shocks, anti-roll bar
Rear suspension	upper and lower A-arms, pushrods, rockers, coil springs, tube shocks, anti-roll bar
Steering	rack and pinion, power assist
Brakes	14.0-inch vented discs front, 13.2-inch vented discs rear
Wheels	18x8-1/2 front, 18x13 rear
Tires	P245/35ZR-18 front, P335/30ZR-18 rear

Performance

0 to 60 mph	3.6 seconds
Top speed	202 mph

FERRARI 360 MODENA

Tradition is at the heart and soul of every Ferrari. The famous Italian company has more than 50 years of building strikingly beautiful automobiles and winning race cars . . . and has its sainted founder, Enzo Ferrari. But if you think the renowned Italian automaker is rooted in the past, you are wrong. Executives and engineers in Maranello are well aware that if they let their minds get mired in yesterday and don't advance, Ferrari could quickly become nothing more than a memory.

Their 360 Modena is the evidence of this forward thinking.

For one thing, it doesn't look like the Ferraris of the past. Pininfarina has designed most street Ferraris since the mid-1950s, and you can see its fine, traditional hand in the rear 3/4 view of the car. However, the front of the car has changed. Gone is the classic central eggcrate grille, replaced by a pair of smaller grilles at the ends of the nose.

Why mess with traditional success? Modern aerodynamics. Ferrari engineers put in more than 5,000 wind tunnel hours fine-tuning the shape of the 360 Modena. By dividing

As with most Ferraris in the past 50 years, the 360 Modena was designed by Pininfarina. The tail carries a resemblance to the car's big brother, the 550 Maranello, while the V-8 engine can be viewed through the large rear window. Under the bodywork is an advanced aluminum frame structure.

When Ferrari developed the 3.6-liter V-8 for the 360 Modena, it upped the F355's horsepower by 20 to 395. While torque was increased by only 7 lb-ft, its curve was greatly broadened, offering the maximum 275 lb-ft from 4,750 rpm up to the 7,500 rpm redline.

the grille and coolant radiators into two parts, they created a center inlet channel for air going under the car. This channel, combined with a smooth, sealed underbody and carefully tweaked upper surfaces, not only produces a low drag coefficient of 0.355, but also endows the 360 with natural downforce that increases with speed. The advantage? A car with excellent high-speed stability, but without the need for external spoilers . . . just like the McLaren F1, but at a fraction of its price.

Ferrari turned away from tradition for another crucial part of the 360, the frame. Production cars from Modena have had steel tube frames, but the 360 marks the automaker's conversion to an aluminum inner structure. Developed with Alcoa, the

frame is a lightweight latticework of castings, extrusions, and carefully formed sheet metal covered by aluminum bodywork. Despite being slightly bigger than its predecessor, the F355, the 360 Modena chassis is 28 percent lighter than the 355's and significantly stiffer.

Ferrari kept and refined the F355's upper and lower A-arm suspensions. The brakes are 13-inch vented Brembos with a sophisticated Bosch anti-lock system that can be turned off for high-performance driving.

Ferrari began with the 355's 40-valve V-8, but increased the displacement to 3.6 liters and added refinements. Horsepower went up by a significant 20 to 395 at 8,500 rpm, but the

Pininfarina updated the traditional Ferrari interior for the 360 Modena, mixing leather and aluminum. This version has the steering column–mounted electronic gearshift paddles, the system having separate center console switches for reverse gear and for fully automatic in-town driving. Another switch controls the firmness of the shock absorbers.

truly important difference is torque. Though upped by only 7 lb-ft to 275, that torque is in a dramatically broadened curve. By 4,750 rpm, the V-8 is already at its torque peak and it stays right there up to 7,500 rpm.

Ferrari will match that V-8 with either of two six-speed gear-boxes: the traditional manual or the F1-style paddle shifter. The great majority of 360 buyers will opt for the paddle, and it's great fun. From a stop, you pull at the right paddle for first gear, push

down on the throttle and quickly accelerate away. To shift up, a quick paddle flip puts you up a gear. Do the same with the left-hand paddle and it's down one gear. Great fun, and in no time you can pretend to be Michael Schumacher in his Formula 1 car. Ferrari claims the F1 star is as quick around its Fiorano test track with the paddle-shifter 360 as with the manual gearbox.

There is, however, a good argument for the traditional. No one has done production car shift gates as crisp, good-looking,

FERRARI 360 MODENA

Base price: $145,000

Specifications

General

Layout	mid-engine, rear drive
Wheelbase (in.)	102.4
Overall length (in.)	176.3
Overall width (in.)	75.7
Overall height (in.)	47.8
Curb weight (lbs.)	3,065

Drivetrain

Engine	dohc 40-valve V-8
Bore x stroke (mm)	85.0x79.0
Displacement (cc)	3,584
Horsepower	395 bhp @ 8,500 rpm
Torque	275 lb-ft @ 4,750 rpm
Transmission	six-speed manual

Body & Chassis

Front suspension	upper and lower A-arms, coil springs, tube shocks, anti-roll bar
Rear suspension	upper and lower A-arms, coil springs, tube shocks, anti-roll bar
Steering	rack and pinion, variable power assist
Brakes	13.0-inch vented discs front and rear, ABS
Wheels	18x7-1/2 front, 18x9-1/2 rear
Tires	215/45ZR-18 front, 275/40ZR-18 rear

Performance

0 to 60 mph	4.3 seconds
Top speed	189 mph (estimated)

For the 360 Modena's front end, Pininfarina turned away from the traditional Ferrari single eggcrate front grille for a pair of smaller side grilles. The area between the grilles is the inlet area for the under-car aerodynamics, which produce excellent high-speed stability without external spoilers.

and easy to use as Ferrari's. Going up or down a gear, there's a wonderful metallic snap—a sound of confirmation—to each cog change.

Regardless of the gearbox, the 360 Modena is a car with two natures. The torquey V-8 is amazingly flexible, allowing effortless around-town driving even with the revs under 1,000 rpm. The car's nicely laid-out cabin is roomy and extremely comfortable, with a stirring sound system and an air conditioning system that will cool you on the most dreadfully hot summer days in Italy. Put the shock absorber ride control switch on soft and just trundle around town like any sport coupe.

Or head out of town, flip the shock switch back to firm, turn off the stereo, and hammer down the throttle. This is what a Ferrari is meant to do, turning in easily in tight turns, ready to be balanced on the throttle before blasting down the next straight, the brakes hauling you down safely corner after corner.

Creating a Ferrari that can drive down a twisting road about as fast as any car in the world is one bit of tradition the company won't change.

FERRARI 550 MARANELLO

Front-engine Ferrari Grand Touring cars have been an important part of the Italian automaker's history since its first days in the late 1940s. Four of Ferrari's victories in the rugged Mille Miglia open road race came in closed-coupe Ferraris powered by V-12s. Generations of great Ferrari GTs followed, adding such famous names as Tour de France, SWB, GTO, and GTB to the company's honor roll.

But then the lineage faded. In the early 1970s, the exotic-car world went mid-engine and Ferrari was with them. To counter Lamborghini's Countach, Maranello created the 1973 365 GTB/4 Berlinetta Boxer with its flat-12 behind the passenger cockpit. This was Maranello's top-line production GT, replaced in 1984 by the Testarossa, a mid-engine line that continued until 1997. Along the way, Ferrari developed its

There's almost a sly smile on the eggcrate grille of Ferrari's 550 Maranello. In addition to giving a classic Ferrari face to the two-seat Grand Touring car, the front end is part of an overall aerodynamics package on the car that includes a clean, flat bottom and short-spoiler tail.

What's inside a $250,000 Grand Touring car? Comfortable, supportive leather-upholstered seats. An instrument and controls layout that is a prototype for how it should be done. A shifter for the six-speed gearbox that is set in a beautifully hewn metal gate.

"smaller" mid-engine V-8 sports car, starting with the 308 in 1975 and continuing today with the 360 Modena. There were also ultra exotic Ferrari mid-engine supercars, the 1987 F40 and 1996 F50.

Impressive as the Testarossa looked and performed, it was a bit of a truck to drive in traffic. Like the Lamborghini Diablo, it was quite wide, more so in the back than the front, making it a bear to maneuver in anything but wide-open spaces. So when it came time to replace the aging "TR" in the mid-1990s, Ferrari went back to its Grand Touring roots and developed an all-new front-engine supercar, the 550 Maranello.

As expected, long-time Ferrari partner, Pininfarina, did the bodywork, which seems to integrate the classic Ferrari

grille in flaring nostrils . . . aggressive without being pushy. With the front-engine layout we again get the classic long hood/short deck proportions, And, by the way, a good aerodynamic package, thanks to the 550's flat bottom and blunt, spoilered tail.

Inside is generous seating for two in a leather-lined cockpit with the wonderful aroma of one of those famous Italian leather shops. The design is a classic: no-nonsense white-on-black gauges in a driver-oriented layout that puts everything from the tall shifter to air conditioning controls just a short reach away.

For the 550 Maranello, Ferrari returned to the traditional V-12, but with the most up-to-date electronics. The model's designation, 550, stands for the displacement of the engine,

Under the Pininfarina bodywork of the 550 Maranello is a chassis with upper and lower A-arms at the front and wide-based H-arms for the rear suspension. Other chassis features include electronically adjustable shock absorbers, huge disc brakes, and variable-assist rack-and-pinion steering.

which is 5,474 cc. With dual camshafts per head and four valves per cylinder, the all-aluminum V-12 puts out 485 horsepower at 7,000 rpm and 419 lb-ft of torque at 5,000 rpm.

Impressive as those numbers are, they don't tell the whole story. More than just powerful, with a 0-to-60 time of 4.7 seconds, the Maranello V-12 is amazingly flexible throughout the power ranges.

What are the tricks? How about advanced electronic engine management? Or computer-controlled variable-length runners in the intake manifold? Or an exhaust system that lessens backpressure as speed rises?

The chassis engineers were just as busy. They started with upper and lower A-arms for the front suspension, using wider-based H-arms at the back. Supplementing the coil springs and anti-sway bars are electronically adjustable shock absorbers. Matched with a 50/50 weight balance, monster disc brakes, and variable-assist rack-and-pinion steering, the Maranello becomes, well, a car for all scenes and seasons.

There was a time when a high-performance car of this sort would have been a single-nature weekend car. Rough riding. Fussy engine. Few creature comforts.

FERRARI 550 MARANELLO

Base price: $204,000

Specifications

General

Layout	front engine, rear drive
Wheelbase (in.)	98.4
Overall length (in.)	179.1
Overall width (in.)	76.2
Overall height (in.)	50.3
Curb weight (lbs.)	3,725

Drivetrain

Engine	dohc 48-valve V-12
Bore x stroke (mm)	88.0x75.0
Displacement (cc)	5,474
Horsepower	485 bhp @ 7,000 rpm
Torque	419 lb-ft @ 5,000 rpm
Transmission	six-speed manual

Body & Chassis

Front suspension	upper and lower A-arms, coil springs, tube shocks, anti-roll bar
Rear suspension	upper and lower H-arms, coil springs, tube shocks, anti-roll bar
Steering	rack and pinion, variable power assist
Brakes	13.0-inch vented discs front, 12.2-inch vented discs rear, ABS
Wheels	18x8-1/2 front, 18x10-1/2 rear
Tires	255/40ZR-18 front, 295/35ZR-18 rear

Performance

0 to 60 mph	4.7 seconds
Top speed	199 mph (estimated)

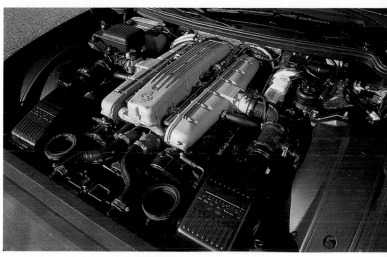

The 550 in the Ferrari's name refers to the engine's displacement, which is 5,474 cc. Power from the all-aluminum V-12 is 485 horsepower and 419 lb-ft of torque, enough to get the 3,725-pound supercar to 60 miles per hour in just 4.7 seconds, and to almost 200 miles per hour.

Not anymore. With the electronic shocks comes a dual-nature chassis, soft enough on its city setting to soak up ordinary road imperfections and divots. Set it on firm, however, and you have a near-race car that corners flat with a neutral attitude that can be tuned with the throttle.

Spin it to the 7,700-rpm redline in any gear, where it makes a wonderful loud and slightly rowdy Ferrari roar. Or slap it into fourth gear at under 1,000 rpm and feel it pull strongly away without protest. You can work the six-speed manual gearbox for every mile per hour or use second or third gear for most all your in-city driving.

And what amenities do you require? A concert-hall sound system? Heating and air conditioning that are as effective as any car's in the world? The 550 obliges.

Best yet, if you have any special requirements, from a favorite color to carbon-fiber seats to a sturdy roll bar, Ferrari will custom build your 550 Maranello.

BUGATTI EB110

To many historians, Ettore Bugatti is one of the half-dozen most venerated men in automotive history. The Italian-born, Alsace-based intuitive engineer is right up there with Henry Ford, Enzo Ferrari, Colin Chapman, Gottlieb Daimler, and Dr. Ferdinand Porsche. All were strong-willed men who created exactly the automobiles they felt the world should have—no compromises—and the results are honored in auto museums around the world.

Bugatti's Type 35 is considered a landmark race car. Some Type 57s are thought to have among the most seductive bodywork ever fixed to an automotive chassis. Bugatti Royales are among the largest, rarest, and most expensive automobiles ever made. And while Bugatti's creations varied from two-seater race cars to the massive Royales, the thing that distinguished them all was a marvelous balance of the science and the art of engineering.

The renowned Bugatti name was revived in the late 1980s with the development of this very exotic mid-engine supercar. Called the EB110, it was to carry on the great line of automobiles created by legendary engineer Ettore Bugatti. The EB110's design was by Marcello Gandini, who did the Lamborghini Countach and Diablo.

So, it was with a great deal of enthusiasm that we all greeted the news in the late 1980s that Bugatti would be revived in the form of an exotic car to match the likes of Ferrari and Lamborghini.

Italian industrialist Romano Artioli was the man behind the ambitious project, though the true source of money was a mystery, which added to the exotic nature of the endeavor. The unveiling of the EB110 in Paris in 1991 was a grand affair of royal proportions that just reeked of big money.

The EB110 seemed worthy of the fuss, a new star in its French blue finish. Marcello Gandini, who gets design credit for the Lamborghini Countach and Diablo, drew the shape of the EB110. The car has an undeniable presence, a miniature of the classic Bugatti horseshoe-shaped grille, and tricks such as a rear spoiler that rises when you get underway to add downforce and expose the engine's intercoolers.

The interior could be a tight fit for taller drivers, but what a nice place to be, all finely stitched leather and polished

In keeping with the spectacular approach to the Bugatti project, the car was unveiled at Le Defense in Paris, followed by a black-tie ball at the Palais de Versailles. Bugattis were assembled in a beautiful purpose-built factory near Modena, Italy, the city that is also home to Ferrari, Lamborghini, and Maserati.

Get in an EB110, and you are surrounded by top-quality leather with polished wood trim. The chassis of the Bugatti is made of carbon fiber, the suspensions have upper and lower A-arms, and the fronts use race car–like pushrod actuation.

wood. You nestle into the seats, the tall center console on your right, with gauges ahead of you and switches to your left, your right, and even on the ceiling.

An advanced carbon-fiber chassis provides excellent stiffness for the suspension and drivetrain. Upper and lower A-arm suspensions are used fore and aft, the fronts with race car–like pullrod actuation of the shocks and coil springs.

As in all Bugattis, the true gem is the engine. The 3.5-liter V-12 has five valves per cylinder (three intake, two exhaust) opened by two camshafts in each cylinder head. Fed by fuel injection and pumped up with a pair of IHI turbochargers to 15.2 psi of boost, the Bugatti achieves 611 horsepower at 8,250 rpm.

With torque measuring 480 lb-ft at 4,200 rpm, Bugatti engineers rightfully specified four-wheel drive and hefty Michelins measuring 245/40ZR-18 front and 325/30ZR-18 rear to get all that power to the pavement.

Launching a car with four-wheel drive isn't easy—even an exotic machine with 611 horsepower—but *Road & Track* got an EB110 from 0 to 60 miles per hour in 4.4 seconds. Drive to all wheels really pays in handling tests, as the Bugatti got through the slalom run at 64.3 miles per hour (a McLaren F1 did 64.5 miles per hour) and set the magazine's then-current record on the skidpad, generating 0.99g of lateral acceleration.

In subjective terms, the Bugatti turned out to be a very civilized-handing car with no evil habits and a surprisingly smooth ride.

The EB110 proved to have what everyone expected in an exotic car, from stunning performance to proud beauty to a price tag (had the car ever been sold in the United States) of $350,000. There was even an impressive new factory for the car in Campogalliano, Italy, just outside the country's exotic car capital, Modena.

BUGATTI EB110

Base price: $350,000

Specifications
General
Layout   mid-engine, four-wheel
                            drive
Wheelbase (in.)   100.4
Overall length (in.)   173.2
Overall width (in.)   76.4
Overall height (in.)   43.9
Curb weight (lbs.)   3,940

Drivetrain
Engine   quad-turbo dohc 60-
                            valve V-12
Bore x stroke (mm)   81.0x56.6
Displacement (cc)   3,500
Horsepower   611 bhp @ 8,250 rpm
Torque   480 lb-ft @ 4,200 rpm
Transmission   six-speed manual

Body & Chassis
Front suspension   upper and lower A-arms,
                            coil springs, tube
                            shocks, anti-roll bar
Rear suspension   upper and lower A-arms,
                            dual coil springs, tube
                            shocks, anti-roll bar
Steering   rack and pinion, power
                            assist
Brakes   13.1-inch vented discs
                            front and rear, ABS
Wheels   18x18 front, 18x24 rear
Tires   245/40ZR-18 front,
                            325/30ZR-18 rear

Performance
0 to 60 mph   4.4 seconds
Top speed   207 mph

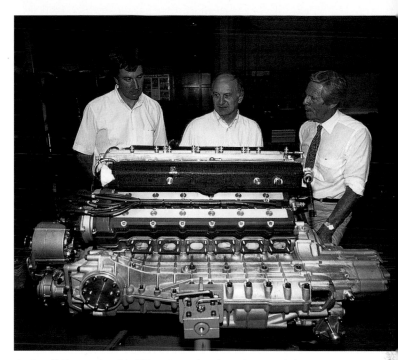

As in all Bugattis, the EB110 engine is quite special, a 60-valve 3.5-liter V-12 sporting an IHI turbocharger for each bank. With 15.2 psi of boost, the engine creates 611 horsepower. Seen with the engine are Michel Bugatti (left), engine designer Paolo Stanzani (center), and famous motoring journalist, Paul Frere.

Sadly, timing and economic conditions didn't cooperate. The exotic-car market stalled and the source of the project's money—whatever it was—dried up. EB110 production was halted and Bugatti went on the block.

Happily, Bugatti did not die. In 1998, Volkswagen bought the bankrupt organization and revived it. The guiding hand behind the purchase? Another brilliant engineer, Ferdinand Piech, chairman of VW-Audi, the grandson of Ferdinand Porsche, and the inspiration behind the Porsche 917. At major auto shows, both VW's design studio and Giorgetto Giugiaro's famed Italdesign began to show new examples of what a new Bugatti could be, either as a hyperexpensive coupe or mid-engine sports car.

The line continues, thanks to VW.

LAMBORGHINI COUNTACH

There has always been something magical about Lamborghini's Countach. Pure enthusiasts gravitate to Ferraris, claiming Maranello's automobiles are better. They may be correct on some levels, but for much of the world's populace what matters most about exotic cars is how they stir your soul . . . and few cars have done it better than the Countach.

Lamborghini beat Ferrari to the mid-12-cylinder-engine market with the Miura in 1966. Another landmark Bertone design, the Miura had begun to age by the end of the decade. Ferruccio Lamborghini went back to Bertone for a new auto-

mobile shape. Unveiled at the Geneva Auto Show in March 1971, the Countach LP500 grabbed all the headlines.

As it turned out, Maranello's experts were at work on a mid-engine supercar and would debut the 365GT Berlinetta Boxer in 1973, beating the Countach to production by a year. But while the famous Boxer has faded a bit into history, the Countach has not.

Bertone's Marcello Gandini gets credit for the Countach's exterior design. Gandini has any number of significant designs to his credit, including the Lancia Stratos and Alfa

Marcello Gandini explained that when designing the Lamborghini Countach, he wanted "people to be astonished when they saw the car." He succeeded, creating possibly THE most recognizable car in the world. While early models were quite clean and pure, later versions grew spoilers and other add-ons.

Romeo Carabo show car, but the Countach is his jewel. He once said he wanted "people to be astonished when they saw the car." He succeeded.

The Countach began as a pure and simple shape. As years passed, the Countach's aluminum body was altered with air scoops, spoilers, and fender flares. Some fans argue that the additions brought an impressive muscular aggressiveness . . . others figure the original shape was best.

Just as Bertone broke new ground with the Countach's exterior, Lamborghini was innovative with the drivetrain. While the Miura's V-12 is mounted transversely (side-to-side), the Countach's is in the more conventional fore-aft location . . . but with a difference.

Instead of positioning the V-12 and gearbox in the expected way—engine behind the passenger compartment, the transmission behind that—they turned the drivetrain around. The five-speed manual gearbox juts into the passenger compartment. The power goes rearward from the transmission via a shaft that passes through the engine sump to the final drive differential. With this layout, the shifter could be mounted directly to the gearbox instead of needing a long complicated linkage from the cockpit around to the back of the V 12.

In its original Countach form, the 4.0-liter V-12 had 375 horsepower, but that was eventually bumped up to 5.2 liters, 455 horsepower at 7,000 rpm, and 368 lb-ft of torque at 5,000 rpm.

This is the view many competitors get of the Countach, going away and accelerating. Debuted at the 1971 Geneva Auto Show, the Countach replaced the groundbreaking Lamborghini Miura, the first serious mid-engine 12-cylinder exotic car. In that era, many automakers, such as Ferrari, Ford, and Porsche, were developing mid-engine designs.

With its engine turned around 90 degrees, the Countach's transmission extends forward into the cockpit, creating a large center console. This widely divides the interior for passenger and driver, the latter facing a classic-looking instrument pod . . . and having the most fun.

Other technical specs include unequal-length upper and lower A-arm suspensions front and rear, with a pair of coil springs and tube shocks per side at the back. Big disc brakes hide inside the Countach's unique alloy wheels.

You pull the Countach's unique doors up to get in, stepping across a wide sill and settling down into the seats. Exotic car seats are often described as form fitting, like a leather-gloved hand. Not this Lambo's, which reminds one more of a chaise lounge from the 1960s. Side support is that wide sill and the tall center console to the right.

You sit low in the Countach, the requisite black-on-white gauges splayed in front. Pull down the door and with a key twist, the car is ready.

Forward into first gear with a metallic thunk and after reasonably light clutch pressure you're away . . . fast. Depending on which form of the Countach you're driving, 60 miles per hour comes up in 4.5 to 5.0 seconds with that unusual big sound of Lamborghini's V-12.

In no time you're whistling along in this wonderful exotic car, putting down the miles and prompting other drivers' smiles.

You must remember two things: One is that you can't see much out of the Countach, and in tight places, it's best to remember how much real estate you're wheeling along. Second, rearward vision is terrible. You need help to back up . . . unless you're as flexible as Lamborghini's factory test drivers. Men such as the famous Valentino Balboni back up a

LAMBORGHINI COUNTACH

Base price: $145,000

Specifications
General
Layout	mid-engine, rear drive
Wheelbase (in.)	96.5
Overall length (in.)	168.0
Overall width (in.)	78.7
Overall height (in.)	42.1
Curb weight (lbs.)	3,263

Drivetrain
Engine	dohc 24-valve V-12
Bore x stroke (mm)	85.5x69.0
Displacement (cc)	4,754
Horsepower	375 bhp @ 7,000 rpm
Torque	303 lb-ft @ 4,500 rpm
Transmission	five-speed manual

Body & Chassis
Front suspension	upper and lower A-arms, coil springs, tube shocks, anti-roll bar
Rear suspension	upper lateral link and reversed lower A-arms, upper and lower trailing arms, dual coil springs, dual tube shocks, anti-roll bar
Steering	rack and pinion
Brakes	11.8-inch vented discs front, 11.2-inch discs rear
Wheels	7.5x15 front, 12x15 rear
Tires	225/50VR 15 front, 345/35VR-15 rear

Performance
0 to 60 mph	4.9 seconds
Top speed	183 mph

While its predecessor, the famous Miura, had a transverse engine, the V-12 in the Countach is located "north-south," with its nose to the back of the car. Early Countachs had a 4.0-liter engine, but this was later increased to 5.2 liters and a very healthy 455 horsepower.

Countach (or, now, a Diablo) while sitting on the wide door-sills looking back over the car; it's more impressive than watching him snake a Countach through tight esses.

However, it is also enjoyable to sit next to Balboni as he pops over the rise at speed on the road to Modena. Just ahead is the famous tight left-hander that has terrified so many customers during test drives, many assuming the car would be catapulted into the field beyond. But the Countach goes slightly nose down as Balboni dabs the brakes at the last moment, slides easily through the corner, and nails the throttle. You take a deep breath and Balboni just grins.

LAMBORGHINI DIABLO VT

It was foggy near Modena, Italy, when they wheeled the all-new Lamborghini Diablo out of the shed for our morning photo session. It was early 1990, and we'd waited almost two decades for the oft-promised-never-delivered successor to the Countach.

It was worth the wait.

Marcello Gandini, who penned the Countach, gets credit for the Diablo's exterior design, though we hear the shape was fine-tuned at Chrysler in Detroit. The interior was all-American,

designed by Bill Dayton while working at Lamborghini in Italy.

Both the exterior and interior beautifully drew on the proportions and design theme of the Countach and updated them . . . softer and more sensuous. While such pieces as the deck lid, engine cover, and sidesills of the Diablo were done in carbon fiber, the main body was aluminum. It fit over a new frame that had square tubes in place of the round tubes used with the Countach. And it was a bit bigger, with the wheelbase

When Lamborghini went to carbon-fiber exterior panels for its Diablo, it also did a minor redesign, including a new lower front chin for the supercar. The parts not done in the lightweight material are the aluminum doors and the steel roof, the latter being part of the car's structure.

Diablo interiors come in several trims; this one is a special version done for the 40th anniversary of the company. All have a broad center console for the gearbox and seats you wiggle over and into before settling down for what should be a great drive.

stretching from 96.5 to 104.3 inches, and overall length growing 10.2 inches to 175.6. The chassis kept the classic upper and lower A-arm suspension layouts.

Like the Countach, the Diablo had the "backward" drivetrain. The "front" of the V-12—now at 5.7 liters and 485 horsepower—was at the very back of the car, the transmission poking forward into the cockpit. This unusual layout proved helpful when Lamborghini developed its VT four-wheel-drive system, which features a viscous coupling and a short

carbon-fiber driveshaft to a front-axle differential. Introduced a few years after the original Diablo, the traction-enhancing four-wheel drive would direct power to the front wheels if the rears ever began to spin more than the fronts.

The Diablo debuted to great excitement and reviews, but its parent company, Chrysler, later sold the small Italian firm, which fell into difficult times. A rebirth came in 1998 when Lamborghini went to Audi, asking to use its V-8 in a new small model. The German company declined, but turned around and

Front-hinged, flip-up doors have been a feature of Lamborghinis since the Countach was debuted. They make getting in and out easier, particularly in tight parking places. This purple Diablo was one of a limited series built to celebrate the automaker's 40th anniversary.

bought Lamborghini. And now, 10 years after photographing the first Diablo, we were back in Italy to do the latest Diablo.

There are mild styling changes, particularly to the nose, but what matters most is that much of the car's bodywork is now tough, lightweight carbon fiber. The only major exceptions are the aluminum doors and the steel roof, the latter a part of the chassis structure.

Carbon fiber shows up in the revised Diablo interior, where it is used extensively on the center console and a new arced dashboard, blending nicely with the leather and aluminum also used inside.

The basics of the suspension didn't change, but the front and rear tracks are a bit wider. The electronically controlled shock absorbers have been improved, and the entire chassis can be better utilized because the Diablo is now stiffer.

The V-12 is opened out to 6.0 liters with horsepower upped to 550 at 7,100 rpm and the torque to 435 lb-ft at 5,500 rpm. The marvelous four-wheel-drive VT system helps spread the power around to all wheels. Get the VT launched properly—rev to 6,000 rpm and side-step the clutch pedal—and the new Diablo smokes its way to 60 miles per hour in just 3.6 seconds. Top speed? Just over 200 miles per hour.

LAMBORGHINI DIABLO VT

Base price: $230,000

Specifications
General

Layout	mid-engine, rear drive or four-wheel drive (VT)
Wheelbase (in.)	104.3
Overall length (in.)	175.6
Overall width (in.)	80.3
Overall height (in.)	43.9
Curb weight (lbs.)	3,865

Drivetrain

Engine	dohc 48-valve V-12
Bore x stroke (mm)	87.0x84.0
Displacement (cc)	5,992
Horsepower	550 bhp @ 7,100 rpm
Torque	435 lb-ft @ 5,500 rpm
Transmission	five-speed manual

Body & Chassis

Front suspension	upper and lower A-arms, coil springs, tube shocks, electronically controlled shocks, anti-roll bar
Rear suspension	upper and lower A-arms, coil springs, tube shocks, electronically controlled shocks, anti-roll bar
Steering	rack and pinion, power assist
Brakes	14.1-inch vented discs front, 13.2-inch vented discs rear, ABS
Wheels	18x8-1/2 front, 18x13 rear
Tires	235/35ZR-18 front, 335/30ZR-18 rear

Performance

0 to 60 mph	3.6 seconds
Top speed	205 mph (estimated)

Diablo V-12s come with either 5.7- or 6.0-liter engines, ranging from 485 horsepower to 550. The engine sits "backward" in the chassis, its transmission jutting forward into the cockpit. The easiest way to get all that power to the ground is the VT four-wheel-drive system.

And all this from a car that's quite civilized. Nuzzle into the clamshell seats and pull down the door. Turn off the combination satellite navigation/television receiver screen so you can concentrate. Reset the electronic shocks from the soft street ride to firm track setting. Get the 6.0 liters burbling behind you. Then onto the circuit.

Not knowing the track layout, we tuck in behind someone who has done it many times and just hang on. Thanks to a broad torque band, there's plenty of power in each of the six gears. Turn-in is ever-so-smooth, and with the four-wheel drive you feel a heightened sense of balance, neither end of the car wanting to dominate. Very quickly you get used to driving the Diablo VT aggressively . . . until you remember this is someone else's $230,000 car.

For all its improvements, the Diablo retains one difficult feature: like the Countach, you can't see out the back. But as my friends at *Road & Track* say, when you drive a Diablo you figure, "What's behind me is not important."

PAGANI ZONDA C12

From the outside there's nothing remarkable about the place. It's another building in still another industrial park, though this one is in Italy's Castelfranco Emilia, a small town just east of Modena. It's no more than a 15-minute drive each to Ferrari, Lamborghini, or Maserati.

This building belongs to Horace Pagani's Modena Design, which has done work for many of the exotic car manufacturers in this fabled automotive Eden, mainly designing and fabricating carbon-fiber components. Upstairs, a studio mixes traditional huge design boards with computers in which body and chassis components can be twirled and tested on-screen. Down in the main shop are huge work areas, including one for laying up carbon fiber, while in another are huge autoclaves for baking the lightweight pieces.

Horace Pagani's dream on wheels, the Zonda C12. Born in Argentina, Pagani moved to Italy to fulfill his dream of creating and building a supercar of his own design. The bodywork is made of carbon fiber in Pagani's own shops, and weighs just 136 pounds.

Detailing, detailing, detailing is the best way to describe the Zonda's interior. Pagani didn't miss designing something into every corner or square inch of the interior—rounded pedals included—and the mixture of leather, aluminum, and carbon fiber gives the car a very contemporary look.

But the most important room in the building is the lobby, because for the moment it contains a Pagani Zonda C12, the car Horace Pagani just had to build.

And here's the remarkable thing: Pagani personally designed the C12's exterior, interior, tub, chassis, and suspension. What's more, he did it the old-fashioned way, by hand on drawing boards before turning the sketches and plans over to his engineers to confirm the design standards in their computers.

In his shops, craftsmen create the Zonda's carbon-fiber tub and exterior body panels, the latter weighing just 136 pounds, 48 of them being the huge rear engine cover. The shape has a jet fighter canopy floating in a race-car lower body inspired by the

Sauber-Mercedes Group C Silver Arrows. The front styling is somewhat predictable, but the rear is a photographer's delight of detailing. The Zonda's aerodynamics have been tested in Dallara's wind tunnel, with a claimed downforce of 285 pounds in front and 330 in back at 125 miles per hour.

Chrome-moly subframes are bolted to the front and rear of the carbon-fiber tub to carry the upper and lower A-arm suspensions and, at the back, the drivetrain. The frames also provide controlled crush for crash tests. Mercedes-Benz supplies the 394-horsepower 6.0-liter or AMG 500-horsepower 7.0-liter V-12, plus electronics, while the gearbox is a ZF six-speed manual.

The reminder of a C12's bought-out components are of equivalent high quality: AP clutch, Brembo ventilated disc brakes, Michelin Pilot tires (255/40ZR-18s front, 345/35ZR-18s back) on OZ wheels, Bilstein shocks, and TRW power rack-and-pinion steering.

While the remarkable detail of the work is obvious in the chassis, it's best seen in the interior, in the leatherwork on the carbon-fiber shell seats, the aluminum instrument pod, and the round brake and clutch pedals. The carbon-fiber surfaces are finished with the care once reserved for the wood in English luxury automobiles.

Whether fitted with the 394- or 500-horsepower V-12, the C12 is a rocket as that horsepower need only accelerate 2,750 pounds. Customers can choose their car's colors and visit the factory for a fitting of what Pagani hopes will be 25 highly personalized cars per year, left- or right-hand drive as you wish. Price? Start at $350,000.

So what is Horace Pagani trying to prove? As a kid, he littered the pages of his school notebooks with automotive designs in his hometown of Casilda (Santa Fe), Argentina. After industrial design studies, he understood he had to go to Italy to realize his automotive dreams. So in 1983, the 27-year-old

Pagani's Zonda C12 design was inspired by Mercedes-Benz's Group C Silver Arrow race cars, with a cockpit meant to mimic that of a fighter aircraft. Using the 550-horsepower V-12, the C12 will rocket to 60 miles per hour in 3.6 seconds on its way to around 190 miles per hour. Price? Around $350,000.

PAGANI ZONDA C12 AND C12 S

Base price:	$350,000

Specifications

General
Layout	mid-engine, rear drive
Wheelbase (in.)	107.5
Overall length (in.)	171.1
Overall width (in.)	80.9
Overall height (in.)	45.3
Curb weight (lbs.)	2,750

Drivetrain
Engine	dohc 48-valve V-12
Bore x stroke (mm)	89.0x80.2 (5,987 cc)
Displacement (cc)	5,987 or 7,010
Horsepower	394 bhp @ 5,200 rpm (C12) or 500 bhp @ 5,500 rpm (C12 S)
Torque	410 lb-ft @ 3,800 rpm (C12) or 540 lb-ft @ 4,100 rpm (C12 S)
Transmission	six-speed manual

Body & Chassis
Front suspension	upper and lower A-arms, coil springs, tube shocks, anti-roll bar
Rear suspension	upper and lower A-arms, coil springs, tube shocks, anti-roll bar
Steering	rack and pinion, power assist
Brakes	14.0-inch vented discs front, 13.1-inch vented discs rear
Wheels	na*
Tires	255/40ZR-18 front, 345/35ZR-18 rear

Performance
0 to 60 mph	3.6 seconds (with 550-bhp V-12)
Top speed	190 mph (estimated)

*na=not available

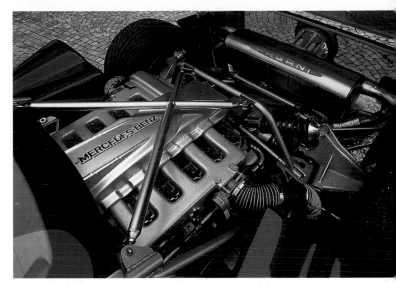

Mercedes-Benz was chosen as the engine supplier, and Pagani offers a choice of two V-12s from the German automaker. The "base" is Mercedes' 394-horsepower 6.0-liter V-12, while the step up is the 7.0-liter AMG edition, hot rodded to 550 horsepower. Both engines come with a six-speed transmission.

Lamborghini fan moved to the Modena area to get a job with that automaker. Already trained in fiberglass methods, Pagani quickly realized that carbon fiber was the future and learned to work with the then-new techniques.

Pagani left Lamborghini in the mid-1980s, but turned his carbon-fiber expertise into a business that has done work for everything from Modena's exotic car makers to major governments.

With the success of these programs came the time, expertise, and funds to begin the sports car. Pagani began work on the car in 1992 and unveiled it at the 1999 Geneva Auto Show, fully certified for low emissions, successfully past its difficult crash test, and with tens of thousands of miles of durability tests already completed—ready for sale.

Is Pagani the next Ferrari or Lamborghini? We'll know in another 10 years, but in the meantime, his car remains a remarkable one-man design feat in a world that sometimes seems overcrowded with design teams.

chapter 3

JAPAN

Wild-looking, hairy chested, high-speed exotic cars do not come naturally to the Japanese. Part of the reason is societal and some of it economic . . . along with a lack of great roads in Japan where you can readily open up a very fast, powerful automobile.

There have been attempts, however. In the early 1990s, Nissan came very close to making a true exotic, a slick-looking all-wheel-drive sports car called the Mid-4 that got well into development before the project was killed. It says a lot about Japanese automakers that Nissan preferred to build the Skyline GTR, a wonderfully nasty-looking four-passenger coupe based on a high-volume model, but modified with twin turbos, all-wheel drive, and the ability to shame many sports cars on a road course.

Individuals have also tried. As an example, for many years the very attractive Made in Japan Gigliato Aerosa was shown at the world's great auto shows. A true exotic with the sophisticated Yamaha-Ford SHO V-8 driveline tucked in behind the driver, the Aerosa never went into production.

Japanese automakers have been willing to build such exotics as the Nissan R390 because they can use them to sell more small cars, but they've never had the courage to put those supercars into serious production. Toyota MR2s and Spyders, Honda S2000s, and years of great Nissan Z-Cars got the nod for the showrooms, but that's the limit.

The Japanese, however, have made a very important contribution to the world of exotic cars, thanks to Honda. Before the debut of the NSX, exotic cars were quick and beautiful, but not very civilized . . . hot in the summer, burdened by questionable cooling systems, and so on . . . weekend cars that might leave you stranded.

Honda, with its exacting engineering and production standards, could never build such a car. So the NSX was not only fast and good looking, but as reliable and comfortable to use as any Accord sedan. Within a generation, other exotic cars had been, for the most part, "NSX-ized."

It's easily arguable that change was a far greater contribution to the exotic car world than still more horsepower and another swoopy-looking body style.

ACURA NSX-T

Acura's NSX is the thinking man's exotic car. While rare, high-performance two-seaters pluck away at our heartstrings, the Honda designed and -built NSX also appeals to your head and, in a way, to your sense of reason.

This is good news and bad. Good because the NSX need not be just the plaything other exotic cars tend to become. For all their emotional appeal, most of these expensive toys turn into weekend wonders. It could be for any of several reasons, from limited interior space to a fussy drivetrain to the fact the car is—like the Lamborghini Diablo—almost impossible to back up without external assistance.

Not the NSX. For while Honda may lack the interest to create a supercar that makes you truly weak at the knees—and that's the bad side of the news—they are equally incapable of *not* building a well-thought-out, sensible automobile. And in doing so, they changed the exotic car world.

Acura's NSX is the automobile that made other exotic carmakers clean up their act. No more excuses. Before the mid-engine Japanese whiz kid came along, companies could get away with creating a high-priced machine with sizzling good looks and tire-shredding horsepower, but they didn't get all the details quite right: marginal air conditioning, too-heavy

Aluminum is used for much of the NSX, from the body to major pieces in the independent A-arm suspensions. Honda used the exotic car as a development ground to learn more about working with this lightweight material.

Opposite: The most important Acura NSX was the first version, which set a new standard of quality in the exotic car world. Ferrari's 348 (seen here with the NSX) was not up to the Honda-made sports car's level and sent the Italian engineers to work, dramatically raising the quality of their automobiles.

pedal pressures, and luggage compartments that would melt lead in the summer.

All that ended with the NSX. Here was a car that came close to the other exotics in all the important areas, from acceleration to handling to a sleek body shape. Given Honda's racing record, it also had a proud competition heritage, which is more than Lamborghini could claim. And yet the NSX was also built to Honda's exacting quality standards, with a cool cabin in the summer, engine noise that entertains the driver without being obtrusive, and a paint finish with no drips.

When Ferrari's first true post-NSX model, the F355, debuted, it had been "Hondaized" into a true two-nature car, both quick and civil. It could be argued that Ferrari did it better. The Italians learned the best parts of the Honda lesson, but kept the Ferrari edge in its cars. Honda, which had dramatically raised the exotic car standards with the NSX, never made the next step forward. By the time Ferrari had moved on one more model to the 360 Modena, Honda still had the NSX . . . by then almost 10 years old.

In all fairness, Ferrari was again copying Honda. By developing the 360 Modena's unit body in aluminum, the Italians were doing something the Japanese had done years before. Add the doors and deck lids, and the Honda's aluminum unit body tips the scale at only 462 pounds. Aluminum is also used for major components of the NSX's upper and lower A-arm suspensions and what many consider the jewel in the NSX's crown, its 24-valve, twin-cam V-6 engine.

Like Ferrari, Honda's reputation began with its engines. And it continues with the NSX V-6—complete with its titanium connecting rods—which comes in two forms. Opt for the six-speed manual gearbox and your V-6 would have 3.2 liters, 290 horsepower, and 224 lb-ft of torque . . . and 0 to 60 in 5 seconds through the very sweet shifter. Choose the four-speed SportShift automatic and its steering wheel-mounted shift levers and you'll have the 3.0-liter V-6 with 252 horsepower and 210 lb-ft of torque. The truly dedicated could, of course, contact Comptech U.S.A., the unofficial NSX racing team for American Honda, and investigate its supercharged, 425-horsepower NSX engine.

What Honda did with the Acura NSX that other exotic carmakers had not managed was to make a fast, mid-engine car that could be enjoyed on a track like a race car, or driven day-to-day as you would any high-quality car.

ACURA NSX-T

Base price: $84,000

Specifications

General

Layout	mid-engine, rear drive
Wheelbase (in.)	99.6
Overall length (in.)	174.2
Overall width (in.)	71.3
Overall height (in.)	46.1
Curb weight (lbs.)	3,090

Drivetrain

Engine	dohc 24-valve V-6
Bore x stroke (mm)	93.0x78.0
Displacement (cc)	3,179
Horsepower	290 bhp @ 7,100 rpm
Torque	224 lb-ft @ 5,500 rpm
Transmission	six-speed manual

Body & Chassis

Front suspension	upper and lower A-arms, compliance pivots, coil springs, tube shocks, anti-roll bar
Rear suspension	upper and lower A-arms, coil springs, tube shocks, anti-roll bar
Steering	rack and pinion, variable electric assist
Brakes	11.7-inch vented discs front, 11.9-inch vented discs rear, ABS
Wheels	16x7 front, 17x8-1/2 rear
Tires	215/45ZR-16 front, 245/40ZR-17 rear

Performance

0 to 60 mph	5.0 seconds
Top speed	168 mph (estimated)

Acura's NSX V-6 has been through several updates and is now sold in two forms. With the manual transmission you get a 3.2-liter, 290-horsepower version of the engine, while the automatic gearbox is matched to a 3.0-liter, 252-horsepower model.

There is nothing wrong with wanting to play Formula 1 driver with the automatic, but in an automobile already so inherently smooth to drive, the manual is really more fun. With traction control on, the NSX is a sweet, safe car to hustle down any twisting road. Turn off the traction control and the NSX takes on a slightly different character, one mastered by your right foot, which now has more control over the car's rear end. In either case, the NSX rides better than most exotic cars and leaves you with a wonderful sense of the road rushing below you.

And you will be in comfort, with seats that hold you in place, good outward visibility, room for an amazing amount of luggage, and, with the 19-pound aluminum targa panel stowed in back, the wind whistling through your hair.

Best yet, the NSX is a relative bargain, priced just above the better Porsche 911s and well below the entry-level Ferrari.

NISSAN R390 GT1

Nissan's R390 GT1 is one of several exotic cars with an important difference: it wasn't really meant to be sold to the public... and how much more exotic can a car get than to be impossible to buy?

Here's what happened. In the late 1990s, the 24 Hours of Le Mans had a class called GT1. To qualify for the class, a car builder was required to create a street-ready machine that could be sold. They only had to build one and they didn't really have to sell it, but the car had to meet street-machine regs.

Was Le Mans a strong enough draw to force an automaker to build such a specialized car? Nissan asked its potential customers that question. The company found that

Nissan discovered that among its customers no single race in the world had the attraction of the 24 Hours of Le Mans. To compete in that famous race, the Japanese company developed the R390. *Photo courtesy of Nissan*

Designed by Ian Callum, who also penned the Aston Martin DB7, the R390 was created to race in the GT1 category. The rules for that class required the company to produce a street-legal version of the car, but did not specify how many, so only a handful of R390s were made. *Photo courtesy of Nissan*

while their car-enthusiast customers put Grand Prix racing at the top of their "favorites" list, the general mass of potential Nissan buyers found Le Mans to be the most important race in the world.

So Nissan decided to attack Le Mans with a car called the R390 GT1. That was in the fall of 1996, and they wanted to be ready for Le Mans the following June. It would be a tight timetable for a pure race car, but Nissan had to build at least that one R390 that was certified for the street, even meeting emissions and crash-safety regulations. They needed help.

England's Tom Walkinshaw Racing (or TWR for short) had extensive experience both at Le Mans, where they won with the Mazda and Jaguar teams, and at producing street-legal exotic cars. So, Nissan went to TWR for assistance with the R390.

The plan was that NISMO (Nissan Motorsports International) would provide the engine for the exotic, while TWR would do the actual car.

Drawing from its experience, TWR created a lightweight carbon-fiber chassis complete with upper and lower A-arm suspensions, rack-and-pinion steering, and huge 14-inch vented disc brakes. Bodywork for the Japanese race car was penned by Ian Callum, who also shaped the Aston Martin DB7 and went on to head Jaguar's design studios.

In Japan, NISMO designed and developed the 3.5-liter twin-turbo V-8 planned for the R390. The lightweight engine block was made from magnesium, while the dual overhead cams opened four valves per cylinder. The R390 was powered

The responsibility for developing and building the body and chassis of the Nissan was farmed out to the Le Mans–winning Tom Walkinshaw racing team. This meant TWR had to design everything from the pseudo-street interior to the carbon-fiber chassis. *Photo courtesy of Nissan*

by 550 horsepower at 6,800 rpm and 470 lb-ft of torque at 4,400, and that was steady, reliable power meant to last for an entire 24-hour endurance race. At the back of the V-8 was a six-speed sequential gearbox.

Inside, the R390 was pure race car. You drop down into seats formed by the center structure and side tanks of the carbon-fiber chassis. Ahead is a typical no-nonsense race-car display of instruments with pertinent information. No frills. One should not expect much in the way of sound-deadening.

That was the basic package that Nissan and TWR certified as street worthy so they could run at Le Mans. And they put a customer price on the car, $1 million.

The 2,420-pound R390 certainly had high-dollar performance, with a 0-to-60 time pegged at 3.9 seconds using gearing that would certainly put its top speed well over 200 miles per hour on Le Mans' Mulsanne straight. Or, presumably, any stretch of open freeway the owner with a great deal of ability and/or courage could find. Wouldn't that tick-off the cops?

NISSAN R390 GT1

Base price: $1,000,000

Specifications
General

Layout	mid-engine, rear drive
Wheelbase (in.)	107.1
Overall length (in.)	185.8
Overall width (in.)	78.7
Overall height (in.)	44.9
Curb weight (lbs.)	2,420

Drivetrain

Engine	turbocharged dohc 32-valve V-8
Bore x stroke (mm)	85.0x77.0
Displacement (cc)	3,495
Horsepower	550 bhp @ 6,800 rpm
Torque	470 lb-ft @ 4,400 rpm
Transmission	six-speed sequential

Body & Chassis

Front suspension	upper and lower A-arms, coil springs, tube shocks, anti-roll bar
Rear suspension	upper and lower A-arms, coil springs, tube shocks, anti-roll bar
Steering	rack and pinion
Brakes	14.0-inch vented discs front and rear
Wheels	18x8 front, 19x10 rear
Tires	245/40ZR-18 front, 295/35ZR-19 rear

Performance

0 to 60 mph	3.9 seconds
Top speed	200 mph (estimated)

While the car was created in England, Nissan made the V-8 engine in Japan. The lightweight engine featured a magnesium block, and while its official horsepower was 550, that power was reliable at race speeds throughout the entire 24 Hours of Le Mans. *Photo courtesy of Nissan*

In reality, it was unlikely Nissan would have sold any R390s. They received queries, but not just anyone would be qualified to drive such a potent automobile. Not only was it a purebred race car, but if retuned for ultimate performance instead of endurance, the turbo V-8 had the potential of up to 1,000 horsepower.

Besides, Nissan and TWR were busy prepping the race cars for Le Mans—and very successfully so. The combination of the English firm's experience and the Japanese engine's power and reliability took R390 GT1s to 3rd-, 5th-, 6th-, and 10th-place finishes in the 1997 24 Hours of Le Mans . . . a race in which finishing one car in the top 10 is impressive.

The GT1 rules changed, and in 1999 Nissan ran its Le Mans project with pure prototypes. This really made more sense, but it is fascinating to consider the place of the R390 and other GT1 cars, such as Porsche's, and that brief time when automakers created some of the most exotic cars ever built.

chapter 4

UNITED STATES

Americans love exotic automobiles. The United States has been the major export market for Ferrari, Porsche, and Lamborghini for years, but it doesn't create its own super-exotic cars. The country has long had the talent, the experience, and the materials to do so, and in the 1930s produced great V-12 and V-16 sedans that rivaled anything in the world. But the United States has always had plenty of cheap, reliable horse-power and inexpensive, readily available fuel, so no one had to break the bank to get ground-pounding power and speed.

Men have tried to make American exotics. John DeLorean took a shot with his stainless-steel, mid-engine sports car, but the effort ended in scandal and lawsuits. The best candidate to be the hands-down U.S. exotic car world-beater, the Vector, had heart-pumping styling and all the speed most drivers could ever control but the Vector suffered from years of poor funding and unkept promises, finally meeting a quiet death in rural Florida.

General Motors took several long, hard looks at doing serious mid-engine exotic cars—the Aerovette, the CERV IV—but could never develop the corporate courage (which is to say,

a winning business plan) to go ahead. GM did own Lotus for a time, just as Chrysler had Lamborghini and Ford runs Aston Martin and Jaguar, but U.S. automakers could just never make a case for home-built exotics.

Chevrolet does, however, build a wonderful Corvette, just as Dodge's Viper is a world-beater in its own class. And how about Carroll Shelby's Ford-powered, U.S.-assembled Cobras?

What do they all share? Good old American engines, with two valves per cylinder and pushrods, based on engines used in rather ordinary cars and/or trucks. And their base prices—minus, perhaps, the Cobra—are in line with Detroit's philosophy of offering the most for a low price.

We do have a U.S. tuner industry. If the stock Corvette and Viper aren't enough, men such as Reeves Callaway and John Hennessey will modify one with enough exotic brakes, carbon-fiber panels, horsepower, and performance to go specifications sheet-to-specifications sheet and price-to-price with any automaker in the world.

But if you're waiting for the likes of GM, Ford, or the Chrysler group to build a true exotic car, don't hold your breath.

DODGE VIPER

Dodge's Viper is every red-blooded American kid's dream car. It's the fastback sports car we sketched in our high-school notebooks. The American answer to imported exotic cars, complete with a big-displacement, bags-of-torque pushrod engine, and an exhaust note that puts even an unmuffled Harley-Davidson to shame. And it has a great—if brief—history.

Even before the 1989 Detroit Auto Show we had a hint that something sporty and remarkable was coming from the Chrysler Corporation. Scrambling to spiff up the image of its Dodge Division, the automaker needed something exciting to tickle our imaginations. But lordy, we never expected what they unveiled: a rugged-looking sports car with an aggressive front end that was almost malevolent. The show car's low

Crank that one-piece hood forward and there it is, the long monster V-10 with its 8.0 liters of displacement, 450 horsepower, and 490 lb-ft of torque. Equipped with a six-speed manual gearbox, the Dodge sports car can leap to 60 miles per hour in just 4.4 seconds.

Opposite: The second-generation Viper changes the proportions a bit and swaps the large one-piece front-hinged engine cover for more conventional fenders and hood. This competition car version confirmed that Chrysler would continue racing the Viper, which has been a consistent winner in international events.

stance was emphasized by a long hood meant to cover—for heaven's sake—an 8.0-liter V-10. Dodge promised not only better-than-Corvette performance, but also a reasonable price.

And here was the best part: Dodge delivered everything it promised.

When the Viper went into production in 1992, it created an instant cult, with potential owners lining up at dealerships to be the first in their neighborhood with the Dodge sports car.

Once you have driven a Viper, it's easy to understand why. You slip down and into the Viper, its tall center console snuggling you into the driving position. It's a nicely laid-out cockpit: the tachometer and speedometer are straight ahead, with the other dials spread out to the right. There's nothing delicate, subtle, or snobbish about the Viper interior, and it's easy to get a good solid grip on the controls—all the better for hanging on.

At the key's turn, the big V-10 starts its odd exhaust note rumble. Into first gear, let out the medium-effort clutch, and the Viper eases away. Nail the throttle and the acceleration will flatten you in the seat, ready to put you back there again when you've hauled it into second gear. In just 4.4 seconds you are

at 60 miles per hour, with 100 coming up in 9.8. Top speed? How about 185 miles per hour at the end of the rocket ride?

Okay, it wasn't a perfect car, and could be a bit of a rough-and-ready drive. The cockpit could be hot inside on a summer's day. The original folding soft top was difficult to use and the side curtains leaked when it rained, but these were all minor inconveniences . . . and they were eventually fixed.

At the 1993 Detroit show, Dodge presented the Viper GTS coupe. Not only did the fastback bring the possibility of comfortable all-weather driving, but it also meant even the roadster inherited the badly needed glass side windows.

The Viper's handling also went through a bit of taming. With all that torque and acceleration, the sports car may be nice and stable, but you can easily take to the edge when driving, and just a little brain fade could slide you over the edge. So you have to use your noggin, but the Viper can also be quite predictable as you use the throttle to measure out just how much you want the back end hanging out.

You don't have to stop at stock Vipers. Several aftermarket tuners will customize your Viper. Texan John Hennessey is

With the Dodge Viper, Chrysler created the throaty, tire-smoking American sports car young men had been dreaming about. The body shape, with its near-malevolent smiling grille, is a classic of long-hood/short-rear-deck proportions, whether it is the removable-top sports version or the closed GT with its kicked-up rear spoiler.

The Viper cockpit is divided into two very separate seating areas by the transmission's tall, wide center console. There is a soft, rounded, welcoming sense to the interior, almost a bit deceiving given the car's super performance.

one of the best at making even faster Vipers with such creations as the Venom 650R. After banging out the V-10 to 8.4 liters and giving it the speed treatment, Hennessey's hot rod Viper adds 200 horsepower for a total of 650. But that can be just a beginning, topping an option list that includes the hidden (Brembo brakes and suspension mods), the almost hypnotic (functional aero packages and eye-popping colors), and the expensive (a final price that would buy you a Ferrari 360 Modena). But the hopped-up Viper will also get you to 60 miles per hour in 3.7 seconds and through the quarter-mile in 11.5 seconds at almost 130 miles per hour.

To its credit, Chrysler also wasn't afraid to put the Viper into serious road racing circles. And it went after the international crowd, winning three successive FIA GT2 championships, nailing down class wins in such famous races as the 24 Hours of Le Mans. Chrysler's finest hour was taking an overall victory in the 2000 24 Hours of Daytona.

The Viper is everything we imagined when we were sketching that dream car in our high-school notes and thinking, "What would happen if . . ."

DODGE VIPER

Base price: $70,000

Specifications

General

Layout	front engine, rear drive
Wheelbase (in.)	96.2
Overall length (in.)	176.7
Overall width (in.)	75.7
Overall height (in.)	47.0
Curb weight (lbs.)	3,380

Drivetrain

Engine	ohv V-10
Bore x stroke (mm)	101.6x98.5
Displacement (cc)	7,990
Horsepower	450 bhp @ 5,200 rpm
Torque	490 lb-ft @ 3,700 rpm
Transmission	six-speed manual

Body & Chassis

Front suspension	unequal-length upper and lower A-arms, coil springs, tube shocks, anti-roll bar
Rear suspension	unequal-length upper and lower A-arms, coil springs, tube shocks, anti-roll bar
Steering	rack and pinion, power assist
Brakes	13.0-inch vented discs front and rear
Wheels	17x10 front, 17x13 rear
Tires	275/40ZR-17 front, 335/35ZR-17 rear

Performance

0 to 60 mph	4.4 seconds
Top speed	185 mph

CALLAWAY C12

It looks like it belongs on a race track. Low and liquid-smooth, the bodywork implies the Callaway C12 sticks to the road like a ground-effects race car. Judging by *Road & Track*'s testing, it comes close to that mark, being one of the rare cars that can generate more than 1.0g of lateral acceleration on a skid pad. Point the C12 straight down the road, however, and it becomes a dragster, the speedo needle whipping past 60 miles per hour in just 4.7 seconds and the 100-mile-per-hour mark just 5.1 seconds later—quick and yet comfortable.

That's the way Reeves Callaway likes his cars.

We first heard from Callaway in 1978, when he began creating turbocharged 3-Series BMWs in a building out in the woods near Old Lyme, Connecticut. Emissions rules had sucked power from automobiles back then, and guys like

When building an automobile that bears his name, Reeves Callaway begins with a stock Corvette. Underneath he adds a modified suspension designed and made in Germany.

The famous small-block Chevrolet V-8 is heavily modified at the Callaway factory in Old Lyme, Connecticut. Among other changes, the cylinder heads and pistons are reworked to modify the combustion chamber shape, and the camshaft profiles are altered. The result is 440 bhp and 420 lb-ft of torque.

Callaway were pumping it back in with turbos. Next came turboed Volkswagens and Porsche 924s that were so impressive because of their added power and superb workmanship that Alfa Romeo hired Callaway to breathe life into its GT6 model. One of these official factory Alfas ended up at General Motors' Milford proving grounds and mightily impressed Dave McLellan's Corvette development group. In 1985, Callaway received the official corporate blessing—an unusual divine approval from GM—to modify Corvettes. He has being doing just that ever since.

When Chevrolet produced the C5 Corvette with its greatly improved chassis and powertrain, it gave Callaway a chance to take an even greater step toward creating more than just modified Corvettes. Although his cars are Corvettes legally converted to conform to the government's emissions and safety rules, there is little in the C12's outward appearance to hint at this heritage. In fact, in Europe the cars are registered as Callaways.

Here's why.

A C12 begins as a set of Corvette bones in Callaway's Leingarten, Germany, factory. Bolted to the 'Vette's stout perimeter frame are new suspensions, upper and lower A-arms developed and hand-fabricated by Munich, Germany's, IVM Engineering. Coil springs/adjustable shock units supplement the stock transverse plastic spring. On go 14-inch-diameter disc brakes, which will later be surrounded by P295/30ZR-19 Pirelli P-Zero tires.

Around this new chassis is custom bodywork designed by Canadian Paul Deutschman and made of fiberglass, carbon fiber, and Kevlar. It's Deutschman who gives Callaways their sleek aero shape, a magic he applies to any of three C12 versions: a fixed-top coupe, a hardtop with a removable central roof panel, and a convertible, which becomes the Speedster model, featuring a unique rear deck lid with headrests.

Callaway also changes the Corvette interior to suit the new exterior. The standard seats are swapped for custom buckets made by Koenig. Like the dashboard, door panels, and center console, the seats are upholstered in a leather of the customer's choice from a wide variety of colors. Custom gauge faces are added, while their surround and parts of the center console get carbon-fiber coverings.

Next comes a trip back to the United States, to Old Lyme for a new engine. The power boffins in the engine shop are world-renowned for their tuning work, having been contracted by Aston Martin to update its V-8 and GM's Holden of Australia to modify the corporation's LT1 V-8s for its Commodore coupes.

For the C12's aluminum Corvette V-8, the shop blueprints the engine and does some serious reworking such as

To finish off the conversion, the company adds custom body panels designed by Canadian Paul Deutschman. With the bodywork arcing out over huge tires, the Callaway C12 takes on a nasty, sit-down-and-shut-up demeanor.

Callaway also modifies the interior of his C12s, with seats custom upholstered from a wide range of leather colors. There are new instrument faces, and the gauges and switches are now set in carbon-fiber accent panels.

machining the heads and pistons to create a new combustion chamber shape, changing the cam profiles, and swapping such stock parts as con rods for beefier pieces. The results were 440 horsepower at 6,300 rpm and 420 lb-ft of torque at 4,800 rpm versus the stock Corvette's 345 horsepower at 5,600 rpm and 350 lb-ft at 4,400 rpm.

Once the buffed-up V-8 is put back in the C12 and bolted to the Corvette's rugged six-speed manual transmission, Reeves Callaway takes the new C12 for a shakedown drive. This is just the sort of personal attention Callaway gives his new cars . . . and what a customer expects when he pays $170,000 to $220,000 for an automobile.

What his money buys is a truly custom-built car. As that price spread implies, there's a lot you can do to personalize your C12. Every C12 owner, however, gets an almost-race car. It has the looks. It has the power. It has the handling. Thankfully it also has an interior that coddles just enough and a surprisingly smooth ride that won't rattle your back teeth.

That's the way Reeves Callaway likes his cars.

CALLAWAY C12

Base price: $178,500

Specifications

General

Layout	front engine, rear drive
Wheelbase (in.)	104.5
Overall length (in.)	191.0
Overall width (in.)	78.7
Overall height (in.)	47.1
Curb weight (lbs.)	3,380 (estimated)

Drivetrain

Engine	ohv V-8
Bore x stroke (mm)	99.0x92.0
Displacement (cc)	5,666
Horsepower	440 bhp @ 6,300 rpm
Torque	420 lb-ft @ 4,800 rpm
Transmission	six-speed manual

Body & Chassis

Front suspension	upper and lower A-arms, transverse composite monoleaf spring, coil springs, tube shocks, anti-roll bar
Rear suspension	upper and lower A-arms, transverse composite monoleaf spring, coil springs, tube shocks, anti-roll bar
Steering	rack and pinion, variable power assist
Brakes	14.0-inch vented discs front, 11.8-inch vented discs rear, ABS
Wheels	19x10-1/2
Tires	P295/30ZR-19

Performance

0 to 60 mph	4.7 seconds
Top speed	200 mph (estimated)

CHEVROLET CORVETTE C5

If this book had been written before the debut of the fifth-generation Corvette, Chevrolet's sports car would not have been included. There have been great Corvettes, such as the original Sting Rays, but the fourth iteration in this line of fiberglass sports car was not among them. So why is the "C5" included? Because project engineer Dave Hill and his Corvette development team took virtually all the complaints made about the previous generation 'Vette and fixed them.

In creating the Corvette C5, Chevrolet put itself back on the supercar map. No, it's not as exotic as a Ferrari or Lamborghini, but the 'Vette provides almost all their performance at a fraction of their price . . . an exotic car for the working person.

With its fifth-generation Corvette, Chevrolet put itself back in the high-performance big leagues . . . though at a minor league price. The body design updated traditional Corvette styling themes with a hint of Callaway thrown in with the tall rear end shape.

Chevrolet began C5 development by redesigning and dramatically stiffening the chassis of the Corvette with such elements as a new steel perimeter frame, an enclosed transmission tunnel, and lightweight crossbraces. Not only did this create a "stiffer" Corvette, but it gave the chassis engineers a better base for the upper and lower A-arm suspensions at each end of the car, the variable-effort rack-and-pinion steering, and the huge disc brakes.

To power the C5 Corvette, engineers created a new engine wrapped around an old philosophy. They kept the fundamentals of the old V-8—the two-valve-per-cylinder pushrod design, 5.7-liter displacement and cylinder bore centers—integrating them into an all-new aluminum powerplant. It's a typically strong GM small-block engine, with 345 horsepower plus 350 lb-ft of torque that will entertain you from 1,500 rpm right up to the 6,000-rpm redline.

Repackaging the interior created a 'Vette that is a pleasure to live with, where previous Corvettes were not. Entry and exit are now easy. The leather seats are like a gentle hand in the center of your back. Controls are well placed and with a nice touch.

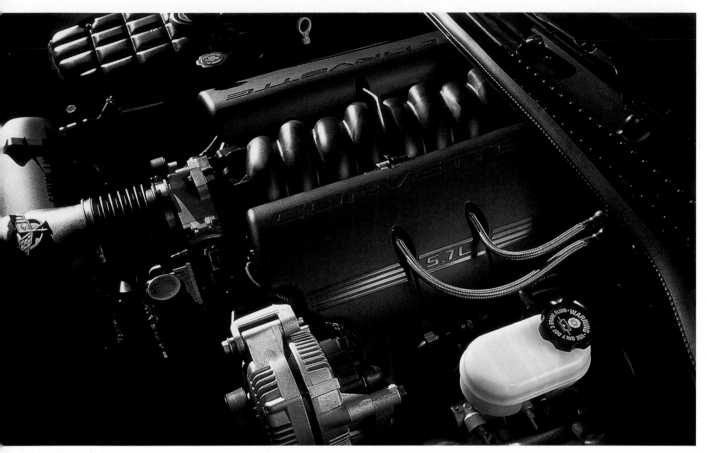

A complete redesign of the small-block V-8 kept traditional elements such as the 5.7-liter displacement and pushrod valve actuation, but advanced the legendary powerplant into the twenty-first century. The all-aluminum fuel-injected engine produces 345 horsepower and 350 lb-ft of low-down torque; manual and automatic transmissions are available.

As a further aid to the chassis engineers, the transmission is part of a rear-mounted transaxle, which led to a 50 front/50 rear-weight balance for the 'Vette.

Designers in the Corvette studio had their chance to clothe the C5 in a new shape. Their efforts took some initial hits from the press, which was looking for something more dramatic. Like many good designs, however, this Corvette quickly became an attractive addition to the sports car ranks. It is also an aerodynamically impressive package, beginning with its low nose and climbing to the tall cut-off tail, producing a 0.29 drag coefficient along the way.

Redesigning created an interior "package" that is much more livable than in past Corvettes. Entry is easy now, no longer requiring you to fall into the seats. The driver and passenger have plenty of room for their heads and elbows. Feet get a break too, as the rear-mounted transmission opens up significant inches of foot room.

Hints of the original Sting Ray's dashboard are the basis for the new layout. Excellent gauges, good controls, and even neat-looking aluminum pedals. Seats that both cushion and support. A very livable cockpit for short spurts or the long haul . . . and a large, usable trunk.

These impressive changes show up in three Corvette models, beginning with the coupe with its removable roof panel for half-open "Targa" driving. The second version of the C5 is the coupe with the fixed top. The third variation is the

Where the fourth-generation Corvette's instrument panel was a disaster, the current model's is an example of how it should be done. The white-on-black gauges are easy to read in high or low light . . . and isn't it a treat to watch that speedo needle twist past 100 miles per hour and keep on swinging?

convertible, where the progress on the C5's chassis and body are most obvious. Quite simply, the last-generation 'Vette's ragtops were rattletraps and the C5s are not. I've been in one with more than 8,000 miles that took on bumpy Michigan secondary road railroad crossings with nary a rattle or a squeak. And the Corvette's top can be put up or down in seconds even though it's a manual with one of the few faults in the new 'Vette: it leaks in heavy rain.

The V-8 rumbles nicely at idle as if wailing impatiently for you to get on with it. Smoothly shift into the first of six gears—or "D" if you prefer the four-speed automatic—and in less than 5 seconds you can be at 60 miles per hour. Another 6.5 seconds and you're at 100 miles per hour.

But there's more than slap-back-in-the-seat acceleration. Despite its price, the Corvette holds its own with megabuck exotics on twisty roads. There's the comfort of initial understeer, but a competent driver can use the throttle to balance the car with the pedal.

So there you have it: an exotic car with value—performance for a price—good looks, a practical interior package, and a proud racing heritage. Proof that you don't have to mortgage your soul to buy a good time in a fast two-seat sports car.

CHEVROLET CORVETTE C5

Base price: $39,000

Specifications

General

Layout	front engine, rear drive
Wheelbase (in.)	104.5
Overall length (in.)	179.7
Overall width (in.)	73.6
Overall height (in.)	47.7
Curb weight (lbs.)	3,230

Drivetrain

Engine	ohv V-8
Bore x stroke (mm)	99.0x92.0
Displacement (cc)	5,666
Horsepower	345 bhp @ 5,600 rpm
Torque	350 lb-ft @ 4,400 rpm
Transmission	six-speed manual

Body & Chassis

Front suspension	upper and lower A-arms, transverse composite monoleaf spring, tube shocks, anti-roll bar
Rear suspension	upper and lower A-arms, transverse composite monoleaf spring, tube shocks, anti-roll bar
Steering	rack and pinion, variable power assist
Brakes	12.8-inch vented discs front, 12.0-inch vented discs rear, ABS
Wheels	17x8-1/2 front, 18x9-1/2 rear
Tires	P245/45ZR-17 front, P275/40ZR-17 rear

Performance

0 to 60 mph	4.8 seconds
Top speed	170 mph

SALEEN S7

Enzo Ferrari. Ferruccio Lamborghini. Steve Saleen?

Why not?

You should know all three names: the first two for their exotic cars, the last for the super Mustangs he has built for the past 17 years, but what do they have in common?

Now they are all exotic car builders. Saleen joins the elite corps with his mid-engine, $375,000 S7.

Unlike Ferrari, Lamborghini, Pagani, and Maserati, Saleen doesn't build his supercar in the greater Modena, Italy, environs, but in rather more prosaic Irvine, California.

Located about 50 miles south of Los Angeles, Irvine is an international automotive center, boasting design studios for Mazda, Mercedes-Benz, and Italdesign, plus the offices of many aftermarket suppliers. It is also the site of the world

Racer and businessman Steve Saleen made his reputation modifying Mustangs, but became a full-fledged automaker with the S7 supercar, which costs $375,000, gets to 60 miles per hour in under 4 seconds, and tops out at over 200 miles per hour.

headquarters for Ford's Prestige Automotive Group, including Jaguar, Land Rover, Aston Martin, and Lincoln.

Dramatically styled with a world-record automotive gill count on its long-tail body, the Saleen S7's design nicely splits the visual difference between road and race car. At 188 inches long, 78.3 inches wide, and 41 inches high, the S7 is a dozen inches longer but 2.5 inches lower than a Lamborghini Diablo and has front-hinged swing-up doors similar to the Italian cars.

Designer Phil Frank did the pen work on the S7, with the aerodynamics tuned and confirmed in the wind tunnel of the University of Glasgow in Scotland.

Why use a tunnel so far from Irvine? The prototype S7 got some engineering assistance from and was built by Ray Mallock's well-known race firm in England. Mallock assembles S7s meant for Europe and the Middle East, with the rest of the world's Saleens being made in Irvine.

While the "S" in the name stands for Saleen, the "7" is for the number of liters in the purpose-built V-8. Although the pushrod engine starts with pieces from Ford's race program, there's a lot of Saleen in there too. For example, the aluminum block is from Ford's race parts catalog, but for packaging reasons has been reworked 8 inches shorter thanks to custom bits

Longer and lower than a Lamborghini Diablo, the S7's wind tunnel–tested bodywork is made of carbon fiber. Under the stunning shape is a tube frame reinforced with aluminum honeycomb panels. The chassis is typical of great exotic cars, with upper and lower A-arm suspensions and Brembo ventilated disc brakes.

For the S7's engine, Saleen engineers begin with an aluminum block from Ford's racing department and highly modify it to 550 horsepower and 520 lb-ft of torque. The dry-sump powerplant features an intake manifold and throttle body made of magnesium and a carbon-fiber air intake.

such as a side-mounted water pump. Among other Saleen pieces are the magnesium intake manifold and throttle body, and the aluminum cylinder heads. Behind the dry-sump V-8 is a six-speed manual transaxle.

Here are the important numbers performance car fans want next: 550 brake horsepower at 6,400 rpm, 520 lb-ft of torque at 4,000 rpm, 0 to 60 miles per hour in under 4 seconds, and a 200+-mile-per-hour top speed, thanks in part to a curb weight of only 2,750 pounds, split 40 percent front/60 percent rear.

Saleen gets that weight to some 600 pounds less than a rear-wheel-drive Diablo, thanks to lightweight chassis construction. The tube frame is supplemented with honeycomb aluminum panels that add rigidity and form front and rear crash safety boxes. Over this goes the carbon-fiber bodywork.

Connolly leather-covered seats sit low in the tub, the driver's set more to the car's centerline, giving the driver a more central driving location and the passenger less of a clamber in over the sill. Instrumentation is simple and rather elegant in its leather-brushed aluminum-and-body-color background. Rearward viewing is by video.

Chassis specs for the S7 are what we would expect from a world-class exotic car. Both the front and rear suspensions use upper and lower A-arms with tube shocks and coil springs.

The interior of the S7 has an asymmetrical layout, with the driver sitting closer to the car's centerline than does the passenger. Fine English leather covers the seats and sets the tone for the rather elegant interior. There is no inside rearview mirror; the car uses a backward-looking video system instead.

Big Brembo brakes hide inside 19-inch forged alloy wheels wrapped with Pirelli P-Zero tires.

Sounds like a race car, doesn't it? And it can be. Saleen's highly successful race team competes with the S7 against international championship-dominating Dodge Vipers and factory Corvettes.

In the exotic-car world it isn't unusual for new projects such as the Saleen to waste away in the oft-promised-never-delivered Never-Never Land of the badly funded for years before fading away. By contrast, the Saleen almost magically appeared on the market in late 2000, ready for sale.

Part of this magic can be attributed to the funding of Tony Johnson and Hidden Creek Industries, a huge automotive parts manufacturing concern. The Saleen's speed-to-market is the result of advanced computer modeling techniques that rocketed the S7 project from first thoughts to finished cars in the remarkably short time of 18 months.

It's nice to see someone building a true exotic car in California, giving potential buyers an American alternative.

SALEEN S7

Base price: $375,000

Specifications
General

Layout	front engine, rear drive
Wheelbase (in.)	106.2
Overall length (in.)	188.0
Overall width (in.)	78.3
Overall height (in.)	41.0
Curb weight (lbs.)	2,750

Drivetrain

Engine	ohv V-8
Bore x stroke (mm)	104.8x101.6
Displacement (cc)	7,000
Horsepower	550 bhp @ 6,400 rpm
Torque	520 lb-ft @ 5,000 rpm
Transmission	six-speed manual

Body & Chassis

Front suspension	upper and lower A-arms, coil springs, tube shocks, anti-roll bar
Rear suspension	upper and lower A-arms, coil springs, tube shocks, anti-roll bar
Steering	rack and pinion
Brakes	15.0-inch vented discs front, 14.0-inch vented discs rear, ABS
Wheels	19x9-1/2 front, 19x13 rear
Tires	275/30ZR-19 front, 335/25ZR-19 rear

Performance

0 to 60 mph	under 4.0 seconds
Top speed	more than 200 mph

chapter 5
GREAT BRITAIN

The best way to understand and appreciate a modern British supercar is to drive an old British supercar. While heritage tends to play an important role with all the builders of exotic cars, it never seems to show through quite the way it does in Great Britain.

A definite straight line can be drawn from Jaguar's famous Le Mans–winning C- and D-Type race cars of the 1950s forward to the 1990s mid-engine XJ220. That vein of history continues right on to the twenty-first century with the XK180 and F-Type Jaguar show cars, unaffected by the fact that these firms are now owned by Ford . . . that's the momentum of British heritage.

An Aston Martin DBS3 or DBR1 racer—also from the 1950s—is the obvious father of the famed DB4GT (James Bond's car), which begot the Aston V8 GTs that eventually led to the Virage and the thinking that led to the modern DB7.

Again it is this matter of heritage, cars so British through-and-through that even if the DB7 began as a Jaguar and was reengineered into an Aston, it still fits in the pattern.

Drive an old Lotus Elite, an Elan, or a Europa—very lightweight, small four-cylinder engine, fiberglass body—and you'll come to understand the ancestry of the 2000 Lotus Turbo Esprit even as it is sold today with a high-horsepower V-8.

You also need to drive these British supercars on British roads. Not broad, booming German autobahns, but the narrow, twisting, hedge-lined roads that are just a few miles from England's exotic car centers, such as Newport Pagnell, Hethel, and Coventry. Like their history, these lanes of macadam are an influential part of English exotic cars.

It's said there will always be an England, and, thankfully, that means there will always be a Jaguar, an Aston Martin, and a Lotus.

MCLAREN F1

During his years as a successful designer of Grand Prix cars, Gordon Murray was famous for his thoughtful and innovative race cars. So, when the engineer turned away from Formula 1 racing and designed an exotic automobile, it only stood to reason that it would be an equally intelligent machine.

Hence, the McLaren F1—what might be termed the Einstein of the exotics.

Peter Stevens gets credit for the shape of the McLaren, which is notable for being different from other exotic cars. Generally, supercars appear to be broad-shouldered and a bit flamboyant with front and rear spoilers designed to

Thanks to lightweight construction, the F1 weighs in at just over 2,800 pounds and, thanks to the BMW power, gets to 60 miles per hour in just 3.4 seconds, through 100 miles per hour in 7.7 seconds, and on to a top speed of more than 225 miles per hour.

Opposite: McLaren's F1 might be called the "thinking man's exotic car" thanks to the fact that it was designed by automotive engineering genius Gordon Murray. The exterior design was created to provide a top speed in excess of 200 miles per hour and yet keep the F1 stable with no external wings or other spoilers.

Gordon Murray asked BMW for a 550-horsepower V-12 to power the new exotic car, but the German automaker managed to coax 627 horsepower and 479 lb-ft of torque from the 6.1-liter, 48-valve powerplant.

add downforce or, in some cases, to add to the "ohh and ahh" factor.

That's not what Murray had in mind. The engineer didn't want his exotic cluttered with add-on aerodynamic devices, so he included them inside the automobile. Instead of being pushed down on the road by air passing over external wings and front lip spoilers, the McLaren is basically pulled down to the road by air channeled under it through a ground-effects undertray diffuser.

There's more to it than that, of course, like a little rear spoiler that pops up during high-speed braking to help keep the aerodynamic center of pressure in balance . . . all of which is leaps and bounds ahead of the simple spoilers that often seem to clutter the exterior of otherwise artful-looking exotic cars.

Murray-thought continues inside, where you find the driver in a seat that is in the middle of the car and somewhat ahead of the passenger seats. There is a variety of reasons for this position. One is to provide a GP driver's perspective when driving. Another is to have the straight-ahead seating-pedal-steering-and-instrument layout of a single-seater, which is almost impossible to achieve in a normal mid-engine exotic.

It's a bit of a step into the driver's seat, but then you settle down cockpit-style, feeling a bit like a fighter pilot. The detailing is superb, like the light gauge faces, the high-tech sound system controls in the center console, the machined pedals, and a red starter button under its flip-up safety cover. No wonder you feel like a jet pilot.

With the passengers sitting to the side and slightly back from the driver, they get an unusual view of the world, one that leaves them feeling slightly vulnerable. Behind the passengers and ahead of the rear wheels are small luggage compartments.

While Williams may be BMW's newest partner in GP racing, their first time around was with Brabham, where Murray was chief designer. So, the engineer went back to his former partners for the engine for his exotic car.

In his talks with BMW, Murray asked for a lightweight, non-turbocharged powerplant that would put out at least 550 horsepower. The company's compact 60-degree V-12 was the logical basis, and engineer Paul Rosche—who worked with Murray in the GP days—led the project. The displacement of the aluminum V-12 is 6.1 liters, and it has such expected features as dual camshafts on each cylinder head, four valves per cylinder, and all the latest electronic engine controls.

What is unusual is the fact that such a large-displacement engine produces not the 550 horsepower or 90.2 horsepower per-liter requested by Murray, but 627 or an impressive 102.8

Among the unusual features of the McLaren is three-across seating with the driver in the middle. The layout makes it more difficult to get in, but being on the centerline gives the driver more of an open-wheel driving experience.

horsepower from each liter. And there's plenty of torque, too, 479 lb-ft available from 4,000 to 7,000 rpm, which is just 500 rpm shy of the redline. Behind the BMW is a six-speed manual gearbox feeding the rear wheels.

Under the skin are upper and lower A-arm suspensions, with rack-and-pinion steering and brakes with no power assist. The McLaren has vented, cross-drilled discs, with the rears fed extra cooling air during high-speed braking.

With Murray's emphasis on saving weight, the F1 scales in at only 2,840 pounds, meaning it is 1.1 inch longer than a Ruf CTR, but weighs 350 pounds less. With that heavy-duty BMW power, a McLaren in U.S. trim gets to 60 miles per hour in 3.4 seconds, to 100 miles per hour in a mere 7.7 seconds, and—if you have the courage and plenty of road—a top speed of some 230 miles per hour.

Although the exotic-car market collapsed after its debut, the McLaren F1 sold out its entire production run of 100. The car was never meant to be sold in the United States, but was eventually put through a rigorous compliance program by Dick Fritz's Ameritech company. While a basic McLaren F1 cost only $890,000, the price of making the car U.S. Feds-ready added $160,000 plus the owner had to pay an $81,120 gas-guzzler tax.

Hey, it's only money.

MCLAREN F1
(U.S. Specification)

Base price:	$890,000 (As certified for sale in the United States)

Specifications

General

Layout	mid-engine, rear drive
Wheelbase (in.)	107.0
Overall length (in.)	168.8
Overall width (in.)	71.6
Overall height (in.)	44.9
Curb weight (lbs.)	2,840

Drivetrain

Engine	dohc 48-valve V-12
Bore x stroke (mm)	86.0x87.0
Displacement (cc)	6,064
Horsepower	627 bhp @ 7,400 rpm
Torque	479 lb-ft @ 4,000 rpm
Transmission	six-speed manual

Body & Chassis

Front suspension	unequal-length upper and lower A-arms, coil springs, tube shocks, anti-roll bar
Rear suspension	unequal-length upper and lower A-arms, coil springs, tube shocks, anti-roll bar
Steering	rack and pinion
Brakes	13.1-inch vented discs front, 12.0-inch vented discs rear
Wheels	17x9 front, 17x11-1/2 rear
Tires	235/45ZR-17 front, 315/45ZR-17 rear

Performance

0 to 60 mph	3.4 seconds
Top speed	230 mph

ASTON MARTIN DB7 VANTAGE

Newport Pagnell is about two hours north of London, and if you drive down its main street into town from the motorway, you can't miss Aston Martin. Set in red brick buildings on both sides of the road, it looks like a movie set for Ye Olde English Motor Manufacturer.

Aston is perhaps the most quaint-looking exotic carmaker in the world, but don't be fooled. This vest-pocket-sized division of the Ford Motor Company builds one of the most delightfully deceiving supercars on the planet. Not in Newport Pagnell, but just outside the small city of Banbury. There, in

An important part of every British exotic car is its heritage. Aston Martin's V-12-powered DB7 convertible in the foreground is a direct descendent of the company's famous DBR1 race car, which won the 24 Hours of Le Mans in 1959. With the DBR1 in the background are its winning drivers, Carroll Shelby (right) and Roy Salvadori.

As in all Astons, the DB7 features Connolly leather upholstery and Wilton carpeting. While there is a standard palette of colors for the car's exterior paint and interior appointments, the automaker will customize customers' cars to their every wish.

the former mill made modern to assemble Jaguar XJ220s, Aston makes DB7 Vantages.

It didn't start out to be an Aston. Originally, the chassis was developed by another Ford division, Jaguar, as its coupe. When it was decided the car was too small to be the needed Jag, it was inherited by Aston to become the DB7, and Jaguar went on to create the larger XJS.

When introduced in 1996, the DB7 had a supercharged inline-six and received high praise from the press. The bodywork was designed by Ian Callum and beautifully carries on the Aston Martin style and image in both coupe and convertible forms. Inside each DB7 is one of those classic English

automobile interiors, with Connolly leather-upholstered seats and just the right array of white-on-black gauges. It is both a comfortable and exciting place for driver and passenger, if a bit tight on space for anyone over 6 feet tall.

One of the few remaining automakers that can custom-build complete cars for its clients, Aston will personally tailor your DB7. Have a favorite color you'd like on the exterior or inside your Aston? Prefer carbon fiber instead of wood on the dash? It's yours for the asking . . . and, of course, the paying.

Standard equipment on every DB7's dashboard is a big red button. Push it when the key is on and you start a powerful mechanical rush up ahead of you . . the reason why the

Vantage qualifies for a book on exotic cars. In 1999, Aston replaced the supercharged six with the first V-12 used in its automobiles.

The V-12 began as a pair of Ford Duratec V-6s that were then blended and built by another Ford subsidiary, the famous race-engine firm of Cosworth Engineering. As installed in the Vantage, the V-12 has a block and twin-cam heads of aluminum alloy, four valves per cylinder, and all the latest in electronic engine management. Just shy of 6 liters, the V-12 boasts 420 brake horsepower at 6,000 rpm and 400 lb-ft of torque at 5,000 rpm.

Aston offers the Vantage with either the five-speed ZF automatic also used in BMW's 750i or the six-speed manual Dodge fits in its Vipers. Either is acceptable, because with all that horsepower and a remarkably wide torque band—85 percent of that 400 lb-ft is available by 1,500 rpm—even the manual DB7 can almost be driven like an automatic.

It's sweet power that's deceptive in its smoothness, so you have trouble believing the watches when the manual-gearbox DB7 hums to 60 miles per hour in just under 5 seconds. The automatic adds only about 0.2 seconds to that timing.

DB7s can be purchased as either a coupe or convertible, with prices that hover around the $140,000 to $150,000 area. Behind the handsome machines are not only the technical might of Ford, but also decades of history, including wins in the world's most famous sports car races.

ASTON MARTIN DB7 VANTAGE

Base price: $140,000

Specifications

General

Layout	front engine, rear drive
Wheelbase (in.)	102.0
Overall length (in.)	184.7
Overall width (in.)	72.0
Overall height (in.)	50.0
Curb weight (lbs.)	4,118

Drivetrain

Engine	dohc 48-valve V-12
Bore x stroke (mm)	88.2x78.8
Displacement (cc)	5,935
Horsepower	420 bhp @ 6,000 rpm
Torque	400 lb-ft @ 5,000 rpm
Transmission	six-speed manual

Body & Chassis

Front suspension	upper and lower A-arms, coil springs, tube shocks, anti-roll bar
Rear suspension	upper and lower A-arms with longitudinal control arms, coil springs, tube shocks, anti-roll bar
Steering	rack and pinion, power assist
Brakes	14.1-inch vented discs front, 13.1-inch vented discs rear, ABS
Wheels	8x18 front, 9x18 rear
Tires	245/40ZR-18 front, 265/35R-18 rear

Performance

0 to 60 mph	4.9 seconds
Top speed	165 mph (limited)

Aston increased the power of its DB7 by replacing the original supercharged inline-six with a 5,935-cc V-12 that has 420 horsepower and 400 lb-ft of torque. The engine's smooth character deceives you into thinking the car could not possibly get to 60 miles per hour in 4.9 seconds . . . but it does.

To go with the power is an upper and lower A-arm independent suspension at each end of the car. The brakes are huge ventilated discs, and the tires are wide and squat. Aston DB7s aren't the sort of automobiles you expect to ride rough and rumbly even on narrow, high-crowned, English roads, and they do not.

But while the DB7 Vantage may slice smoothly down Britain's famous hedgerow lined lanes, it won't abandon you when the going gets twisty. Let the roadway cut sharply left or right, or should it suddenly rise or drop out from under you, the Aston stays firmly planted. It may lean a bit more than hard-edged exotics—that goes with the smoother ride—but it will never deceive you.

Aston Martin's DB7 Vantage won't raise the hair on the back of your neck like some exotics. It will not growl or snarl or overtly tempt you to lay twin black streaks of rubber every time you leave a stop sign. Then again, it isn't as demanding as those hard-edged exotics, so you cannot only cover ground at a great rate, but be exhilarated without being exhausted at the end of the road.

JAGUAR XJ220

"It makes sense that a Jaguar XJ220's speedometer reads up to 220 miles per hour, and right now the white needle is just shy of that mark. Davy Jones, whose usual Jaguar seat is an IMSA XJR-14 race car, is strapped into the leather-covered driver's seat next to me. We're a couple of feet this side of what now looks like a solid steel ribbon of double Armco barrier. There are 542 turboed horsepower humming behind us and 8 miles of banked circle arcing ahead . . ."

According to the technicians at Fiat's Nardo high-speed circle in southern Italy, Davy had the Jaguar pegged at 218 to

Some would argue that Jaguar's XJ220 was the sleekest, prettiest supercar from the 1990s. Designer Keith Helfet was responsible for the shape, which takes traditional Jaguar design thinking, from the old D-Type to the sensational mid-engine XJ13 race car, and blends it into a road machine.

220 miles per hour. It was quite a ride I was taking for *Road & Track*, strapped snugly in the passenger's seat wearing a racing suit and helmet, watching Davy make little corrections to allow for minute track imperfections.

And what is the most lasting memory of that high-speed run? That of all the exotic cars of the past two decades, Jaguar's XJ220 was the limousine of the lot. Not a rough-edged, raspy pseudo race car. Never the twitchy ill-behaving beast. But just the sort of supercar one would expect of the company that has both won the 24 Hours of Le Mans and built decades of comfortable XJ sedans.

Jaguar's XJ220 began as an after-hours project of Jaguar employees led by Director of Product Engineering Jim Randall.

The highly regarded engineer wanted to build a Group B Jaguar a la Porsche 959. Suppliers donated materials. Company designer Keith Helfet, working with studio head Geoff Lawson, contributed the exterior design, while Nick Hull did the interior.

The resulting XJ220 concept car was unveiled at the 1988 Birmingham Show: long, sleek, silver, V-12, four-wheel drive, 200-mile-per-hour top speed . . . and such a hit that Jaguar decided to build the car.

Lacking the manpower and facilities to build a series of mid-engine exotic cars, Jaguar turned the project over to JaguarSport, which it jointly ran with Tom Walkinshaw's TWR.

Developing the XJ200 for production necessitated changes.

Supercar interiors tend to have a more exotic look, but the Jaguar's is elegant . . . as a Jaguar should be. Nick Hull designed the XJ220's interior, including seats that are as speed-worthy as they are sumptuous. To keep the low-roof interior from causing a confining "bunker effect," the roof has a tinted glass panel.

The only disappointment in the XJ220 is its engine. It is certainly powerful enough, with 542 horsepower and 475 lb-ft of torque, but the turbocharged V-6 has a rather agricultural sound and rattle to it. The powerplant is, however, well displayed and viewed through a large glass engine cover.

Sadly, the V-12 had to go, its place taken by a 3.5-liter twin-turbo V-6. The four-wheel drive was replaced with two-wheel drive. The car was shortened by 10 inches in length—8 from the wheelbase—cutting weight some 700 pounds to 3,025 pounds. Shortening the XJ220 did nothing to harm the looks of the XJ220, which has all the beauty and grace expected of a Jaguar . . . plus an aerodynamic drag coefficient of 0.36.

The interior is appropriate to Jaguar's reputation, with the closest thing to comfy overstuffed seats you'll find in a supercar. The full array of gauges includes a few, like the clock and turbo boost gauge, fitted to the door. There are luxuries, such as air conditioning, electric window lifts, and an Alpine stereo with a 6-CD changer. And to keep the low roof from creating a "bunker effect" interior, a smoked glass roof lets in the light.

The turbo V-6 was adapted from Jaguar's XJR-10 and -11 race cars, but traces its history back through the Rover Metro 6R4 rally car. In the super Jag, the dry-sump V-6 has twin cams, four valves per cylinder, and a pair of turbos to produce 542 horsepower at 7,000 rpm and 475 lb-ft of torque. Behind the turbo V-6 is a five-speed manual transmission.

Jaguar's factory for the XJ220 was a converted ancient mill in Bloxham outside Banbury where Aston Martin DB7s would later be made. Inside, it looked like an assembly line of race cars. In one end came chassis tubs made of aluminum honeycomb and paneling. A steel roll cage, upper and lower A-arm suspensions fore and aft, and 90-liter fuel cells were installed. On went AP racing discs brakes with neither power assist nor ABS. Add the drivetrain and aluminum body panels and bolt-on Speedline wheels fitted with Bridgestone Expedia tires.

Out the other end went 350 finished XJ220s . . . to a troubled existence. Between the time when prospective owners—many of them speculating in supercar futures—plunked down $75,000 deposits on the $500,000 Jaguars and the start of production at Bloxham, the market for supercars went in the tank. Buyers backed out, lawsuits flew. Jaguar wasn't able to sell all of its XJ220s until mid-1999. By the end of the century, XJ220s were appreciating back to their original price.

Those who took possession of their XJ200s got what might be the prettiest of the supercars: elegance in a class where racy beauty is the norm. They got precise supercar handling balanced by possibly the smoothest ride in the genre. A rush to 60 miles per hour in the brief span of 3.8 seconds, the V-6 spoiled only by a rattling engine noise that sounds too agricultural.

And an appropriate top speed of 220 . . . just ask me, I've been there.

Previous pages: **Jaguars are supposed to look sleek, and the XJ220 does just that. The acceleration from the 3.5-liter turbo V-6 gets the 3,234-pound supercar to 60 miles per hour in 3.8 seconds, and we can personally attest to the fact the great cat can get to well over 200 miles per hour.**

JAGUAR XJ220

Base price: $500,000

Specifications
General

Layout	mid-engine, rear drive
Wheelbase (in.)	103.9
Overall length (in.)	194.1
Overall width (in.)	87.4
Overall height (in.)	45.3
Curb weight (lbs.)	3,025

Drivetrain

Engine	turbocharged dohc V-6
Bore x stroke (mm)	94.0x84.0
Displacement (cc)	3,496
Horsepower	542 bhp @ 7,000 rpm
Torque	475 lb-ft @ 4,500 rpm
Transmission	five-speed manual

Body & Chassis

Front suspension	upper and lower A-arms, coil springs, tube shocks, anti-roll bar
Rear suspension	upper and lower A-arms, coil springs, tube shocks, anti-roll bar
Steering	rack and pinion
Brakes	13.0-inch discs front, 11.8-inch discs rear
Wheels	9x17 front, 14x18 rear
Tires	255/45ZR-17 front, 345/35ZR-18 rear

Performance

0 to 60 mph	3.8 seconds
Top speed	220 mph

LOTUS ESPRIT

Among the world's exotic cars, the Lotus Esprit is the grand-daddy. The old man. The survivor. In an automotive world in which everything seems so new and ever changing, the Esprit is, well, no spring chicken.

And yet if you put a new Esprit in about any parking lot in the world, it will draw a crowd of admirers. They aren't interested in the car's history. All they know is that it looks like a supercar . . . and it is.

Famed designer Giorgetto Giugiaro drew the original Esprit show car introduced in 1974, the year the Lamborghini Countach went into production. It was two years before the Esprit was in showrooms, but that still puts its on-sale date

Although it is still an exciting-looking exotic car, the basic Giugiaro-designed shape of the Esprit has been around since 1974, proving that good design is lasting.

two years before Mario Andretti won his Formula 1 championship in a Lotus in 1978.

The original Esprit was a fairly basic car. There was a mid-engine, backbone chassis—a Lotus trademark—with independent suspension front and rear. Power came from the company's 2.0-liter four through a five-speed manual gearbox. The body was formed of fiberglass and smelled of it, so when you worked your way down and into the seat of an early Esprit, there was a certain kit-car aroma to it. Fit and finish were okay, but not up to Ferrari standards.

Lotus founder and designer Colin Chapman was famous for keeping things mechanically simple and light, and the Esprit suffered in some ways for that, at least in the way of finish and amenities.

But what a treat to drive. Light and precise, the Lotus would scamper along the narrow, hedge-lined roads around the company's Hethel, England, factory like a jackrabbit that can quickly and confidently stop, start, jink left, and scamper right, always ahead of the fox.

Over the decades, the Esprit went through many changes. Come 1981 there was a significant power boost with the first Turbo Esprit and its 2.2-liter 210-horsepower turbocharged four. Using some of the money earned when it developed the failed DeLorean gullwing sports car, Lotus upgraded the entire

Under the Esprit's fiberglass body is the classic Lotus backbone frame, with the sort of independent-suspension chassis expected from a company so renowned for its fine-handling automobiles.

Esprits have always been comfortable cars, with the driver nestled in a leather-covered seat between the tall center console and the door. And with the large sunroof, the car has a very open feeling, making the Esprit a delight for a quick, fair-weather drive.

chassis. Within a decade, that same turbo engine would put out some 264 horsepower in the United States.

While the original wedge shape of the Esprit survived, as the car moved though the 1990s, it was modified, made smoother, and filled out in the right places, like a well-trained athlete. So despite its age, the fiberglass-bodied Esprit has remained visually contemporary . . . and has probably the nicest-looking rear wing in the exotic car business.

What really kicked the Lotus in the modern times was the Type 918. That is the company's code name for an all-aluminum V-8 of its own design that debuted in the Esprit in 1996. Don't forget, in addition to being an automaker, Lotus is

famous for its engineering, one example being the Corvette ZR1 V-8.

For its own supercar, Lotus developed a 3,506-cc V-8 with four valves per cylinder and a pair of turbochargers. While most companies go to outside firms for items such as fuel injection and engine management systems, Lotus created its own. And true to the Colin Chapman pursuit of light weight, the entire engine weighs only 485 pounds, "dressed" and ready to install.

In the Esprit with its five-speed manual gearbox, you'll be at 60 miles per hour in 4.4 seconds. Stay in fifth to the redline and you'll see the speedo needle hovering around 178 miles per hour.

At the 1996 Geneva Auto Show, Lotus unveiled the latest engine for the Esprit, a lightweight 3.5-liter, 32-valve, twin-turbo V-8 with 350 horsepower, which is enough to power the car to 60 miles per hour in just 4.4 seconds.

To go with all the added power, Lotus has continually developed the backbone chassis of the Esprit. The front suspension has upper and lower A-arms, while the rear design uses upper and lower transverse links with trailing arms. Brembo ABS disc brakes are inside the alloy wheels fitted with squatty profile Michelin Pilot SX tires.

Lotus hasn't forgotten the interior. Although the fundamental layout is as it was in the late 1970s, this Esprit bears no resemblance to that ancestor, thanks to Connolly leather seats and walnut trim, with sound and air conditioning systems to coddle you.

And at a price in the mid-$80,000s, the Lotus Esprit V-8 is a relative bargain . . . all that luxury and power, but without losing the jackrabbit senses of that original Esprit.

LOTUS ESPRIT

Base price:	$85,250

Specifications

General

Layout	mid-engine, rear drive
Wheelbase (in.)	96.0
Overall length (in.)	172.0
Overall width (in.)	73.5
Overall height (in.)	45.3
Curb weight (lbs.)	3,043

Drivetrain

Engine	dohc 32-valve V-8
Bore x stroke (mm)	83.0x81.0
Displacement (cc)	3,506
Horsepower	350 bhp @ 6,500 rpm
Torque	295 lb-ft @ 4,250 rpm
Transmission	five-speed manual

Body & Chassis

Front suspension	upper and lower A-arms, coil springs, tube shocks, anti-roll bar
Rear suspension	upper and lower transverse links, trailing arms, coil springs, tube shocks, anti-roll bar
Steering	rack and pinion, power assist
Brakes	11.6-inch vented discs front, 11.8-inch vented discs rear, ABS
Wheels	17x8.5 front, 18x10 rear
Tires	235/40R-17 front, 285/35ZR-18 rear

Performance

0 to 60 mph	4.4 seconds
Top speed	178 mph

JAGUAR

JOHN HEILIG

Acknowledgments

William Lyons was a genius. He had the foresight to create a product—initially assembling that product out of readily available components—that the public fell in love with and bought. With the profits gained from these simple products, he developed more complex products and established an automobile company that has persisted for over 70 years.

That company, of course, is Jaguar. And while Lyons began by building motorcycle sidecars with his neighbor, William Walmsley, the cars he created toward the end of his life were exotic sports cars and luxury sedans that had no equal in the world.

Like most youths of the 1950s, I loved the legend of Jaguar. I had an MG budget, but a Jaguar was always the goal. Eventually, I was able to buy an aged 3.4 sedan (for $300) that at least brought me some of the thrill of owning the sports cars. But despite the fact that the 3.4 appeared to have been built with quarter-inch-thick steel in the fenders, the transmission was fragile and broke. I wasn't up to attempting the repairs or restoration, so I traded it in on a more practical economy car.

Today, the products of Jaguar are luxury sedans and one of the best sports cars in the world, the XK8. Things haven't changed much over the last 45 years. In 1989, Ford stepped in and rescued what is one of the last bastions of a once-thriving British automobile industry. The company that has survived after the Ford take-over is not emasculated, as many feared. It is, instead, stronger than ever and retains a level of independence that permits it to continue to develop its sedans and sports cars with a distinctly British flavor.

Many people helped in this project, most particularly Chris Gennone of Communication Dynamics International, who was its catalyst and who provided support, fact-checking and editorial assistance. Another source of great moral, editorial and photographic support was Len Alcaro of Jaguar Cars North America, who checked the manuscript and also made cars available to photograph.

Special thanks must be given to Don Vorderman, who graciously allowed me to use portions of his unpublished work on Bill Lyons. Also, thanks to Margaret Harrison for her photographs and to the Automobile Quarterly Photo and Research Library for supplying photographs when the original source dried up.

Car owners whose vehicles are in here include the late Jim Spooner, and Les Jackson, Jaguar Cars of North America,

As with anything I do, this couldn't have been completed without the love and support of my wife, Florence, our three daughters, Susan, Sharon and Laura, and their honeys. Well, it could have been completed, but it wouldn't have been worth it.

The Prewar Years

There would never have been a Jaguar car if there had never been a William Lyons. And Lyons might never have begun his life's work if there had not been a William Walmsley. Lyons, who was eventually to be knighted for his work with Jaguar, was designer, engineer, visionary and activist for Jaguar and the companies that would precede it. When he retired in 1972, the company lost its driving force and spirit, and lost its way for a couple of years. That it has been able to revive itself in the past 25 years is a credit to the organization that Lyons created and the men who worked so hard to save it, particularly John Egan, who would also be knighted.

1932 SS1 FIXED HEAD COUPE
The SS1 was the first full automobile built by William Lyons and William Walmsley. Introduced in October 1931, the SS1 had a modified 6-cylinder Standard chassis supplied by John Black of the Standard Motor Company. The underslung frame provided for a low body. Lyons wanted a body that was even lower than the production car, but Walmsley signed off on the slightly higher version when Lyons was in the hospital with appendicitis.

Don Vorderman, former editor of *Automobile Quarterly*, said of Lyons: "Had he done nothing else but serve as chief stylist at Jaguar, had he done nothing more than supervise the development of the SS100, or the XK120, or the prewar or postwar saloons, his place in the pantheon of automotive design would be secure. The remarkable fact is that he did all of these cars and a dozen or so more while simultaneously directing the operations of a major automobile company.

"A varied assortment of talents were present, all functioning smoothly and independently within him. Lyons' exquisite sense of design was merely one, but perhaps the most evident of his gifts. He also oversaw the engineering and advertising departments. He orchestrated their racing programs. He was a diplomat, too, having to deal with unions and successive governments that were all too often inclined to interfere with this or that aspect of his business.

"Of course he didn't create these legendary designs entirely on his own. There were a number

William Lyons' love of motorcycles is what led to the formation of Jaguar Cars. Lyons met William Walmsley, who had established a small factory to build motorcycle sidecars in the garage behind his home. Lyons bought a sidecar from Walmsley, and the two decided to go into business together to make sidecars. They grew the business to include building of custom bodies for Austin chassis, and eventually began designing their own cars on Standard chassis. From these Standard Swallows the Jaguar was born.

of talented people to assist him, most notably Malcolm Sayer, but while he was there, Bill Lyons had the first and last word on the design of every car Jaguar built." But we're getting ahead of ourselves.

William Lyons was born September 4, 1901, in the village of Blackpool. His father was an Irish musician who visited Blackpool one year as a member of an orchestra that was hired for holiday entertainment. Lyons Sr. never returned home, because he met and fell in love with a local girl,

Minnie. They were married and William Sr. opened a music store and sold pianos. When William Jr. was born, his father's music business was well-established.

As a youth, Lyons apprenticed at Crossley Motors Ltd. When he was 18, he began working for Brown and Mallalieu, a local car dealer, as a junior salesman.

Like most youths of the era, Lyons liked motorcycles. England had not yet been blessed with a "people's car" like the Model T Ford, so young dandies from middle-class families would buy motorcycles and attach sidecars as basic transportation.

Lyons first met William Walmsley when Walmsley's family moved into the same Blackpool neighborhood. Walmsley had been developing a small business in the family garage building sidecars for motorcycles. Lyons, who had owned an early Harley-Davidson, discovered Walmsley's business and bought a sidecar. The two eventually decided to join forces in 1922, but Lyons was still under the legal age of 21 required to acquire loans from banks. They had to wait until September 4, 1922, before founding the Swallow Sidecar Company with £1000 (around $5,000). The factory was at 7-9 Bloomfield Rd., in Blackpool.

Swallow Sidecars built as many as 10 zeppelin-shaped sidecars a week, fitted to chassis built by Montgomery's of Coventry. The most expensive chassis they sold cost £30.

In 1924, the same year Lyons married Greta Brown, Tourist Trophy entrants with Swallow sidecars finished second, third, and fourth in the annual motorcycle race on the Isle of Man.

Two years later, the company moved to larger premises in Cocker Street. It changed its name to the Swallow Sidecar & Coach Building Company because they had begun offering repairs to auto-

The original Swallow factory was in Blackpool, where "side cars and light car bodies" were manufactured, and coaches were painted and trimmed. The small Austin Swallows are lined up in front of the factory, showing their trim bodies that attracted someone who wanted the economy of an Austin Seven but not its utilitarian looks.

mobile bodies. This was all in preparation for a new business that would commence in January 1927, but which began with the introduction of the Austin Seven in 1922.

The Austin Seven was a genuine British car for the mass market, but it also proved to be a very good chassis on which to build custom bodies. Called the Seven because of its taxable horsepower, the little Austin was simple in design and execution. Lyons knew that he could buy a chassis for little money and could build a custom-bodied car for a reasonable asking price. The factory cars were also plain and wouldn't provide any competition for a custom design.

Lyons and Walmsley bought an Austin Seven chassis in 1927 for £100 and built their first car, designed by Lyons. It was a two-seater sports model with a top that was hinged at the rear. When this application proved to be awkward in the wind, the hinging was moved to the front for production models. Success of the Austin Swallow

The Swallow sidecars were aluminum, torpedo-shaped and relatively aerodynamic. They provided the youth of the 1920s with a means of transporting themselves and a companion, since there was no equivalent of the inexpensive Model T Ford in England at the time. Later, the Austin Seven would serve that purpose, so Lyons was fortunate that he was born at the right time.

was assured when Henley's of London, a large Austin dealer, ordered 500 cars.

In mid-1928, a four-door Swallow sedan joined the lineup, also built on an Austin Seven chassis. Once again, the company changed its name, to the Swallow Coachbuilding Company,

1935 SS1 AIRLINE SALOON
Before they were Jaguars, William Lyons built the SS1, which was the first car totally designed by the Swallow Coachbuilding Company, predecessor to Jaguar. The SS1 was built on a modified 6-cylinder Standard chassis, supplied to Lyons and William Walmsley for this purpose. With a low-slung chassis and the engine set back 7 inches from where it was in the Standard, stylish bodies were possible. This body is an Airline Saloon, or sedan. Airline designs were the fastbacks of the 1930s, and similar products from companies such as MG remain stylish to today. *Margaret Harrison*

indicating future intent. Swallow still built motor-cycle sidecars, and would through World War II, but automobiles would play a larger and larger role in the company's affairs.

"The (Swallow) bodies were attractive," wrote Ken Purdy. "They ran to split windshields, external sun visors, wire wheels, and good options in two-tone paint jobs—but the running gear under them was never up to the performance the coach-work seemed to promise."

In November 1928, Swallow moved to Coventry, England, in the center of the British automobile industry. It was the equivalent of a new American automobile manufacturer moving its operations to Detroit. The building was an old artillery shell-filling factory.

Swallow built cars on chassis supplied by Austin, Wolseley, Morris, Swift, Standard and the Fiat 509. Eventually, designs on the Morris chassis were abandoned when Morris began building a more sporty version of its own cars and called it MG.

In May 1931, John Black, managing direc-tor of the Standard Motor Company, agreed to sell a modified 6-cylinder Standard chassis to Swallow for the creation of Swallow's first total design, the SS1. Standard agreed to modify the

1936 SS1 AIRLINE DROPHEAD COUPE
SS Cars Ltd. built several body variations on the SS1 chassis. This Drophead Coupe is what is referred to in the United States as a convertible, with a removable top. Some drophead coupes had landau irons framing the C-pillar area of the top, but in the case of the SS1, the top is simpler. The Airline coupes were powered by 2,143 and 2,663 side valve 6-cylinder engines that were derived from the Standard 16 and Standard 20, respectively. *Margaret Harrison*

1936 SS1 AIRLINE SALOON
This SS1 Airline Saloon has a different rear treatment than the 1935 SS1 Airline Saloon. The rear styling is more conventional, with a square addition to the body for the trunk. *Margaret Harrison*

1934 SS1

By the time the 1934 SS1 was produced, the wheelbase had been extended 7 inches. The company had gone public in 1933, and co-founder William Walmsley had left. Lyons was in full control now, and the roofline of the 1934 SS1 reflected his taste more.

chassis by adding 3 inches to the wheelbase and stuffing in a higher axle ratio for more top speed—but of course, less acceleration. The frame was underslung and the engine was set back 7 inches. The first SS1 cars were introduced in October 1931 at the London Motor Show, along with the SS2, which was essentially an SS1 with a 30-inch shorter chassis. Incidentally, nobody is certain as to the exact meaning of "SS," since it was never well-defined. It could have stood for "Swallow Sports," "Standard Swallow," or "Swallow Side-car," but neither Lyons nor Walmsley ever revealed what they were thinking.

Vorderman, an owner of numerous Jaguars, wrote, "It was with the announcement of the SS1 late in 1931, based on still another manufacturer's running gear, that Lyons burst out of obscurity to become one of the most respected figures in the British automobile business, a position he would occupy with dignity and grace for the rest of his life."

"The SS1 of 1932 knocked the British industry on its collective ear," Vorderman continued, "offering what journalists began calling 'The car with the 1,000 pound look'—that's nearly the price of a contemporary Bentley chassis—but it cost only £310. It was about that time that people began asking each other the question that would follow Jaguars around for years to come, 'How can they do it for the money?' The truth is that there was a great deal of profit to be made in the building and selling of coachbuilt motorcars in those days. In creating the SS1, Lyons had simply selected a proven, inexpensive chassis from the Standard Motor Company, had it slightly modified to his own specifications and then set up a production line to mass produce hand-built bodies for it, hundreds at a time. Simple."

The SS1 was known primarily for its style, rather than its performance. Both the coupe and two-door sedan had long hoods, flowing fenders, wire wheels and low rooflines. Actually, Lyons wanted a roofline that was even lower than the one that appeared on the cars, but Walmsley signed off on a more practical version when Lyons was in the hospital with appendicitis.

Based on the Standard 16 horsepower chassis, it was officially known as the SS Sixteen. Later, a larger 20 horsepower engine was also offered.

In 1933, the company's name was changed again, to SS Cars Ltd. William Lyons was named Chairman and Managing Director. In 1934, he proposed going public with the company. William Walmsley didn't share Lyons' ambition, and resigned amicably, turning total control of SS Cars over to Lyons. Walmsley was a practical engineer who was as happy tinkering with his model railroad trains as he was with cars.

The 1933 version of the SS1 had a 7-inch longer wheelbase and an underslung chassis, which gave a lower seating position and the lower roofline that Lyons had originally wanted.

The shorter SS2 that appeared at the same time as the SS1 was known as the "little brother" to the bigger car. The car was powered by 9, 10 and 12 horsepower Standard engines. The SS2 retained some of the panache of the bigger car, albeit in a more compact fashion.

Lyons introduced his first sports model, the SS90, early in 1935. It was soon followed by the more powerful SS100. Between the introductions, Lyons was also hard at work thinking of a new name for the cars. One of the names he considered was "Sunbeam," but the Rootes organization had secured the rights to that name. "Jaguar" was eventually chosen. But first, Lyons had to obtain permission from Armstrong-Siddely, another Coventry firm that had a tradition of giving big cat names to their airplane engines—Cougar, Cheetah and Lynx, for example.

The first car to carry that name, SS Jaguar, was a sedan version of the SS90 with wire wheels. A Tourer version of the car was also introduced in 1935. In September, the SS Jaguar 100 was advertised as "an entirely new SS for 1936." Priced at £385 ($1,900), and available in 1½ (1608cc) and 2½ (2662cc) liter versions, it generated more than 100 horsepower with the larger engine.

The extra power was derived from a head design by Harry Weslake, who was England's greatest expert on cylinder head design and who was working as a consultant to Lyons. His overhead valve head for the Standard six increased the power of the 2.6-liter engine from 70 to 100 horsepower. Working for Jaguar as chief engineer was William Heynes, who joined the company in 1935.

British writer John Stanford, in *The Sports Car*, said in 1962 of the first cars to bear the Jaguar name: "The introduction . . . of the first Jaguar series saw the beginnings of a really well-merited rise to spectacular success. Like the modern Jaguars, they were the work of William M. Heynes; and had very robust pushrod o.h.v. engines, well-chosen gear ratios, and rigid, rather stiffly sprung chassis. From the beginning, an open short-chassis version was available with 2½- or 3½-liter engine, at a very low price. The opulent and slightly flashy

1937 SS100
The SS100, introduced in 1935, was the first sport car introduced by Swallow. At this time, William Lyons was thinking of a new name for his company. Later versions of the SS100 would reflect that name—Jaguar. The SS100 was available in 1 1/2- and 2 1/2-liter versions, with the latter generating more than 100 horsepower. An SS100 could go 100 miles per hour, and the car was victorious in many races, hillclimbs and rallies.

lines, with their rakish swept wings and exaggerated long bonnets, have dated somewhat to modern eyes; and with the engine well forward in the very short chassis, handling was apt to leave some room for improvement. None the less, performance was available in full measure, both versions having top speeds closely approaching 100 miles per hour with considerable refinement."

American writer Ken Purdy wrote: "The SS1 and SS2 passenger cars were backed up by sports models—SS90, SS100—because Lyons, whose grasp of the fundamentals has never been less than brilliant, knew that competition effort was vital to sales, particularly in Europe and particularly then. A good SS100 would do 100 miles per hour and the model had notable successes in rallies, hill climbs, and sports car races. An SS100 won the International Alpine Trial of 1936 (and again in 1948) and the 1937 Royal Automobile Club Rally. The car would not only run, it had visual appeal to burn—a happy amalgam of the design points that were the desiderata of the day: big flat-lens headlights, flaring fenders, louvers all over the hood, curved dashboard carrying saucer-sized main instruments, a saddle gas tank hung astern. Only a few SS100s were made and the survivors are all classics." Tommy Wisdom and his wife Elsie (or "Bill") won the 1934 Alpine Trial in a factory-sponsored car.

In 1937, a 3½-liter version of the SS Jaguar 100 was introduced and immediately earned its stripes in competition. Sammy Newsome set the fastest time at the Shelsley Walsh hill climb in a 3½-liter SS100. Tommy Wisdom won the Long Handicap race at Brooklands in the same car.

"The SS100 is certainly one of the best looking sports cars ever built," wrote Don Vorderman. "Its swooping wings, extremely low build, its long, louvered bonnet, excellent cockpit and lavish instrumentation were the perfect expression of the sports car of the 1930s. The fact that it wasn't nearly as fast as it looked and had whimsical mechanical brakes seemed to have little effect on people's enthusiasm for it. A little more than 300 SS100s were made from 1936 into 1940, and according to the Jaguar Register, most of them are still around, arousing lustful thoughts among a new generation of car fanciers and appreciating at a dizzying rate."

For the 1938 model year, SS Jaguar sedans changed from wood frames to all-steel construction. The 3½-liter engine joined the sedan lineup that year as well. In a trend away from sportiness,

the spare tire was moved from its location on the fender to under the floor of the trunk.

Purdy: "To give the first SS Jaguar the performance its appearance called for, Lyons had asked the designer Harry Weslake to modify Standard's side-valve engine into an overhead-valve unit and had brought in W.M. Heynes to oversee engineering, the beginning of an enduring association with the company for both men. Heynes was a vice-chairman when he retired, full of honors, in 1969. Like the SS1 that had gone before it, the new SS Jaguar sedan looked more expensive than it was: a poll of dealers at its introduction showed an average price guess of £632 ($3,000), but the sticker was only £385 ($1885). The model was another smash success (it was called the poor man's Bentley, sometimes admiringly, sometimes not), and when everything stopped for World War II in September 1939, the firm was turning out 250 cars a week."

Jaguar's oldest established American dealership opened in 1938. Hugh Weidinger's Hempstead Motors on Long Island in New York became an imported car dealership that year and continues today, despite the death in 1995 of its founder. Hempstead Motors sells Jaguars and Mercedes-Benz today, among others but not in the same showroom.

As the 1930s drew to a close, SS Cars Ltd. was a growing company whose products had developed a strong following in England and had earned recognition in the United States as well. Unfortunately, that growth would be put on hold for six years when Great Britain declared war on Germany on September 3, 1939. SS Cars continued to use its remaining stocks of raw materials to build cars as late as the spring of 1940. In the last full year of car production before switching over to war production.

Chapter Two | # The 1940s

During the war, Swallow Sidecars, which was still a subsidiary of SS Cars, made more than 10,000 sidecars for British army motorcycles. In addition, the company built 50,000 trailers for the war effort in three different weight classes. Before hostilities began, SS had begun building wing tips for Stirling bombers. Another major effort was the repair and modification of Armstrong Whitworth "Whitley" bombers. Planes would be trucked to the Foleshill plant, where they would be repaired. After repairs were completed, they would be trucked to a local

1948 JAGUAR MARK IV DROPHEAD COUPE
The 1948 "Mark IV" Jaguar sedans and Drophead coupes were postwar versions of the prewar 3 1/2-, 2 1/2- and 1 1/2- liter versions. Although never officially recognized as the Mark IV by the factory, the postwar versions of these cars acquired these names. This Mark IV was powered by a 3 1/2-liter inline 6-cylinder engine that was soon overshadowed by the 6-cylinder XK engine that Jaguar had been developing during the war. This Drophead Coupe was capable of a top speed of 90 miles per hour.

airfield for tests. When the Whitley was taken out of service, SS repaired the "Welington." The company also made components for the Supermarine "Spitfire," Avro "Lancaster," DeHavilland "Mosquito" and Airspeed "Oxford" planes. As the war wound down, SS also built the complete center section of the Gloster "Meteor," which was England's first operational jet-powered fighter.

Toward the end of the war, Walter Hassan, who had joined SS cars from Bentley in 1938, and Claude Bailey designed two lightweight vehicles that were to be parachuted into battle. Called the VA and VB, they were both built with unibody construction and had 4-wheel independent suspensions. The VA was powered by a rear-mounted 1096 JAP motorcycle engine with chain drive. The VB had a Ford 10 horsepower engine and used a 3-speed transmission in a more conventional layout. Because of its rear-mounted engine, the VA had excellent traction, and the front end could be lifted by one man. Neither car pro-

1947 JAGUAR MK IV SEDAN
The first cars Jaguar built after the war were pre-war designs, the Mark IV 3 1/2-liter sedan. This Australian example shows the big headlights typical of pre-war cars, combined with a decidedly vertical architecture, as exemplified by the grille. The sweeping front fenders connect all the way to the rear, offering vestiges of running boards. *Margaret Harrison*

ceeded beyond the prototype stage because the development of transport aircraft went so quickly that it was possible for them to carry heavier loads, and air-drop full-sized Jeeps into battle, rather than specially designed lightweight vehicles.

Because of its location in England's industrial sector, Coventry received a lot of attention from German bombers. The center of the city was the focus of several Luftwaffe blitzkrieg raids. Ken Purdy wrote: ". . . the cathedral in Coventry, England. It had been burned and blown into rubble (during a ten-hour raid) on the night of November 14, 1940, by 500 Luftwaffe bombers in the longest raid England took during the war. Work to rebuild began the

All Jaguar sedans throughout the history of the company have exhibited long hoods, flowing fenders and short rear decks. This 1947 Mark IV 3 1/2-liter Sedan is typical of prewar designs converted to early postwar production. This angle also shows the semaphore turn signals, recessed door handles for both front and rear doors, and the wire wheels so beloved by William Lyons. *Margaret Harrison*

next day, the architect Sir Basil Spence planning the new cathedral on the site of the old, forming some of the standing ruins into it; the cornerstone was laid by the queen sixteen years and a bit later."

As for Jaguar, Browns Lane, 3 miles away from the cathedral, was only badly damaged once. Part of the roof of a newly constructed building on

Swallow Road was damaged. Don Vorderman recounts part of Jaguar's legend that has "Lyons and his chief engineer Bill Heynes . . . on air raid watches during World War II, mapping out their postwar plans. At times the obstacles must have seemed nearly insurmountable, with Coventry all but obliterated by the ten-hour air raid. The plan-

1947 JAGUAR MK IV SEDAN
Jaguars, especially the sedans, have featured the "leaper" hood ornament. Safety legislation of the 1980s dictated that such "unsafe" ornamentation should be removed to prevent injury to pedestrians. The leaper remains on select Jaguar sedans of the 1990s. *Margaret Harrison*

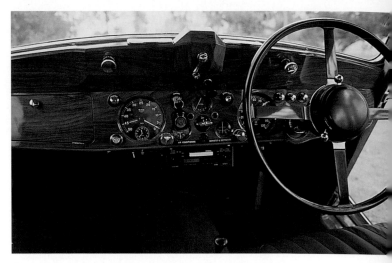

Part of the tradition of Jaguar cars has been the wood trim and leather upholstery. Wood-trimmed dash fascias date back to the earliest days of the company, as evidenced in this 1947 Mk IV sedan that was essentially a prewar car rushed into postwar production. This right-hand-drive Australian model also shows some interesting remnants of prewar design, such as the crank to open the bottom of the windshield, and a starter that is separate from the ignition. This car has been modified with the addition of a modern sound system. *Margaret Harrison*

ning continued, and when peace finally came, Jaguar was ready, though unfortunately the rest of the country was not." The company emerged from the war with a larger factory, expanded to increase war production.

One of Lyons' first actions as the war drew to its inevitable conclusion was to change the name of his company once again. SS Cars wasn't a popular name because "SS" had developed a strongly negative reputation during the war, thanks to Hitler's storm troopers (Schutzstaffel). Lyons responded by changing the name to Jaguar Cars Ltd., the name by which it has been known, in one form or another, for over half a century.

His next move was to get out of the sidecar business. Swallow Sidecars was sold, making Jaguar an automobile company once and for all.

Tube Investments bought the Swallow name, and continued producing sidecars until 1956, when it was absorbed by Watsonian, a Birmingham company that also made sidecars and had supplied William Walmsley with his first chassis in 1920. In the mid-1950s, Tube Investments dabbled briefly in the production of the Swallow Doretti sports car.

Lyons' final move was to buy the tooling that built the Standard 2½ and 3½-liter engines, making Jaguar a complete manufacturer. New equipment would be used to build the XK engines that were designed during the war.

The British government decreed that in order for manufacturers to obtain the raw materials necessary to return to production, 50 percent of that production must be exported. Car manufacturers in particular were urged to build vehicles for

Proper sedans of the 1930s carried fully equipped tool sets. In the case of the 1947 Jaguar Mk IV, which was a prewar design rushed into postwar production, the tool kit was included in the trunk and had the tools fitted into the case. Of interest, besides the important tire iron, screwdrivers, wrenches and hammer for wire wheel knock-offs, there is a pump to inflate tires, an oil can, and wire-cutter pliers. *Margaret Harrison*

export, especially to the United States, which was cash rich. Consequently, Jaguar added left-hand-drive cars to the mix late in 1945.

Jaguar was one of the first British manufacturers to return to production and was under way in July 1945. The first cars were modified prewar models. It wasn't until 1948 that a new model was introduced, the Mark V, which was available in sedan or convertible form with a 2½- or 3½-liter engine. This was the first Jaguar with independent front suspension and hydraulic brakes. As Ken Purdy wrote, "It was no ball of fire in performance and it had irritating detail flaws (for one, a heater

that couldn't cope with a brisk autumn day in Connecticut, never mind a Minnesota winter)." People loved the car anyway.

In 1946, Frank Raymond Wilton "Lofty" England joined Jaguar as service manager. He earned his nickname because of his height. England would lend his considerable organizational skills to Jaguar's racing program in the 1950s and would eventually become managing director of the company.

Lyons traveled to the United States for five weeks in 1948, appointing sales and service agents for Jaguar cars. With the government's export policies and Jaguar's potential for sales in the U.S.,

1948 JAGUAR MARK IV DROPHEAD COUPE
Besides the Saloon, or sedan, Jaguar also built Drophead coupe versions of the Mark IV. Still carried over from the prewar version of the car, the Drophead Coupe offered open-air driving. When compared with the SS1 Airlines, the grilles of the Mark IV Drophead Coupes seem taller and more massive. This is true, as the cars themselves were bigger. All were powered by the 2,663 cc 6-cylinder engine, that was now a Jaguar engine, since the factory that built the engines had been taken over from Standard by Jaguar. Note the large headlights, smaller "fog" lights, running lights on the fenders and landau irons on the top. *Margaret Harrison*

establishment of these agents was a smart move. Max Hoffman on the East Coast and Charles Hornburg on the West Coast were named the U.S. distributors. At the time, Jaguar sold 238 cars in the United States in 1948 and 158 in 1949. This was in an imported car market of 15,442 and 11,858, respectively. Incidentally, all the cars imported in those years were either British or French.

All the efforts of the company were not devoted entirely to the war during the struggle. William Heynes, who joined the company in 1935 as chief engineer, and Walter Hassan spent some of their time developing a new engine that would be used in Jaguar cars after the war. They worked on developing these "X" or experimental engines and were up to "XK" when they found a design they felt would work, a double overhead camshaft 6-cylinder of approximately 3.4 liters capacity. The XK engine proved to be the basis of Jaguar engines for more than 30 years after the end of hostilities.

The engine that Heynes and Hassan developed during the war was initially intended for a

This Australian Mark IV Drophead Coupe differs from the black one in that this car has the running lights on the fenders and the rear-view mirrors have been moved from the fender tops to the doors, where they are more practical. Both cars exhibit classic prewar Jaguar styling, with long flowing front fenders sweeping back to the rear fenders, which allows vestiges of running boards on both sides. *Margaret Harrison*

new sedan, which was to be a successor to the Mark V, but the new sedan wasn't ready in time. Therefore, Lyons and crew installed the engine in an aluminum-bodied sports car that was intended to be a stopgap low production vehicle. Since it had the 3.4-liter XK engine and engineers figured the car was capable of a top speed in the neighborhood of 120 miles per hour, it was named "XK120." The car was introduced in October 1948 at the London Motor Show. To confirm the car's potential—and its name—test driver Ron Sutton took an XK120 to the Jabbeke

autoroute in Belgium (a favorite high-speed test track for auto companies) and traveled 132.596 miles per hour over the measured mile. Actor Clark Gable was one of the first buyers of an XK120 after he met Lyons at a cocktail party in Hollywood. In his bylined article in the May 1950 *Road & Track* he claimed to have driven the car 124 miles per hour.

As John Stanford wrote in *The Sports Car*, "That such an engine could be made in large numbers at a relatively low price, and also run, as some have done, for 100,000 miles without over-

1949 JAGUAR MK V

Jaguar introduced the "interim" Mark V sedan when the XK engine that was supposed to go into it was still not ready for production. Hence, the Mark V was powered by the older 3 1/2- and 3 1/2-liter engines that were based on the old prewar Standard engines. What was most significant about the Mark V, though, was its modern chassis, an independent front suspension. The Mark V used 16-inch wheels rather than the 18-inch wheels of its predecessor. Styling was slightly more modern than the Mark IV, with headlights fared into the fenders.

122

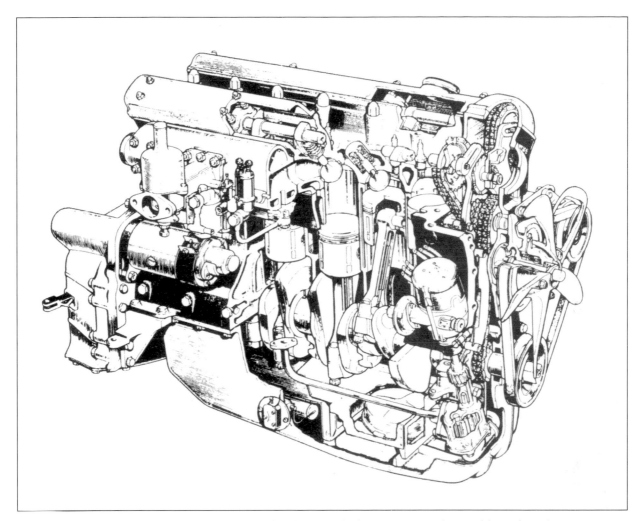

In 1948, Jaguar introduced the 3.4-liter double overhead cam 6-cylinder "XK" engine that would transform the company from building modified cars on another's chassis with Jaguar engines, into a full-scale automobile manufacturer. The XK engine had been designed by Lyons, Chief Engineer William Heynes, engine designers Walter Hassan and Claude Bailey while they were on fire watch duty during World War II on the roof of the factory in Coventry.

haul is perhaps the greatest proof of the advances made in design and production in that era."

The XK engine had a bore and stroke of 83 x 106 mm for a capacity of 3,442 cc. and delivered 120 bhp at 5,000 rpm. In experimental form it ran for 24 hours at 5,000 rpm with occasional bursts to as high as 6,000 rpm. The engine's strength may

be attributed to the robust and large-diameter seven-bearing crankshaft and the reliability of the valve gear, with two chain-driven camshafts operating two valves per cylinder.

This engine was installed in a box-section frame with great torsional rigidity. The front suspension incorporated torsion bars, while the rear

used semi-elliptic leaf springs. On the first cars, a V-shaped windshield was fitted, but a small "aero screen" was available for racing. In the rear was a nice-sized luggage compartment, although a 25-gallon fuel tank could be fitted in place of the original equipment 15-gallon tank for longer runs.

After Jaguar built 240 cars with aluminum bodies and demand for the XK120 was still strong, the company switched to steel bodies. In all, from 1948 to 1953 when the XK120 was replaced by the XK140, more than 18,000 were built, with less than 600 going to the home market, confirming the government's export policy.

A 2.4-liter 4-cylinder version of the XK engine was also planned, with the idea of installing it in a "XK100" sports car, but the car was never built. The engine was developed later.

XK120s proved their worth on race tracks. One of the first recorded victories for the car was in the 1949 *Daily Express* race at Silverstone, when Leslie Johnson won and Peter Walker finished second. Johnson also drove the XK120 to its first sig-nificant U.S. success in 1950 when he finished second to George Huntoon's Ford-Duesenberg Special in the SCCA's Palm Beach races. John Fitch, who would go on to success as a Mercedes-Benz team driver, was a class winner at Bridgehampton in an XK120 in 1950, as was Erwin Goldschmidt at Westhampton. In June 1950, Clark and Haines finished 12th in Jaguar's first Le Mans effort.

One significant victory, for both car and driver, occurred in August 1950, when a young Stirling Moss won the Tourist Trophy race in Northern Ireland. Here was a major victory for the car and an equally important win for the driver who was soon to make his mark as one of the greatest racing drivers in history.

Jaguar finally introduced the Mark VII sedan (there was no Mark VI because Bentley had a model by that name) with the 3.4-liter XK engine at the London Motor Show in October 1950. When the car was later put on display at the New York Auto Show, dealers placed more than $20 million in orders.

JAGUAR

Mark VII

S4170

At ports of entry:
sales tax, white-wall tires,
automatic transmission
and license extra.

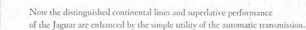

Now with
automatic transmission

Now the distinguished continental lines and superlative performance
of the Jaguar are enhanced by the simple utility of the automatic transmission.

Exclusively designed for Jaguar by Borg-Warner, this automatic transmission adds a final
note of distinction to a car already acclaimed for old-world craftsmanship and sports car performance.

Visit your local dealer and enjoy the thrill of a demonstration in the 1953 Jaguar
with automatic transmission. *Then you'll know that Jaguar is the one fine car for you.*

HOFFMAN MOTOR CAR CO., INC.
Importer East of the Mississippi
487 Park Avenue, New York

CHARLES H. HORNBURG, JR., INC.
Importer West of the Mississippi
9176 Sunset Blvd., Los Angeles

Guaranteed factory parts and complete service at dealers in most major cities

THE FINEST CAR OF ITS CLASS IN THE WORLD

 XK-120 Sports Coupe,
sedan comfort with
racing car performance

 XK-120, world's fastest
production car,
132.6 miles per hour

 XK-120 Convertible,
handsomely appointed—120
miles per hour performance

2-251F

Chapter Three | The 1950s

After the less-than-successful first effort at Le Mans in 1950, Jaguar returned a year later with a new car. Labeled the XK120C (or C-type, the "C" was for Competition), the car was a sleek, lightweight, aerodynamic version of the road car. One writer called the C-type body "purposeful-looking and stark." The aluminum body was designed by Malcolm Sayer, who would go on to design other great Jaguar sports cars. The space frame chassis carried an uprated 220 horsepower version of the 3.4-liter XK engine. To reach this level, the compression ratio was raised to 9.0:1 and high-lift camshafts were fitted. A wide choice of gear and axle ratios was available. There was torsion-bar suspension front and rear. The C-type

1953 JAGUAR XK120M
The XK120M (the "M" was for Modified) had an improved 3.4-liter XK engine that delivered 190 horsepower, as opposed to the 160 horsepower of the original. The extra power came from race-bred high-lift camshafts and 8.0:1 compression ratio pistons.

won at Le Mans in 1951 at the record average of 93.5 miles per hour. The car driven by Peter Walker and Peter Whitehead led a team of three cars to overall victory, and the car driven by Stirling Moss and Jack Fairman was leading when the engine failed.

Later in the year, Moss repeated his Tourist Trophy win in Northern Ireland, this time driving a C-type, with Peter Walker finishing second. The car driven by Tony Rolt and Leslie Johnson finished third.

Jaguar expanded on the business side as well, buying the neighboring Daimler factory on Browns Lane, Coventry. Daimler was a company that had descended from the original Daimler company of Germany. While the German company was renamed Daimler-Benz after the 1926 merger of Daimler and Benz and eventually became Mercedes-Benz, the British company retained the Daimler name and regularly supplied limousines and sedans to the Royal Family. Jaguar's purchase of the

1953 JAGUAR C-TYPE
In 1951, Jaguar launched an assault on Le Mans with the XK120C, or C-type. The "C" was for Competition. The C-type was a pure racing car, with a space frame chassis made up of steel tubing and an independent rear suspension. The aerodynamic body, designed by Malcolm Sayer, was built of aluminum. Jaguar won the 1951 Le Mans 24 Hours with a C-type driven by Peter Walker and Peter Whitehead. When the 1952 cars retired due to overheating, the car was redesigned slightly for the 1953 race and was made 120 pounds lighter. This 1953 version represents the cars that finished first, second, fourth and ninth in the 1953 race.

factory and the name added significant prestige to the company.

In 1952, the merger of the British manufacturing companies Austin and Morris into the British Motor Corporation had little immediate impact on Jaguar, although BMC did build and distribute Austin-Healey sports cars, which were priced below the XK120.

Jaguar's 1952 Le Mans effort wasn't as successful as 1951, because a new streamlined body designed by Sayer developed cooling problems. All three works cars retired. Later in the year, Phil

JAGUAR XK120 FIXED HEAD COUPE
Jaguar's XK120 Fixed Head Coupe, introduced in 1951, had a remarkable resemblance to the Bugatti Atlantique coupe. Both had long hoods, sweeping fenders, "bullet" headlights, split windshields, and cramped cockpits. The similarities weren't accidental, because William Lyons was an acknowledged fan of the Bugatti and wanted his car to look like it. This XK120 is owned by Les Jackson.

Hill won one of his first races in a C-type sponsored by Jaguar West Coast distributor Charles Hornburg Jr.

The cooling problems were solved for the 1953 Le Mans race. Disc brakes were also added to the cars, which were 120 pounds lighter thanks to the use of lightweight electrical equipment and air-craft-style fuel tanks. With an even more powerful version of the 3.4-liter engine, (Weber carburetors replacing SUs) and a redesigned rear suspension that incorporated a Panhard rod and a torque arm, C-types finished first, second, fourth and ninth, led by the team of Tony Rolt and Duncan Hamilton.

Jaguar had introduced a Fixed Head Coupe (hard top) version of the XK120 in 1951. A Drop Head Coupe version followed in May 1953. The Drop Head was more closely related to an American convertible, with wind-up windows and more creature comforts than the original Open Roadster. The top could be raised and lowered in a matter of seconds, and its bracing structure was completely concealed by a padded and fully lined mohair top. Inside, the Drophead Coupe had a walnut-veneer dash and door trim as did the Fixed Head Coupe.

The Fixed Head Coupe bore a striking resemblance to the Bugatti Atlantique, with the long

JAGUAR XK120 FIXED HEAD COUPE AND XK8 CONVERTIBLE
Jaguar's first Fixed Head Coupe, the XK120, and its newest sports car, the XK8, sit side-by-side in an Alexandria, Virginia, courtyard, displaying the advances in automotive design in 50 years. The XK120 is a "vertical" design, while the XK8 is more "horizontal," showing more attention to aerodynamics. The XK120 is owned by Les Jackson.

hood, horseshoe-shaped grill and flowing hood and fenders. The resemblance is no coincidence. Lyons was an avowed fan of Bugatti designs. In fact, according to XK120 FHC owner Les Jackson, there are reports that when Lyons was informed that the seating capacity in the FHC was cramped, he said he didn't care as long as the Bugatti-like lines were retained.

Jackson also notes that "the design department apparently ran out of pencils when they got to the back of the car." Where the front two-thirds of the car is a pleasant combination of sweeping lines and compound curves, the rear is bland, and appears to have been copied from an Austin-Healey 100 or the yet-to-be-produced MGA.

Despite the use of disc brakes on the Le Mans winning C-type, the XK 120 and later 140 were still supplied with drum brakes. One other feature that indicated the direction the sedans would follow was the addition of a 3-speed automatic transmission for the Mark VII.

1954 JAGUAR XK140
When Jaguar began offering a Borg-Warner 3-speed automatic transmission in the XK140, it may have offended some sports car "purists," but the company was recognizing what modern producers of sport utility vehicles are realizing; not all vehicles are driven the way they are built to be driven. Many XK140 owners used their cars for sporty driving, rather than racing. They would appreciate the convenience of an automatic transmission, especially if they were driving in the Fixed Head Coupe, with its superior weather protection.

Now ... the convenience of Borg-Warner
automatic transmission
available in the **Jaguar XK-140**
convertible and hardtop coupe.

1957 XK140
Successor to the XK120 was the XK140, introduced in 1954. The prime exterior difference between the XK120 and the XK140 was in the grille; the 140 had fewer vertical slats. The 140's bumpers were also heavier. With an engine that had been moved forward in the chassis by 3 inches, and additional modifications to the chassis, the seats were moved forward, which created more room in the car. The XK140 also benefited by the installation of the 190 horsepower version of the 3.4-liter XK engine. Power was raised to 210 horsepower by a Special Equipment, or SE, version that used C-type cylinder heads.

In October 1954, the XK120's successor, the XK140, was announced. The XK140 used rack-and-pinion steering, replacing the recirculating ball steering box of the XK120. The most distinguishing physical difference between the XK120 and XK140 was the latter car's new grille with fewer vertical bars and heavier front and rear bumpers. The XK140 also had greatly improved brakes but they were still drums. It soon became a familiar sight on highways and race tracks. Improvements were made in the engine compartment as well, with a new "C-type" cylinder head developing 210 horsepower from the 3.4-liter engine.

Also introduced at that London Motor Show was the Mark VII M sedan, with a 190 horsepower version of the 3.4-liter engine, a new front fascia with better headlights and driving lamps, and restyled bumpers.

The C-type was replaced as the factory race car by the D-type in 1954, also known as the XK120S Series 4. The D-type's Le Mans initiation wasn't quite as successful as the C-type's, though. It finished second in the 1954 race. A C-type finished fourth. But the D-type came back to win in 1955, 1956 and 1957, the last two years in Ecurie Ecosse-owned cars.

The 1955 cars were 7.5 inches longer than the 1954 cars and had a tonneau cover over the

136

1955 JAGUAR D-TYPE 3.8
Replacing the C-type as the company's racer was, the D-type. This car had monocoque construction, as opposed to the space-frame construction of the C-type, with a magnesium alloy tub. While the D-type finished second to a Ferrari in the 1954 Le Mans race, it was credited with winning the disastrous 1955 event, in which more than 80 people were killed. D-types repeated his success in 1956 and 1957, the latter race being under the colors of Ecurie Ecosse, a private racing team.

While the C-type was successful at Le Mans in its first effort, the D-type had no such luck. In 1954, it finished second to a 4.5-liter Ferrari. Success came in the tragic 1955 race, however, when the D-type won after Mercedes-Benz withdrew. Jaguar repeated its win in 1956 with a factory-back D-type and in 1957 with a private entry D-type.

"passenger" seat with a fin behind the driver's head. The cars used higher wraparound windshields and the exhaust exited out the rear. Six cars were built.

Unfortunately, Jaguar's 1955 win was tainted by the accident with Pierre Levegh's Mercedes-Benz 300SL that caromed off Lance Macklin's Austin-Healey and into the crowd, killing more than 80 people. A Mercedes was leading when the company withdrew from the race, handing it to Jaguar.

The D-type was even lighter and more potent (250 bhp) than the C and had an unorthodox frame built around a central welded fabrication. Forward of this center section was a sub-frame to support the engine and front suspension.

Jaguar announced in October 1956 that it was withdrawing from racing as a factory team, but would continue to support private entries.

At the 1955 London Motor Show in October, Jaguar introduced a compact sedan, the 2.4, with a 112 horsepower 2.4-liter version of the venerable XK 6-cylinder engine. With a price of £895 ($1,500) plus tax, the economical sedan offered speeds of over 100 miles per hour and seating for five people in a luxurious leather-lined interior with a walnut-veneer dash.

The year 1956 was important for Jaguar in other ways as well. In recognition of his vast contributions to the British automobile industry, as well as national pride in winning Le Mans with cars from his company, William Lyons became Sir William Lyons early in the year when he was Knighted by Queen Elizabeth II.

That same year, Jaguar introduced the Mark VIII sedan, which was more luxurious than the Mark VII which preceded it. The Mark VIII used walnut veneer throughout the passenger compartment, including two picnic tables for rear seat passengers. In addition, the car had three cigar/cigarette lighters for smoking passengers, clocks for front and rear passengers, and a veneered magazine rack for rear seat passengers in cars with a bench front seat. Under the bonnet was the 210 horsepower version of the 3.4-liter XK engine.

the car . . . the Jaguar XK-140 hardtop coupe . . . about to depart from
the Plaza 'midst a modest cloud of admiring glances. For this version of the fabulous "XK"
(there are three models) is considered by automotive aesthetes to be one of the
all-time gems of motor car design. The XK-140 HARDTOP is particularly favored
by business and professional men who make a *pleasure* of the *necessity* of
driving. Cozy, comfortable, luxuriously appointed . . . and, of course,
pure JAGUAR in performance. With additional rear seating accommodation,
priced at approximately $3,900.

For the traveler, may we suggest that you ask your dealer about the "Visit Europe Delivery Plan."
Jaguar Cars North American Corporation, 32 East 57th Street, N. Y. 22, N. Y.
(Importer east of the Mississippi)
Charles H. Hornburg Jr., Inc., 9176 Sunset Blvd., Los Angeles, Cal.
(Importer west of the Mississippi)

the Jaguar Mark VII

The stately four door MARK VII SEDAN represents a pinnacle of automotive craftsmanship. Among its many virtues is the ability to carry six people swiftly over great distances . . . in supreme luxury.

The MARK VII is at home on any road . . . in town or country. Throughout the world it is frequently seen proudly bearing license plates marked *Corps Diplomatique*.

The MARK VII is available with automatic transmission and standard equipment includes such amenities as a sliding sun roof, double fuel tanks to allow tremendous luggage capacity . . . lavish yet tasteful use of hand-rubbed walnut panelling and glove leather upholstery.

It is a car that gives its passengers as much pleasure as the owner behind the wheel.

SPECIFICATIONS

- **Engine:** Six cylinder 3½ litre twin overhead camshaft Jaguar XK engine developing 190 H.P. Twin S.U. horizontal carburetors.
- **Transmission:** Borg Warner automatic transmission. Four speed synchromesh gearbox with optional overdrive available on special order.
- **Suspension:** Independent front suspension; transverse wishbones, torsion bars and telescopic shock absorbers. Rear: Half elliptic springs controlled by telescopic shock absorbers.
- **Brakes:** Vacuum servo-assisted hydraulic. Friction lining area 179 sq. ins.
- **Steering:** Recirculating ball. Adjustable steering wheel.
- **Wheels:** Steel disc wheels with Dunlop 6.70 x 16 in. tubeless tires.
- **Fuel Supply:** Twin S.U. electric pumps. Capacity 20½ gallons in two tanks of 9½ and 11 gallons. Turn-over switch on instrument panel.
- **Electrical:** 12 volt 64 amp/hour battery.
- **Instruments:** 120 mph speedometer, tachometer, ammeter, oil pressure, water temperature and fuel gauges, electric clock.
- **Body:** Four door all steel six seater with sliding roof. Built-in heater, defroster and windshield washers. Upholstered in finest quality leather over foam rubber. Polished walnut panels.
- **Luggage Accommodations:** Capacious 17 cubic foot trunk with spare wheel fitted inside.
- **Dimensions:** Wheelbase 10 ft.; overall length 16 ft. 4½ ins.; width 6 ft. 1 in.; height 5 ft. 3 ins.; dry weight 3696 lbs.

1956 2.4, XK140, MARK VII

Jaguar's 1956 brochure showed the versatility of the company, with offerings of a compact sedan—the 2.4, a thoroughbred sports car—the XK140, and a large sedan—the Mark VII. The XK140 and Mark VII were powered by the 3.4-liter XK 6-cylinder engine, while the new 2.4 used a smaller version of the same engine. The 2.4 offered 30 miles per gallon and 100 miles per hour performance in a compact sedan that could comfortabley carry five passengers. The XK140 was the second-generation postwar Jaguar sports car, combining knowledge gained from the XK120 as well as three wins at the Le Mans 24 Hours race. The Mark VII was a full-size sedan with seating for six in "supreme luxury."

1956 XK140 FIXED HEAD COUPE

Jaguar's XK140 Fixed Head Coupe offered the ultimate for the "Man About Town." Here was a sports car of the highest magnitude, yet it was also a closed coupe that would protect the driver and his passenger from the elements. And a rear seat was available. The price was a reasonable $3,900.

1957 JAGUAR XKSS
When Jaguar withdrew from factory racing in 1956, it still had some spare D-type chassis lying around the factory. The solution was to take the cars, equip them with road gear to make them "street legal," and sell them as production cars. These cars were called the XKSS. Unfortunately, a fire in the Jaguar factory on February 12, 1957, wrote the final chapter on the XKSS shortly after the first one had been written. With only 16 cars completed, the remaining stock of XKSS chassis were destroyed in the fire, as well as several sedans. Jaguar returned to production within a week, but the XKSS was never revived.

With the end of factory-backed racing, there were a few D-type chassis lying around the factory. Lyons had an excellent idea what to do with them. The solution was to add bumpers, a muffler and top to the cars to make them suitable for road use and sell them to the public as the XKSS. With a list price in the United States of $5,600, it was expensive, but desirable. Unfortunately, a fire at the Browns Lane factory on February 12, 1957, destroyed most of the XKSS cars that were being built, leaving a production run of just 16. Limited production of regular cars returned to Browns Lane in just two days. Less than two weeks later, the company introduced the 3.4 sedan, which was a larger-engined version of the 2.4. Full production also returned to Browns Lane shortly, but without the XKSS.

The next version of the sports car was the XK150, which was introduced at the New York Auto Show in March 1958. The engine was the 210 horsepower version of the XK 3.4, but servo-assisted four-wheel disc brakes were now available for stopping. The transmission was a 4-speed manual, but a 3-speed automatic was available. An "S" version of the XK150 became available later, with a three-carburetor version of the 3.4-liter engine tuned to D-type specifications and developing 250 horsepower. This

1957 JAGUAR XK150
The XK150 was the ultimate expression of the XK line. While it was heavier and wider than the XK120 and 140, it had a curved one-piece windshield that improved the styling, and power options that helped the 3.8-liter XK engine develop as much as 265 horsepower to improve performance. The XK150 also had wind-up windows, which forced the elimination of the low-cut doors of the XK140.

With sedans as its bread-and-butter line, Jaguar sports cars have always played second fiddle. The problem for the ad people was how to turn this into an advantage. Make it exclusive! Only 7,500 XK150s would be sold in the United States, making it exclusive. And what a car it was. Four-wheel disc brakes, one-piece windshield, roll-up windows and a sensible convertible top made the XK150 as comfortable as any sedan, with a lot more performance than most sedans could offer.

car was only available with a manual transmission, however. All these had rack and pinion steering and disc brakes.

In October 1959, the new 3.8-liter XK engine became available for the XK150. In standard form, this engine developed 220 horsepower, but in "S" tune it pumped out 265 horses.

Along with the XK150, Jaguar also introduced its latest large "Saloon," the Mark IX in October 1958. Powered by the 3.8-liter XK 6-

cylinder, and with standard disc brakes and power steering, the Mark IX was a true luxury sedan.

Jaguar introduced Mark 2 versions of the 2.4 and 3.4 sedans in 1959, along with a 3.8-liter version of the compact sedan, also designated Mark 2, even though there was no "Mark 1" 3.8. As they should have, the Mark 2 versions were improved versions of the original cars. Larger glass area gave the A-pillars a slimmer, more attractive line. A wider rear track, designed to improve handling, also eliminated the

Successor to the XK140 was the XK150 (left), with a slightly more bulbous body, but improved interior room. Introduced in 1957, it was built until 1961, by which time it had become the most prolific range ever built by Jaguar to that time. The cockpit was widened by 4 inches and a curved one-piece windshield was fitted in place of the flat two-piece affairs of the XK120 and 140. Top speed for the original XK150 was in excess of 135 miles per hour. In 1959 and afterward, the XK150 was powered by the 3.8-liter version of the XK engine. In standard form this engine developed 220 horsepower, while in "S" form, power was up to 265 horsepower. This XK150 is pictured next to an XKS.

"pinched in" look of the original cars. Up front, standard fog lights were fitted in place of the air intakes. The bigger 3.8 liter engine made the cars more competitive in touring car races and rallies. Automatic and manual gearboxes were offered.

Mark 2s had enviable racing records in British sedan racing, until Ford brought Galaxies over with big honking V-8 engines that Jaguar simply couldn't compete with. Among the drivers were Roy Salvadori, Graham Hill, Jack Sears, Colin Chapman and American Walt Hansgen. Jack Coombs prepared many Mark 2s for racing, including Hansgen's. He recalled Hansgen for this writer when we did an article on the Mark 2 for *Automobile Quarterly*:

"Walt Hansgen was the most exciting driver I have ever seen. I had him over here and he drove my Mark 2. He would go into Woodcote Corner [at Silverstone] absolutely sideways. I asked him what speed he was going and he said, 'John, it's a bit difficult to tell you. I haven't got time to look at the instruments. I'm a little busy.' But Walt was the best Mark 2 driver. He just chucked it sideways. He was a great character."

Jaguar closed out the 1950s in strong form, with a wide variety of cars to offer in a wide variety of classes, from sports cars to large sedan. The following decade, though, would see a period of turmoil for the company, both in the marketplace and in the corporate offices.

Jaguar

Versatile beauty. Responsive as a sports car yet meticulously fitted with all the appurtenances of supreme comfort. Tailored for family driving.

1959 JAGUAR 3.4 SEDAN

The 1959 Jaguar 3.4 Sedan offered everything a Jaguar owner would want in a compact sedan. For less than $4,600, a buyer could obtain performance of an XK150 (or at least the same engine and transmission of an XK150) with the traditional luxury of a Jaguar sedan, all in a compact package. There was no mistaking a Jaguar coming at you down the highway, either. With its oval grille and vertical chrome slats flanked by two huge headlights, there was nothing that looked quite like a Jaguar 3.4.

JAGUAR MARK IX SEDAN

Jaguar's Mark IX Saloon, or sedan, was introduced in October 1958, and would be the last "old style" sedan built by Jaguar. The next generation Mark X would be a longer, lower, more aerodynamic vehicle. The Mark IX, though, was a true large luxury sedan, with leather upholstery, walnut veneer dash and the powerful 3.8-liter XK double overhead cam 6-cylinder engine. The Mark IX also had power steering and front disc brakes for stopping. Skirts over the rear wheels aided aerodynamics slightly. As evidence of the market Jaguar was hoping to compete in with the Mark IX, compare this car with a Rolls-Royce of the era and note the strong similarities. The only major difference is in the grille. *Margaret Harrison*

TOP RIGHT
1961 JAGUAR XK150

The last year of production for the XK150 was 1961, when this car was built. The XK150 was available with the 3.8-liter engine that offered exhilarating performance. A choice of transmissions was also offered, with a four-speed manual (with or without overdrive) as standard and a Borg: Warner three-speed automatic as optional. Special Equipment XK150s were available with wire wheels, dual exhausts, fog lamps and windshield washers.

RIGHT
1960 JAGUAR MARK IX

The Jaguar Mark IX sedan showed little exterior change from the Mark VIII. Under the skin, however, there were several changes, prime of which was the installation of a 3.8-liter double overhead cam 6-cylinder engine rated at 225 horsepower. This was also the first Jaguar sedan to be offered with standard front disc brakes and power steering. The engine offered more power, the disc brakes offered the opportunity to stop the two-ton sedan more easily, and the power steering made it possible to handle it more easily.

The 1960s

Jaguar had established its American ties early, beginning with Lyons' 1948 trip to the United States to set up sales and service agents. Lyons' relationship with importer Max Hoffman soured when Hoffman rejected Lyons advice and began importing Mercedes-Benz cars in 1953. That same year, Jaguar hired Johannes Eerdmans, to set up an import company in Manhattan.

In May 1960, Jaguar bought the Daimler factory at Radford in Coventry for £3.4 million, which became the main production center for engines and suspension units.

1963 JAGUAR E-TYPE

Few cars have had the impact on the world of automobiles as the Jaguar E-type, introduced in 1961. Its sleek aerodynamic lines were unlike anything seen on the road until that time. Designed by Malcolm Sayer, the E-type (or XKE in the United States) was powered by a 265 horsepower 3.8-liter XK engine at first that gave it a top speed in the neighborhood of 150 miles per hour. The E-type also had 4-wheel disc brakes, with the rear brakes mounted inboard.

Jaguar bought Coventry Climax in 1963, gaining an important engine developer. Some rumors said the only reason Lyons bought Coventry Climax was to regain the services of Walter Hassan, who had left Jaguar to work there. By 1965, Jaguar Cars Inc. had become the Jaguar Group, with 20 different companies under the corporate umbrella, including Daimler, Coventry Climax and Guy trucks.

In order to reduce his involvement with the company, Sir William named 16 "executive directors" in June 1966. One month later, Jaguar merged with the British Motor Corporation to form British Motor Holdings (BMH). The idea of the merger, at least in Jaguar's mind, was that BMC's size and assets would provide Jaguar with a sound financial and engineering base. While Sir William still remained in titular control of the company, corporate interests dictated many moves. Lyons relinquished the role of Managing Director to "Lofty" England early in 1968.

The gentlemen are discussing automotive performance. But, as Jaguar owners, they should know better than compare the speed of the new XK-E with that of the 3.8 Sedan, since speed alone has never been the criterion of excellence in judging Jaguars. How, then, you may ask, does one choose between the XK-E and the 3.8 Sedan? Both offer dramatic acceleration, phenomenal performance and superb handling. Therefore, let your own personal require-ments be the basis for your choice between the two. If there are two of you, then by all means investigate the new XK-E. But, if family needs dictate a roomier vehicle, then avail yourself of the comforts and spaciousness of the 3.8 Sedan. Both are, after all, thoroughbred Jaguars. For more information on both of these fine automobiles, consult your nearest Jaguar Dealer, or write JAGUAR CARS INC., 32 East 57th Street, New York 22, N. Y.

The Jaguar XK-E vs. the 3.8 Sedan

1961 XK-E AND 3.8 SEDAN

Both the XK-E (or E-type) and the 3.8 Sedan were powered by the venerable 3.8-liter XK 6-cylinder engine. By 1961, when this ad appeared, the engine was almost 15 years old. It would continue in operation into the 1980s. While the E-type offered stirring sports car performance, the 3.8 Sedan would take the same engine/transmission combination and put it in a compact five-passenger sedan. Nissan called its 1990s Maxima "the four-door sports car." It is a definition that Jaguar could have used 30 years earlier.

Unification of the British automobile industry continued in 1968 when BMH and Leyland Motor Corporation joined, forming British Leyland Motor Corporation. Sir William was named deputy chairman of BLMC under Lord Stokes. The new corporation joined 95 percent of the British-owned motor industry under one banner.

Johannes Eerdmans had been president of the successful Jaguar Cars North America since 1954. He held this position through the formation of British Leyland and retired in 1969. Graham Whitehead, as president of British Leyland Motors Inc., replaced him as Jaguar's U.S. chief.

On the automotive side, the 1960s were highlighted by the introduction and development of the E-type (or XKE in the United States). Rumors of a new and full-blooded Jaguar sports car grew through 1960. Introduced at the Geneva Salon in March 1961, the E-type was an instant success. Designed by Malcolm Sayer, it had some of the lines of the D-type and prototype E2A racer that followed it. But here was a completely new road car with a look unlike any other. The car was introduced in two forms—Open Roadster (or convertible) and Fixed Head Coupe. It was the latter, with its dramatic fastback styling and faired-in headlights, that the public fell in love with.

Powered by a 265 horsepower version of the XK 3.8-liter engine, the E-type had performance

1961 JAGUAR E-TYPE

Jaguar's E-type (or XK-E) hit the sports car world like an A-bomb. It offered stirring styling in both Coupe and Roadster forms, but it was the Coupe that elicited the most excitement. Fastback styling was still fairly new to most Americans, and when they saw the E-type, they went wild. The back door opened to reveal a healthy storage compartment, while the nose tipped forward to reveal the three-carburetor 3.8-liter XK 6-cylinder engine.

to match its good looks. The engine and gearbox were mounted in a detachable fabricated subframe with box-section frame members carrying the coachwork.

The coupe could go from 0-60 miles per hour in seven seconds and had a top speed of 151 miles per hour. It handled, too. The front suspension was by wishbones and torsion bars. Telescopic

Newest of Jaguars: The classic Mark X luxury sedan

As of today, the fine-car connoisseur has nothing left to wish for. Because here, with the introduction of the new Jaguar Mark X Sedan, is luxury rarely equalled; performance without peer. Under way, new monocoque construction and independent rear suspension afford a ride that is nothing short of phenomenal. Appointments are of the finest, and typically Jaguar. Seats are of the finest glove leather, with those in front fully reclining. Cabinet work is of hand-crafted walnut, mated and matched. Walnut tables, each with a vanity mirror, fold rearward from the front seat-backs. Standard equipment includes power-assisted steering, two independent brake systems (power-assisted), dual fuel pumps and lockable dual fuel tanks, automatic transmission with intermediate gear-hold for passing. Look for the Mark X at your Jaguar dealer's or write JAGUAR CARS INC., 32 East 57th St., N. Y. 22, N. Y. Jaguar Technical Service and Parts Headquarters, 42-50 Twenty-First Street, Long Island City 1, New York

1962 JAGUAR MARK X

The 1962 Mark X offered the consumer pure Jaguar luxury and performance at a reasonable price; reasonable when you compare it to a Rolls-Royce which offered slightly more luxury and less performance at a higher price. The Mark X Sedan offered leather seating ("glove soft"), hand-crafted walnut cabinetry, including walnut tables with vanity mirrors on the backs of the front seats, monocoque construction and a fully independent suspension.

1962 JAGUAR E-TYPE

The essence of the Jaguar E-type was its three carburetor double overhead cam XK 6-cylinder engine. William Lyons always was concerned with the esthetics of his automobiles, whether from the outside or the inside. Consequently, his engines always dazzled the eye when you opened the hood. The 4.2-liter (230.6 cubic inch) engine developed 265 horsepower at 5,500 rpm, or 1.15 horsepower per cubic inch. And yet the XK-E was still elegant enough to accommodate a young lady in a fur coat.

shock absorbers were at all four corners. It is in the final abandonment of the conventional heavy rigid rear axle that this car broke most with Jaguar tradition. The rear suspension was mounted on a sub-frame and was by two pairs of coil springs with universal-jointed half-shafts located by radius arms and transverse links. Dunlop disc brakes were all around, with the rears mounted inboard.

At the time, the sports car market in the United States was a full one, with MGA, TR4, Austin-Healey 3000 and Alfa Romeo at the lower end and the Daimler SP250 somewhere in the middle. The E-type had a list price of $5,595 for the convertible and $5,895 for the coupe.

In the E-type's race debut, Graham Hill drove an Equipe Endeavour car to victory over Roy Salvadori in John Coombs' similar car at Oulton Park. It was the first of many wins for the sleek car.

The year 1961 was a watershed year on the sedan front as well. Jaguar introduced the Mark X in October at the London Motor Show. Here was a sleek modern sedan to replace the classic Mark IX, with a monocoque body that was longer and lower than its predecessors, but built on the same wheelbase. The Mark X used the 265 horsepower 3.8-liter XK engine and independent rear suspension of the E-type to record some impressive statistics for a big car; 0-60 miles per hour in under 11 seconds and a top speed of 115 miles per hour. A 4.2-liter version of the same engine powered the 1965 car, introduced in 1964. While this engine had the same nominal horsepower, a 10 percent increase in torque made it a better performer. Top speed was up to 122 miles per hour.

The same 4.2-liter engine made its debut in the 1965 E-type. Externally, the only distinction between the original cars and the 4.2 was a small badge on the trunk lid. Inside, there were new seats that were more comfortable and the elimi-

Five minutes behind the wheel will tell you why the 1964 Jaguar XK-E is the new standard by which all sportscars are compared.

For one thing, it doesn't look like any other car you have ever seen. And it is capable of phenomenal speed and acceleration.

Yet its handling qualities give you the relaxed confidence of always being in complete command,

whatever the road, speed or driving conditions.

What's more, the 32 unique performance and luxury features of the XK-E are on each car when you buy it. With many other sports cars, they are added "extras."

A few of these features; the race-proven engine; "Monocoque" body; all-around independent suspension; four-wheel disc brakes;

bucket seats fully covered with genuine leather; completely instrumented dash panel.

See and drive the Jaguar XK-E. Roadster: $5,525 P.O.E. Coupe $200 more. (If you're going to Europe, inquire about Jaguar's money-saving Overseas Delivery Plan.) There are Jaguar dealers coast-to-coast. Jaguar Cars Inc., New York 22, N.Y.

The 1964 Jaguar XK-E

The sportscar.

1964 JAGUAR E-TYPE

The 1964 Jaguar E-type (or XK-E) Coupe was priced at $5,525 in the United States. As such, it was probably one of the best values for the dollar. It offered the most aerodynamic body of its time, with wire wheels, leather seats, 4-wheel disc brakes, fully independent suspension and monocoque construction.

nation of brushed aluminum trim on the dash and transmission tunnel. Even with the automatic transmission installed after 1966, the E-type 4.2 would accelerate from 0-60 miles per hour in under 9 seconds and reach a top speed of over 136 miles per hour.

In October 1963, Jaguar introduced improved versions of the 3.4 and 3.8 Mark 2, calling them the 3.4S and 3.8S. These cars were 6 inches longer overall to accommodate the independent rear suspension. This extra length was used to good advantage by increasing the luggage capacity and providing for dual fuel tanks. Interior room improved as well, with the real benefit going to rear seat passengers.

Jaguar introduced yet another variation of the E-type, the 2+2 Coupe, in March 1966. Built on a chassis that was lengthened by 9 inches, the new car had rear seats that were usable by children or one adult on a long run. In addition, the roofline was raised 2 inches, which improved rear headroom. The extra 220 pounds of weight raised 0-60 miles per hour acceleration times to 8.3 seconds, though.

In a marriage between the large sedans and the compact versions, Jaguar introduced the 420 and 420G in October 1966. This car retained the general profile of the S-Class cars, but with a rectangular grille reminiscent of the Mark X. "Eyebrows" over the four headlights were another carryover from the S-type, although American versions had four equal-size headlights. In Europe the inner lights were smaller in diameter. The engine in the 420 was a two-carburetor version of the E-type's three-carburetor engine, delivering 245 horsepower.

While the 420 was derived from the S-Types, the 420G was clearly a derivative of the Mark X. The 420G had a wheelbase that was over a foot longer than the 420 (120 inches vs. 107.3 inches) and was 14.3 inches longer overall (202 inches vs. 187.7 inches). Walnut veneer was used on the dash, which was one of the last to feature toggle switches for controls. These "unsafe" switches would soon be replaced by the "safer" rocker switch variety. The chrome horn ring would also disappear shortly.

At the New York Auto Show in the spring of 1968, Jaguar displayed the Piranha, which was a Bertone-bodied E-type 2+2. The chassis was modified slightly to take D-type wide-rim wheels and wider tires. After appearing at the show and another in Montreal, the car was auctioned by Parke-Bernet

1965 JAGUAR E-TYPE

By 1965, when this E-type was built, the engine capacity had been increased to 4.2 liters, although power was still 265 horsepower. Engine capacity was increased by increasing the bore by 5 mm. A new block was thus needed, which also required a new crankshaft. Jaguar used the cylinder head from the 3.8-liter engine, which did not match exactly with that of the 4.2. Inside, the only difference between this car and the original were new, more comfortable seats and the elimination of the polished aluminum trim around the dash and transmission tunnel.

1967 JAGUAR 3.4 SEDAN
While Jaguar had always built large sedans, the 2.4 and 3.4 (and later 3.8) were the company's first "mid-size" sedans. The first sedans were introduced in 1957, with "Mark 2" versions introduced two years later. The Mark 2 cars offered better visibility with more glass and thinner A-pillars. The 3.4-liter inline six engine developed 210 horsepower, giving it one horsepower per cubic inch displacement. The Mark 2 3.4 was then one of the world's first muscle cars. Wire wheels were offered as a factory option.

1966 JAGUAR E-TYPE
By 1966, when this Series III Jaguar E-type was built, federal regulations had eliminated the faring over the headlights and created a "chromier" grille. The car still retained its aerodynamic lines, although a more vertical windshield detracted somewhat from this. In order to overcome this loss of aerodynamics, the Series III cars were equipped with a 5.3-liter V-12 engine, the first production V-12 to appear since the Cadillacs of the 1930s. The engine was rated at 250 horsepower in the United States, and could be mated to a 4-speed manual or 3-speed automatic transmission.

Galleries. It brought $16,000 at a time when Jaguars were selling for $5,500 to $6,500.

While the large 420G remained in production, all the other Jaguar sedans were made obsolete with the introduction of the XJ6 in September 1968. Through the 1960s, Jaguar was building two completely different lines of sedans in addition to a range of three sports cars. This created a terrific strain on the company's resources. The solution was the XJ6, a mid-size sedan that replaced both existing sedan lines. It was a hit from the start. Here was a car that looked like the 420, but was sleeker and moved Jaguar in a new direction. With the traditional "Jaguar look," it was both trim and modern. While not as big as the Mark X, it was comfortable enough for five adults and offered infinitely better handling

and overall performance. Before the XJ6, Jaguar was a producer of sports cars and high performance sedans; after the XJ6 it was a producer of luxury cars.

Powered by the 4.2-liter XK engine that delivered 245 horsepower, the XJ6 made its mark by having low levels of noise, vibration and harshness years before "NVH" became a watchword for car engineers. Adding to the package were low-profile radial tires,

which, with the independent front and rear suspensions mounted on sub-frames, added to the car's road silence. The dash featured burl walnut trim, eight round instruments and an imposing array of ten toggle switches splayed across the bottom of the dash.

Economy versions of the S-Type—the 240 and 340—were introduced in October 1967. While they retained the basic styling of the Mark 2 sedans,

1967 JAGUAR 340
In 1967, Jaguar introduced "economy" versions of the Mark II sedans, dubbed 240 and 340. This 340 was powered by the venerable 3.4-liter dohc XK six. While the exterior "bathtub" lines of the 340 were almost identical to those of its predecessors, economy was introduced with Ambla vinyl, rather than leather, upholstery. The bumpers were single chrome bars rather than the double bars of the Mark II sedans, and wire wheels were no longer available. The owner of this 340 is Jim Spooner.

the 240 and 340 were truly low-price versions of a medium-priced car. For example, while the 2.4 and 3.4 had leather upholstery, the newer cars were trimmed in Ambla vinyl. The bumpers were slimmer single chrome bars, as opposed to the double bars of the Mark 2. And wire wheels were not available; steel discs were the order of the day. The 240 did get a power boost, though, from 122 horsepower of the original version to 133 in the 240.

Late in 1968, Jaguar introduced the Series II E-type, with modifications made necessary by U.S. Federal Safety regulations. The glass fairings on the headlights were removed in 1967 and the toggle switches replaced by rockers. For the Series II, the headlights were moved forward and the bumpers made more sturdy. A connection with history disappeared when the ears had to be removed from the wire wheel knock-offs, again as a safety measure. Clean air regulations dictated a replacement of the S.U. carburetors with Zenith-Strombergs, which

were cleaner. Thus restricted, the engine now delivered 246 horsepower vs. 265 in the "SU" version.

In the United States, Jaguar headquarters were located on the 12th floor of 32 East 57th Street, New York, where they had been since the late 1950s. Graham Whitehead was named president of Jaguar's U.S. operations in October 1968. Jaguar moved its headquarters to the British Leyland offices to Leonia, New Jersey. Jaguar would retain the location after the dissolution of British Leyland in the 1970s.

Briggs Cunningham had persuaded Jaguar to sell him the E2A prototype car, which was an evolutionary step between the D-type and E-type. Cunningham raced the car at Le Mans with no success, then brought it back to the United States. Painted in Cunningham's white-with-blue-stripes racing colors, it won at Bridgehampton with Walt Hansgen at the wheel. Cunningham then retired the car to his collection in California and sold it to the Collier Museum in Naples, Florida, in 1988.

Jaguar compact sedans, from the 3.4 through the 3.4 Mark II to the final iteration of the 340, were powered by the 3.4-liter dohc XK six. By the time the engine was installed in the 1967 340, it was more than 20 years old, but it had only reached middle age. The engine would continue to power Jaguars into the 1980s, although enlarged ultimately to 4.2 liters capacity. Crammed in the 340, though, it was a service nightmare even in an era of minimal additions for air conditioning and emissions controls.

The 340 was conceived and delivered as an "economy" version of the 3.4 Mark II compact sedan. These economies reached inside the car in the form of vinyl upholstery rather than the original leather and thinner padding in the seats. The burl walnut veneer dash, however, was retained from the Mark II sedans, as were the traditional round, white-on-black instruments. From the left, the instruments are speedometer, tachometer, water temperature, oil pressure, fuel level and battery amperage. Beneath the dash was a small tray that was useful for carrying maps.

With a rear end similar to the Mark I sedans, the only difference exhibited with the 340 was a thinner chrome bumper and chrome farings around the taillights. Even with the smooth rear end that has none of the aerodynamics of modern sports sedans, the Mark IIs and 340s were potent racing cars at the hand of such luminaries as Graham Hill and Roy Salvadori.

Chapter Five

The 1970s

The decade of the 1970s would see Jaguar, and all manufacturers, forced to deal with ever more stringent U.S. Federal safety and emissions legislation. These regulations would cripple engine performance until designers learned how to cope by offering more efficient fuel injection systems. In addition, styling would suffer to some degree with the addition of stronger bumpers and minimum headlight heights.

Jaguar had responded to these rules in the 1960s by modifying the E-type's headlights, for

1978 JAGUAR XJ6
While Jaguar has been revered and respected as a producer of high-performance sports cars, it is the Jaguar sedans that have been the bread-and-butter cars. Jaguar introduced the XJ6 in 1968, which was a successful marriage between the compact Mark 2 range and the larger 420 sedans. Powered by a 4.2-liter XK 6-cylinder engine, the XJ6 packaged traditional Jaguar values in a sedan that was years ahead of its time. Five people could ride in comfort in the XJ6, which used the same subframe-mounted rear suspension of the E-type, as well as the E-type's inboard rear disc brakes.

example, in the Series II cars. As that decade ended the glass headlight fairings had disappeared and more substantial bumpers changed the front fascia.

To improve the power situation, Jaguar introduced the Series III E-type in March 1971 with the first V-12 engine in series production since the Lincolns of the 1940s. The 5.3-liter V-12 in the E-type delivered 272 horsepower in Europe and 250 in the U.S. The introduction of the V-12 also meant universal use of the 9 inch-longer "2+2" wheelbase on all models.

The V-12 engine was based on a 5.0-liter concept used in the XJ13 racing prototype. The production version was an all-aluminum 5.3-liter engine with single overhead cams on each bank of cylinders. It was capable of propelling the E-type to 100 miles per hour in 15.5 seconds. Automotive writers all over the world have called the Jaguar V-12 "one of the world's great engines." In fact, its existence was denied for years by Jaguar until it was eventually restored after a

1971 JAGUAR E-TYPE V-12

The ultimate expression of the E-type was the 1971 Series III with the 5.3-liter V-12 engine. Some writers said the trend toward a heavier car with the aerodynamic concessions brought about by federal regulations reduced the sportiness of the E-type. Still, it was the only serious production vehicle with a V-12 engine and it still had the E-type panache. A Series III Roadster tested by *Road & Track* achieved a top speed of 135 miles per hour and went from 0-60 miles per hour in 7.4 seconds. What offended the purists, though, was the availability of a 3-speed Borg-Warner automatic transmission as well as a 4-speed manual gearbox.

1971 SERIES III JAGUAR E-TYPE V-12

Putting a V-12 engine in the E-type made it a whole new kind of cat. True, the windshield wasn't as sharply raked as in the Series I E-type, and the mouth now had a proper grille and bumper overriders to protect it, but the presence of the first V-12 engine since the 1930s was more than enough to offset exterior physical deformities. The 5.3-liter engine developed 314 horsepower, or almost one horsepower for each of its 326 cubic inches. This "ultimate cat" also had 4-wheel disc brakes, a fully independent suspension and power-assisted rack-and-pinion steering for better control.

crash during testing. The crash scotched any racing plans for it.

The engine had more than adequate power for the job and was smooth to boot. Power was listed as 272 horsepower vs. 265 for the latest 4.2-liter XK six. Two comparison tests by *Road & Track* show the performance difference. In 1969, *R&T* tested an XKE 2+2 with the 4.2-liter six and hit a top speed of 119 miles per hour and 0-60 miles per hour in 8.0 seconds. When the magazine tested a Series III Roadster with the V-12, the top speed was 135 miles per hour and the 0-60 time had dropped to 7.4 seconds. And the roadster was 300 pounds heavier than the 6-cylinder 2+2.

The V-12 had first seen the light of day in the XJ13 prototype. This mid-engined car had a four-cam version of the engine (production V-12s would have one cam per bank). With a possible goal as a future Le Mans competitor, the XJ13 was extensively tested.

As installed in the Series III E-type, the V-12 had a bore and stroke of 90 x 70 mm for a capacity of 5,343 cc. There was one chain-driven camshaft per bank of cylinders. The block and crankcase was aluminum. Cooling was by two electric fans. Fuel injection was tried, but the initial versions of the engine used four downdraft Zenith-Stromberg carburetors.

On the styling side, the Series III E-type had a grille of horizontal chrome strips over a larger air intake, necessitated by the V-12 installation, and bumper overriders to protect it. More significantly, a more vertical windshield detracted from the cleaner lines of the original E-type.

Sir William Lyons retired from Jaguar on March 3, 1972, ending a 50-year association with the

1966 JAGUAR XJ13 CONCEPT CAR
Even when Jaguar withdrew its backing from an official factory racing team, there had been discussions about the development of a V-12 engine. The test bed for that engine became the XJ13 concept car of 1966. XJ13 was designed by Malcolm Sayer and was a mid-engine configuration with a similarity to the E-type and other sports-racing cars of the era such as the Lola/Ford GT40 and McLaren-Elva. The car's existence was denied by Jaguar for many years, until it was time for the announcement of the production V-12. Unfortunately, XJ13 crashed during the filming of a commercial and was badly damaged. It was rebuilt in 1972 and began making public appearances in 1973.

company he founded. At his retirement he said he still believed that "motoring should be a joy and not a choice." Sir William was now 70 and reluctantly left his company in younger hands. Those hands belonged to F. R. W. "Lofty" England, who was 60 and had joined the company in 1946 as service manager. He was responsible for much of Jaguar's success at Le Mans. England's reign was a short one, however, as he was replaced in September 1973 by 34-year-old Geoffrey Robinson, appointed by the British Leyland board. Lofty England retired in 1974.

England was met with a strike when he first took office. The strike was caused by a change by the BL management of the way workers were paid. In the past, Jaguar workers were paid on a piece-work basis, where they were paid for the amount of work they did. BL changed that system to a day-rate payment basis. This was anathema to the way Jaguar had done business in the past and a 11-week strike crippled the company.

In July 1972, the V-12 engine became available in the XJ6 sedan, creating the XJ12. With a 241 horsepower (U.S. specs) engine lurking beneath the hood, the XJ12 was capable of a top speed of almost 140 miles per hour. The XJ12 also was equipped with power-assisted 4-wheel disc brakes, with the front brakes ventilated and

1973 JAGUAR V-12
The Series II E-types lost some of their aerodynamic penetration to a more vertical windshield and uncovered headlights. But still they were unmatched by any other cars on the road at the time. With the 5.3-liter V-12 engine under the hood, the E-type could accelerate from 0-60 miles per hour in 6.8 seconds and reach a top speed that was illegal in any state in the union. But with the smoothness of the V-12, you could also cruise at 10 miles per hour in top gear and accelerate to cruising speed.

1976 JAGUAR XJC COUPE
When Jaguar introduced the Series II XJ sedans, the company also introduced coupe versions in both six and V-12-engined versions. The cars were introduced in 1973, but weren't available until 1974. The reason for the delay was that the pillarless door design did not seal perfectly at high speed. By 1976, the Coupes also had to compete with the new XJS. Add to this the fact that the Coupes cost $750 more than the Sedans, and sales weren't what was expected.

the rear brakes mounted inboard, as in the E-Type, to reduce unsprung weight. Long wheelbase versions of both the XJ6 and XJ12 were introduced just two months later. These cars offered an extra 4 inches in wheelbase and 2 inches in overall length to improve rear seat leg room. With a 4-inch longer rear door, entry and exit also became easier.

Series II versions of Jaguar's entire XJ sedan line were introduced in September 1973. These redesigns were required to satisfy U.S. safety regulations which dictated a front bumper height of 16 inches. Since this would have put the bumpers in the middle of the XJ grille, the front end was redesigned. And as some reporters of the scene noted, the change lightened the look of the Jaguar

PRESENTING THE SUPERB NEW JAGUAR XJ-S

1976 XJS
Jaguar introduced the XJS in 1976, saying it had "the performance and handling of the more expensive sports cars and the quietness and comfort of luxury sedans." Maybe it was the quietness and comfort that made purists dislike the XJS. However, it was powered by the same 5.3-liter V-12 that had powered the E-type. Standard equipment included an 8-track AM/FM stereo sound system and a heated rear window.

front end, while similar changes to cars including the MGB and Triumph Spitfire served to destroy the looks of the cars.

The dash of the Series II XJ was also redesigned to replace the confusing, if handsome, array of rocker switches in front of the driver with a more logical arrangement. Instruments were now clustered in front of the driver in a redesigned instrument panel.

Two-door versions of the XJ sedans—XJ6C and XJ12C—were introduced along with the Series II sedans. Due to a combination of problems, these cars did not sell well and were discontinued in 1975. With their windows down, these 2-door "hardtop" coupes looked like convertibles with their tops raised. This look was enhanced by the standard vinyl top of the coupes.

One of the reasons for dropping the XJ coupes was the introduction of the XJ S sports coupe in September 1975. Initially shown at the Frankfurt Auto Show with a V-12 engine, the XJ-S was the last product to show the design hands of Sir

1977 JAGUAR XJS

By 1975, the E-type had been around for almost 15 years and was getting stale. Jaguar needed a new sports car to replace it, but the era of sports cars was also getting stale. The car that replaced the E-type was the XJS, which was introduced in September 1975. Powered by a 5.3-liter V-12 engine, the XJS was a 2+2 coupe with controversial "flying buttresses" around the rear window. While its styling was not universally admired, the XJS would survive for over 20 years and become the most-produced Jaguar sports car of all time.

William Lyons and Malcolm Sayer, who had died in 1970. This sports coupe filled the hole vacated by the E-type, which was discontinued in February 1975. But it was not a sports car in the sense the E-type coupes were. Rather, the XJ-S was more of a grand touring coupe in execution and use, although performance versions of the car did have some racing successes in the United States and Europe.

In true sports car tradition, though, the original XJ-S had a plain interior with leather upholstery. The car would remain essentially unchanged until 1982,

SIR WILLIAM LYONS (LEFT) AND SIR JOHN EGAN (RIGHT)
John Egan took over the reins of Jaguar in 1980, when Sir Michael Edwardes was appointed chairman of British Leyland. Sir William Lyons had an opportunity to meet Egan shortly after the latter took over. Egan was knighted in 1986 for his efforts in resuscitating Jaguar and saving it from the liquidators.

1978 XJ12
The most elegant Jaguar sedan was the XJ12, with the 5.3-liter V-12 engine, 3-speed GM automatic transmission, 4-wheel disc brakes, independent suspension all around, and such traditional Jaguar touches as walnut interior trim, leather seats and power-assisted rack-and-pinion steering. Dual fuel tanks made every trip to the gas station a thrill for the attendant, as did oil changes with the gleaming chrome head covers on the V-12 engine.

tion operating, which meant that the NEB had a major voice in day-to-day operations. Geoffrey Robinson resigned as managing director of Jaguar. Lord Ryder left the NEB in 1977, but the damage had been done. Michael Edwardes was named to head British Leyland (BL) in 1977 with a brief to restore it to profitability by virtually any means. A BL operations committee ran Jaguar until Bob Knight was named managing director in 1979. John Egan was hired as managing director by Michael Edwardes in 1980 and Knight retired at that time.

The Ryder Report's misguided attempt to centralize design, engineering and management functions by British Leyland nearly destroyed the spirit that existed in the individual car companies. At Jaguar, a core of people, primarily in engineering, kept the spirit of the company alive as well as the future model program.

when a High Efficiency version appeared. There were complaints about the styling of the XJ-S. which featured "buttresses" around the rear windows that limited rearward vision somewhat.

Powered by a 5.3-liter V-12 engine rated at 244 horsepower, the XJ-S had a top speed of over 135 miles per hour and looked as if it was going that speed even when standing still. One of the reasons for this was a unique styling feature of "flying buttresses" that swept from the roofline to the tail of the car. While these controversial buttresses aided the stability of the XJ-S at speed, they did reduce rearward vision.

Earlier in 1975, a British government report by the National Enterprise Board (NEB), named after its author, Lord Ryder, proposed uniting all British Leyland car manufacturing under one umbrella group, BL Cars. Government funding had to be provided to keep the crippled corpora-

GROUP 44 V-12 E-TYPE AT ROAD ATLANTA
Jaguar's return to racing in the United States was under the banner of Bob Tullius' Group 44 on the East Coast and Joe Huffaker on the West Coast. The Tullius effort was the more successful. Tullius first raced a V-12-engined E-type and was successful in his second year out, winning an SCCA National Championship.

Tullius went to a highly modified XJS after the E-type and won the SCCA's Trans-American Sedan Championship. All Group 44 cars were noted for their pristine finish. With Quaker State as a prime sponsor besides British Leyland, the cars were painted white with two shades of green as a bottom color.

Bob Knight, among others, fought to keep Jaguar engineering dedicated to Jaguar, rather than part of a corporate homogenization. While this ran counter to the aims of the Ryder Report, it was successful and Jaguar engineering remained independent. One of their tactics was to design the engine bay of the forthcoming XJ40 sedan so that it was too narrow to accommodate a Rover V-8, as BL wanted, and they would have to use a Jaguar straight six. Of course, when Jaguar eventually decided to add a V-12 to the line, this plan backfired.

On the competition front, Jaguar Cars Inc. in the United States supported two racing efforts, one under the tutelage of Bob Tullius' Group 44 on the East Coast and the other under Joe Huffaker on the West Coast. Tullius and Lee Mueller in the Huffaker car both drove E-types, with Tul-

1979 XJ6/12, XKS (S-TYPE)
By 1979, Jaguar was calling the XKS the "S-type" in an attempt to place it in the lineage of the C-type, D-type and E-type. The XKS wasn't a sports car in the classic sense; it had far more refinement and probably as good performance as most sports cars. The XKS used the 5.3-liter V-12 engine, which was enough to give it a certain panache. That engine was also available in the Jaguar Sedan, be it XJ6 or XJ12. In these two cars, Jaguar offered stirring performance and unmatched luxury.

lius' overall effort being the more successful. He finished second in the SCCA runoffs at Road Atlanta that year.

Tullius won the SCCA championship in 1975, competing against the likes of Corvette. He switched to an XJ-S in 1976 and won the SCCA's Trans-Am Sedan Championship in 1977 and

1979 JAGUAR XJ-S
"The most extravagant Jaguar ever built" was the elegant 1979 XJ-S. This was the street version of the car that, in Bob Tullius' hands, won five Trans-Am races in its first season. Yet here was also a four-passenger car with fully independent suspension, 4-wheel disc brakes, power rack-and-pinion steering and Jaguar's 5.3-liter V-12 engine.

1978. In the latter year he won seven of ten races. Tullius' final Trans-Am effort was in 1981 when he finished second, but by then the company's efforts were trending toward sports racing cars.

Another competition effort gave Jaguar a record that is likely to stand forever. It was in the 1979 Cannonball Baker Sea-to-Shining-Sea Memorial Trophy Dash from Darien, Connecti-cut, to Los Angeles. Begun by *Car and Driver* Editor Brock Yates early in the decade, it was both a tribute to the erstwhile Cannonball Baker, who set coast-to-coast records in the early years of the century in a variety of cars from Stutz to Cadillac, and it was also a challenge to the national 55 miles per hour speed limit. Yates and a group of competitors would try to be the first to reach Los Angeles.

In the fifth running of the event in 1979, Jaguar dealers Dave Yarborough and Dave Heinz ran the Cannonball in an XJ-S V12 coupe. They covered the 3,000-mile distance in 32 hours, 51 minutes, for an average speed of 86.7 miles per hour. Since it was also the last running of the Cannonball, Heinz' and Yarborough's record will stand forever.

Jaguar closed out the decade of the 1970s with the introduction of Series III versions of the XJ sedan range. With a new roofline and rear window to improve rear seat headroom, the Series III cars showed subtle styling changes which served to perfect the XJ design. Besides the roofline, the side windows slanted in slightly to a narrower roof, the windshield was slanted more sharply, and the wing windows were eliminated. Up front, the horizontal chrome bars of the grille were replaced by vertical bars, which continue to the 1997 models.

In Europe, the new XJ-S became available in 1984 with a choice of engines: a new 3.6-liter six, or the 5.3-liter V-12. In the U.S., however, only the V-12 was offered. Initially rated at 289 horsepower, power output grew to 295 horsepower in 1981. When fuel consumption concerns threatened to kill the V-12, the "Fireball" cylinder head of Swiss engineer Michael May was incorporated into the 1982 "HE" or High Efficiency versions of the engine.

Chapter Six

The 1980s

The 1980s began with Jaguar doing business as usual; moving through a period of rediscovered independence; and ending dramatically with the company under control of Ford and producing the fastest production car of the time. Jaguar returned to the scene of its greatest triumphs at Le Mans and took the prize home twice. On the sad side, founder Sir William Lyons died in February 1985.

Administratively, Jaguar Cars Ltd. ended its unhappy alliance with British Leyland by going public on June 29, 1984. Hamish Orr-Ewing was named chairman of the company, only to be ousted in 1985. John Egan continued through the decade as managing director, retiring in 1990.

1980 JAGUAR XJS
While Jaguar sales were suffering under the confused management of British Leyland in the early 1980s, the XJS continued to carry the banner of Jaguar sports cars. Bob Tullius campaigned an XJS to win the 1978 SCCA Trans-Am Sedan Championship in the V-12-engined car. A 6-cylinder version of the XJS was to come in 1985, but this 1980 car still used the elegant 5.3-liter V-12.

Jaguar production increased from 14,000 at the beginning of the decade to more than 50,000 in 1988, before the U.S. stock market crash of October 1987 put a crimp in all luxury car sales. American sales reached a peak of 24,464 in 1986

In 1984, 178 million Jaguar shares were offered on the British stock market for the first time, with the exception of a "Golden Share" held by the British government to protect the company from a takeover. The offering caused a rush on the London Exchange on August 3, 1984, when there were offers for eight times as many shares as were available. The price of the shares went to £1.88 ($2.94) within a week. In the United States, the over-the-counter price rose to $9.50 in early 1987.

A takeover at the time seemed unlikely. Profits rose to £120.8 million ($189 million) in 1986 and continued near the £100 million ($150 million) mark for several years. A new Engineering Centre was opened at Whitley, Coventry, in 1988. Jaguar Cars Inc., moved to new headquarters in the United States in June

171

1989 JAGUAR VANDEN PLAS MAJESTIC
Along with the introduction of the new AJ6 engine, Jaguar also introduced the Majestic version of the XJ6 Vanden Plas sedan in 1989. The Majestic only came in Regency Red and included a magnolia leather interior, alarm system and diamond-polished alloy wheels. It also included all the standard Vanden Plas features, such as a limited-slip differential, self-leveling suspension, and folding burl walnut picnic tables on the backs of the front seats.

1990. The new home office was located in Mahwah, New Jersey, in the north-central area of the state, near the New York border.

But all was not completely well. Profits dipped to £47.5 million ($74 million) in 1988, and £1.4 million in the first six months of 1989. In 1989, new competitors appeared from the Far East in the form of luxury cars introduced by the three major Japanese auto manufacturers: Honda's Acura, Toyota's Lexus and Nissan's Infiniti divisions.

John Egan realized that he no longer had the resources to fund product development on his own. Late in 1988, Egan met with Donald Petersen of Ford. Discussions broke off when it was apparent that Ford wanted a majority interest in Jaguar. Egan next went to General Motors. These discussions were more fruitful and GM agreed to an arrangement whereby it would buy 30 percent of Jaguar, but would leave the company independent.

After the brief courtship between Jaguar and GM during 1988, Ford came back into the picture and announced on September 19, 1989, that it would buy 15 percent of Jaguar's stock. Under American regulations and Jaguar articles of incorporation, this was the limit. Such a move also had to be made public. Three weeks later, GM made the same announcement. All this speculation fueled interest in Jaguar shares on the stock market, raising the price from around $5 to around $13.

FASTMASTERS JAGUAR XJ220
While the XJ220 didn't make it to production, approximately a dozen of these cars were used for a one-year racing series called FastMasters. Retired drivers such as Bobby Allison, Parnelli Jones and Jack Brabham raced in events that were companion races to NASCAR or CART events. The series proved to be popular and had TV sponsorship, but the costs of maintaining the cars far exceeded the public relations value.

On October 31, 1989, the British government withdrew its "Golden Share," permitting full takeover of Jaguar. GM had only wanted a minority interest in Jaguar; Ford had decided it wanted the whole package. Ford's offer was now the only acceptable one. On November 2, 1989, Ford purchased Jaguar for £8.50 ($13.28) per share or $2.5 billion (£1.6 billion). The transaction became official on January 1, 1990, when Jaguar Cars Ltd. became a wholly owned subsidiary of the Ford Motor Company.

John Egan told employees of Jaguar North America, "In 1980 when I became chairman of Jaguar, the company was worth nothing. It was a case of revive Jaguar or close it. In 1984, after four years of sales growth worldwide, when we floated our shares, the new worth was approximately $500 million. That in itself was not a bad turnaround. Now in 1989, the Jaguar board has approved an offer from Ford Motor Company of approximately two and one half billion dollars for Jaguar. That represents a five-fold increase in value since 1984."

Jaguar supported two competition efforts through the early years of the decade, but ended the decade backing just one team worldwide. Bob Tullius and Group 44 continued to be the corporate standard-bearer in the United States. After winning SCCA National Championships in the V-12-powered E-type and two Trans-Am Sedan Championships in the XJS, in 1982 Tullius received permission from Mike Dale of Jaguar Cars to build a prototype racer to compete in the International Motor Sports Association's GTP series in the United States. The car was the XJR-5 (XJ for experimental Jaguar, R for racer, 5 because it was the fifth Jaguar racer for Tullius). The body was designed by Len Dykstra, while the V-12 engine was derived from the 5.4-liter unit used in the XJ-S. In developed 525 horsepower. It its first race, the XJR-5 finished third at Road America. Its first win came in 1983 at Road Atlantic.

1988 LE MANS 24-HOUR VICTORY
Jaguar returned to the Le Mans winner's circle in 1988 with a three-car team of Tom Walkinshaw Racing cars sponsored by Silk Cut and Castrol. The winning car was driven by Johnny Dumfries, Jan Lammers and Andy Wallace, and the three remaining Jaguar cars in the race crossed the finish line after 24 hours in formation.

In Europe, Jaguar support went to Tom Walkinshaw Racing. Walkinshaw raced an XJ-S in the European Touring Car championship and won the title in 1984. Although Tullius spearheaded Jaguar's return to Le Mans in 1985 with a 13th place finish, it was TWR which would be competing in the World Sportscar Championship, which included Le Mans. An XJR-5 was shipped to TWR for analysis, but Walkinshaw had already commissioned a new design from Tony Southgate. Christened XJR-6, the car finished third in its first race at Mosport. Its first win was at Silverstone in May 1986. Group 44 and TWR would continue to build XJR racers, with Group 44 getting the odd numbers and TWR the even numbers.

Group 44 debuted its new car, XJR-7, at Daytona in 1985, where it finished fourth. Tullius and Chip Robinson won the December Daytona

three-hour race that year, however. They won two more races in 1987, after it was announced that TWR would also campaign for Jaguar in the United States in 1988. The final race for Group 44 was at Watkins Glen, where there was an emotional "good-bye party" after the race.

For TWR, the 1987 car was the XJR-8, with a 7-liter V-12. The car won eight of ten world championship races and the World Championship of Sports Cars. In 1988 TWR won the Daytona 24 hours and brought Jaguar back to the winners' podium at Le Mans, after 31 years. The driving team of Johnny Dumfries, Jan Lammers and Andy Wallace was successful for Jaguar and TWR.

In February 1990, a TWR XJR-12 won the 24 Hours of Daytona in its first race, driven by Lammers, Andy Wallace and Davy Jones. Jaguar repeated its Le Mans win in 1990 in a car driven by John Nielson, Price Cobb and Martin Brundle. Lammers, Wallace and Franz Konrad finished second in another XJR-12.

In production cars, Jaguar developed a new 3.6-liter 6-cylinder engine that debuted in September 1983. Dubbed the AJ6 (for Advanced Jaguar), this engine would be used initially in the sport coupes, but would later also be used in sedans.

With a capacity of 3,592cc and dual overhead camshafts, the AJ6 was only slightly larger than the XK engine developed during World War II that had been so instrumental in Jaguar's resurgence. Compression ratio for the AJ6 was 9.6:1 and it developed 221 horsepower at 5,000 rpm initially with four valves per cylinder. Eventually, 2.9-liter, 3.2-liter and 4.0-liter versions of this engine would be developed, with the different capacities dictated by changing the stroke from 74.8 to 102 mm, but keeping the bore at 91 mm.

The first cars to use the AJ6 were the 1984 XJ-S line of cars (coupe and cabriolet). The cabriolet was the surprise car. Considered doomed by safety regulations, convertibles were making a small comeback in the automotive marketplace. Jaguar's XJ-SC was a Targa top model with a folding rear window and, as such, wasn't a "real" convertible. But it was Jaguar's first open-topped car in eight years. A later V-12-powered model followed.

In 1986, a true XJ-S Convertible would be announced with a price tag of $50,000. This was not a "factory" car, but was, in fact, an after-market "chopped top" version built by Hess & Eisenhardt in Cincinnati. Customers would buy an XJ-S coupe and have it delivered to H&E, where it would be modified and delivered back to the buyer in 45-60 days. The total price included a three-year, 36,000-mile warranty.

Hess & Eisenhart was one of America's premier coach builders who had built Cadillac limousines since 1936 and had created both Cadillac and Buick convertibles for those manufacturers. Prior to World War II, H&E had built cars designed by Darrin for movie stars.

Two years later, Jaguar introduced its own XJ-S V-12 convertible, with a draft-proof automatic top and stiffened body to eliminate flexing. The XJ-S convertible also had a glass rear window, which incorporated defroster wiring.

This one was built with design assistance from Karmann in Germany, who had designed and built such cars for Volkswagen, Audi and Ford of Germany. Karmann would design and tool the metal expansion frames and folding mechanism. Jaguar would make and fit the fully lined convertible top.

Jaguar had been developing a new sedan for several years. It was not a great secret that the car, code-named XJ40, would be a great new Jaguar sedan. What was a secret, though, was its final name, XJ6. While confusing to those who followed the industry closely, XJ6 was a logical name

to continue for the sedan. Powered by the AJ6 engine, the new XJ6 debuted in September 1986. At the launch, it was announced that the only thing in common between the new XJ6 and its predecessor was the horn button. Comparisons between the BMW 7-series and the Mercedes-Benz S-Class were natural, with the general opinion that the Jaguar and BMW outclassed the S-Class, primarily on the basis of their sportiness

In September 1989, a 4.0-liter version of the AJ6 engine was installed in the XJ6. While horsepower increased from 221 to 235, the real reason for the larger engine was an increase in torque, which went up dramatically from 249 pound feet for the 3.6-liter engine to 285 pound feet for the 4.0. The engine was mated to a new ZF four-speed automatic gearbox with "Sport" and "Normal" modes. Inside, the XJ6 had an instrument panel that returned to round analog gauges in a walnut-trimmed dash.

Jaguar and TWR formed a joint venture, JaguarSport, which developed the XJR-S, introduced in 1989. This car was based on the production XJ-S V-12 coupe, but the 6.0-liter engine now developed 318 horsepower and was mated to a GM three-speed automatic transmission. With a top speed of 160 miles per hour, the XJR-S had a stiffer suspension with better front and rear springs and gas-filled shock absorbers. In addition, the wheels and tires were widened, with the rear tires being wider than the fronts.

Inside, there was Doeskin leather with contrasting piping on the seats, a JaguarSport steering wheel. One hundred Le Mans Celebration cars were specially built and numbered, with Number 2 going to Jan Lammers. His Le Mans-winning Jaguar carried number 2.

A later product of this joint venture would be the 1994 XJR sedan, with a supercharged 6-cylinder engine.

CASTROL JAGUAR AT DAYTONA 24-HOUR
In 1990, Jaguar returned to the winners circle again at Le Mans, proving that the 1988 win was no fluke. The TWR team started out the year with a win in the Daytona 24 hours race.

Perhaps the most exciting Jaguar of the decade was the XJ220 concept car. Likely based loosely on the XJ13 concept car, the XJ220 was powered by a 500 horsepower version of the 6.2-liter V-12 engine. Top speed was estimated at over 200 miles per hour, with a 0-60 time of 3.5 seconds. It was unveiled on October 10, 1988, at the Birmingham International Motor Show and caused a sensation.

The frame was built of bonded aluminum with a steel roll cage. The fact that it was 4-wheel drive resulted from a close association with FF Developments, which was a Coventry-based engineering firm owned by 1953 Le Mans winner Tony Rolt. Double wishbones were used for the 4-wheel independent suspension with the rear coil springs in a nearly horizontal position.

But it was also a Jaguar, so it had Connolly leather upholstery and trim on the dash and doors, air conditioning, power windows, adjustable steering column, remote-control locking, heated seats and a CD player. The styling was intended to evoke memories of the XJ13 and E-type.

JaguarSport announced a production run of 220 to 350 cars, depending on demand. The price of the cars was £290,000—about $500,000—and a deposit of £50,000 was required with the order. Firm orders were received from enthusiasts such as Mick Jagger and Elton John, among others.

The production version differed from the concept car in that the engine would be a twin turbocharged version of the V-6 engine used in the XJR-10 and XJR-11 race cars, but detuned to 500 horsepower from 750 horsepower. The production car would also have rear-wheel drive instead of 4-wheel drive. Top speed was still in the 200 miles per hour range, with a 0-60 time of 4.0 seconds.

Jaguar cars also suffered from quality and assembly problems at the end of the decade, just as Customer Satisfaction was becoming a watchword in the industry. With a work force accustomed to doing its job in a more traditional manner in older factories, attention to detail had slipped. Ford's influence would bring tougher quality control guidelines to the factory floor and would bring Jaguar's quality levels, as well as Customer Satisfaction Index values, back to more acceptable levels.

In the United States, sales slipped to 3,023 in 1980, the lowest level they would ever reach. Then vice-president of sales Mike Dale told his staff that they would be wise to explore the job market, because the future of the company was truly questionable. That Dale's predictions were off is attributable to the Series III XJ sedans. Sales were back up to 18,044 by 1984 in a remarkable recovery.

The
1990s

Chapter Seven

Jaguar showed in the 1990s that it was a company that could rebound and still innovate. Customer Satisfaction Index (CSI) ratings rose from a low of 25th overall in 1992 to 9th overall in 1996, an increase attributable to better production methods and a better corporate attitude toward its customers.

Jaguar was also honored when an E-type roadster was made part of the permanent display at the Museum of Modern Art in New York in 1996, recognizing the car's contribution to the world of automobile styling. Only the third automobile to enter the museum's collection, the Malcolm Sayer-designed car was the showpiece

1996 XJR
Originally introduced in 1995, the XJR carried a Roots supercharged version of the 4.0-liter V-6 that delivered 322 horsepower and 378 pounds-feet torque. The XJR was developed as a joint venture between Jaguar and Tom Walkinshaw's JaguarSport. It represented Jaguar's first supercharged car. Besides superior performance, the XJR also offered increased levels of luxury over the XJ6, with maple wood trim and a wood-and-leather steering wheel.

of a four-month exhibit, "Refining the Sports Car: Jaguar's E-type." Terence Riley, chief curator, Department of Architecture and Design, said," Since 1972, when the Museum acquired its first car, a Cisitalia 202 GT, we have been committed to expanding this facet of the design collection. We developed a wish list of ten to twelve cars, with the E-type at the top. Because of the E-type's beauty and sculptural quality, its functionality, and its seminal impact on overall car design, it perfectly suits the criteria of a landmark design object."

In March 1990, Sir John Egan announced that he would be leaving Jaguar in June of that year after ten years as managing director. His contributions to the company were recognized with his Knighthood, conferred in 1986. Egan also presided over the difficult transition from independent company to Ford subsidiary. After his retirement, Bill Hayden was appointed chairman and chief executive at Jaguar by Ford.

179

1990 JAGUAR XJ6
For the 1990 XJ6 sedan, Jaguar introduced a 4.0-liter version of the AJ6 engine that was based on the original 3.6-liter AJ6. The XJ6 showed only minor changes from the 1989 edition, as the changes were made in the engine compartment. The influence of Ford management had yet to be felt in the design and development of Jaguar cars. Teves anti-lock brakes replaced the Girling/Bosch units formerly used. Quad round headlights were retained on the base model, but rectangular headlights were used for the Vanden Plas, Sovereign and Majestic.

Hayden, a career production man, announced that the pursuit of quality would be unrelenting, and he set out to achieve this on all fronts. The work force was streamlined and contracts re-negotiated to achieve greater worker commitment to building better products. Investments were made in manufacturing facilities, creating improvements in everything from welding to final painting. An increased number of computer-controlled processes ensured accuracy. More robots on the line also contributed to increased accuracy. Quality standards were set for suppliers as well, and new suppliers were found for parts that didn't measure up. Ford's buying power helped reduce costs.

White coated inspectors, who stood at the end of the line to evaluate cars, were replaced by fault diagnosis on the line itself. Problems were solved at the source so that finished cars could be driven away directly to the transporters. The Uniform Product Assessment System (UPAS) was instituted to ensure that finished Jaguars met the standards of the luxury car buyer, not just production guidelines.

1991 VANDEN PLAS
Only minor changes were reflected in the 1991 XJ6 and Vanden Plas. Both offered leather seats and burl walnut trim, but the Vanden Plas added boxwood inlays in the woodwork and the traditional picnic tables on the rear of the front seats. For 1991, the Vanden Plas was identified by a fluted grille surround and trunk plinth, which were reminiscent of British Daimlers.

In the United States, Jaguar Cars Inc. president Graham Whitehead also retired in 1990 after almost 22 years at the helm. Whitehead had also presided over drastic changes at Jaguar, since he joined the company right after the merger with British Leyland. He was replaced by Mike Dale, who had an equally long tenure and who was responsible for Jaguar's U.S. racing efforts under Bob Tullius. Dale himself was an SCCA champion, driving an Austin-Healey Sprite to that title in 1973.

Dale would direct the company from new North American headquarters in Mahwah, New Jersey. The new facility among the lush foliage of northern New Jersey was a distinct contrast to the Leonia headquarters, which had been inherited from British Leyland Motor Holdings.

On the competition side, Jaguar won Le Mans in 1990, with a TWR XJR-12 driven by John Nielson, Price Cobb and Martin Brundle. It was Jaguar's second win in three years and seventh win overall. The competition season had begun on a strong note as well, with the TWR car winning the Daytona 24 Hours.

In the first half of the decade, Jaguar products were very much the result of Jaguar management; it was only in the latter half of the decade that the influence of Ford began to be felt. Therefore, the company followed a conservative tack with its early vehicles. The first vehicle to be announced was the 4.0-liter version of the XJ6 sedan in September 1990. The engine was based on the 3.6-liter AJ6 engine. Two new models in the sedan range were the Sover-

1991 XJ-S CLASSIC EDITION
Jaguar's 1991 Classic Edition XJ-S Coupe and Convertible both used a 5.3-liter V-12 engine for power, coupled with a 3-speed automatic transmission. The engine was rated at 263 horsepower at 5,350rpm. The XJ-S rode on a 102.0-inch wheelbase and was 191.7 inches long. It weighed 4,050 pounds, but the big V-12 could move it along at a brisk pace. In 1992, Jaguar warranties would increase from three years/36,000 miles to four years/50,000 miles, showing significant confidence in the improved quality of the line.

eign and Vanden Plas Majestic, giving Jaguar four sedan models, all based on the XJ6. The Vanden Plas was an upgrade from the XJ6, with limited-slip differential, self-leveling suspension, headlight washers with heated nozzles, footwell rugs, heated front seats, folding burl walnut picnic tables on the front seat backs, leather-covered seat backs, rear arm rest storage, fog lights and rear reading lamps. The Sovereign added a power sunroof, burl walnut inlays and rear head restraints. The Majestic, which only came in Regency Red, added a magnolia leather interior, diamond-polished alloy wheels and an alarm system.

Base engine for the 1991 XJ-S Coupe and Convertible was the 5.3-liter V-12. A production version of the XJ220 was announced early in 1991, with a turbocharged 3.5-liter V-6. It was priced at £290,000. Jaguar took £50,000 non-refundable deposits on the car and had a full order book. But when the bottom fell out of the collector car market and investors realized that the value of the XJ220 would not appreciate as much as they

had hoped, they tried to reclaim their deposits. Lengthy lawsuits resulted, with Jaguar eventually ending up retaining the deposits.

The last Series III XJ12 sedan left the line at the end of 1992 and went straight to Jaguar's museum. This sedan/engine combination had helped maintain Jaguar's sense of individuality for 20 years, through periods of turmoil. While the V-12 engine may not have been the most practical in an era of fuel crisis and government-mandated fuel economies, it gave Jaguar a definite "halo effect" car whose value far outweighed its negatives.

In 1993, a new sedan range was offered, with approximately one-third new body panels. The changes were made to alter the rigidity for air bag installation. This year, Jaguar identified the Vanden Plas sedan with fluting around the grille and trunk plinth previously used on the short-lived Majestic. This fluting resembled that used on Daimlers. Late in the year, the XJ12 returned with a 6.0-liter V-12 engine.

By 1994, models in the United States were the XJS convertible and coupe with 4.0-liter 6-cylinder and 6.0-liter V-12 engines, the XJ6 and Vanden Plas sedans with 4.0-liter 6-cylinder engines, and the XJ12 sedan with the 6.0-liter V-12. Passenger-side air bags were installed on all models. Prices ranged from $51,750 for the XJ6 to $79,950 for the XJS 6.0L convertible.

By 1995, the first fruits of the Ford investment were realized with a restyled sedan line, a more powerful 6-cylinder engine, and the introduction of Jaguar's first supercharged car, the XJR sports sedan based on the XJ6. The XJR was powered by the 4.0-liter inline six of the XJ6, but with a Roots-type supercharger and a lowered compression ratio. Still, the XJR posted impressive numbers; 322 horsepower at 5,000 rpm and 378 pounds feet torque at 3,050 rpm. XJR carried a price tag

Jaguar's 1994 line was one of the most comprehensive in the company's history. All cars added passenger-side airbags to the driver's side airbags that had been installed since 1993. The sedans were refined with cellular phone pre-wiring, a remote trunk release, and Pirelli P4000E tires on diamond-turned 7x16 aluminum wheels. The XJS line comprised four models, with 4.0-liter 6-cylinder and 6.0-liter V-12 engines in coupes and convertibles.

1996 XJ12

1996 was the last year for the XJ12 sedan. The V-12-engined variation of the X300 was powered by a 6.0-liter engine that was a derivation of the previous 5.3-liter version. With a longer stroke, power was increased as was mid-range torque. The bodyshell had been modified in 1992 to accommodate the V-12 engine, with about 60 of the 140 new or modified panels associated with the V-12 installation. While many of the panels were required for the V-12 engine installation, several were also necessitated by the installation of a driver's-side airbag, including the required chassis stiffening.

of $65,000, just $6,600 more than the base XJ6.

The sedan line was based on the Series III or X300 as it was known internally. The base engine for the sedans was the AJ16, a 4.0-liter inline six based on the AJ6. It developed 245 horsepower, a 10 percent increase over 1994. Exterior styling of the new sedans was smoother and more aerodynamic. As in previous years, grille design differentiated the models.

For 1996, long wheelbase versions of the X300 sedans were introduced. The X300 LWB sedans rode on a 117.9-inch wheelbase, compared to the standard 113.0-inch wheelbase. In 1996, this chassis was used only for the Vanden Plas and XJ12, but in 1997, with the discontinuance of the V-12-engined car, it became available on XJ6L and Vanden Plas. A short wheelbase XJ6 remained in the line and the XJR kept the short wheelbase as well.

Nicholas Scheele joined Jaguar from Ford of Mexico in 1992 as Chairman and CEO, with the same commitment to quality improvement

1996 XJS
In its last full year of production, the 1996 XJS was offered only as a convertible and only with the 6.0-liter V-12 engine. Coincident with the discontinuance of the XJS, the V-12 engine was also discontinued. The engine of choice for Jaguar's new sports car would be a 4.0-liter V-8, the first V-8 in Jaguar's history. Still the XJs served a useful purpose in Jaguar's history. While not a pure sports car, it provided a continuation of Jaguar sports cars between the E-type and 1997 XK8.

as Hayden. Since taking office, he has pressed for further improvements, including the 21-day installation of a completely new "overhead" sedan assembly track at Browns Lane.

Ford has been relatively true to its initial promise to allow Jaguar to be Jaguar. When the purchase was announced, automotive analyst Maryann Keller said the buy-out was cheap for Ford, because it would have cost them more to develop their own line of luxury cars.

In December 1989, Jack Telnack, Ford vice president of design, told the International Motor Press Association that Ford's plans were to keep Jaguar's uniqueness. Although he also said, "There are so many things that can be done with the XJ6. The proportions are great and the car has a very distinctive silhouette. I would have killed to have that kind of tread and the cowl in that location and the low hood. And now it's right in our laps. We could . . . really clean it up and simplify it."

Chapter Eight | # XK8

On the product side, Jaguar returned to the world of exciting sports cars in March and April 1996 with the introduction of the XK8 coupe and convertible, introduced at the Geneva and New York auto shows, respectively. They collected universal praise from all who saw and drove the cars. Nick Scheele said, "The XK8 reaffirms Jaguar's heritage of outstandingly beautiful sports cars. The dynamic style of the XK8 convertible and coupe can only begin to communicate the driving experience in store."

Powered by Jaguar's first V-8 engine, known as AJ-V8, the XK8's introduction meant the departure of its predecessor, the XJS. First intro-

duced in 1975, the XJS was Jaguar's best-selling sports car, with sales of approximately 112,000 units, and was in production longer than any other Jaguar, 21 years.

The AJ-V8 4.0-liter engine is a product of Jaguar's Whitley Engineering Centre in Coventry. It is only the fourth all-new engine designed by Jaguar. It is a four cam, 32-valve, 90-degree V-8 of 3,996 cc capacity that delivers 290 bhp at 6,100 rpm and 284 pounds feet torque at 4,250 rpm. Eighty percent of peak torque is available between 1,400 and 6,400 rpm. At its introduction, the engine represented best-in-class performance in a variety of measures, including specific power output, power density (engine weight versus power), powertrain rigidity and friction levels. Development of the AJ-V8 engine began in the mid-1980s with internal engineering studies that arose out of Jaguar's new-found independence from British Leyland. The first running prototype was produced in November 1991. The engine was benchmarked

The Jaguar XK8 has a wide oval grille that is reminiscent of the E-type. In addition, the modern halogen headlights offer greater candlepower than the sealed-beam headlights of the E-type, while returning to the classic fared in look of the past. The "power bulge" in the hood adds structural stiffness to the panel as well as a muscular look to the first new Jaguar sports car in 30 years.

JAGUAR XK8 COUPE

The 1997 Jaguar XK8 Coupe was introduced at the 1996 New York International Automobile Show to rave reviews. It is a classic aerodynamic design that harkens back to the original E-type of the 1960s with a wide oval grille, fared-in headlights and stunning lines. The XK8 is also powered by Jaguar's first V-8 engine, dubbed AJ-V8. It is only the fourth all-new engine designed by Jaguar. The car and engine were both designed in England. Design of the cars began in the early 1990s, but engine development began in the mid-1980s.

The smooth rear lines of the Jaguar XK8 Coupe hide a respectable 11.1 cubic foot trunk. In addition, there is carrying space behind the front seats. The two rear seats offer head and shoulder room that is only slightly less than that afforded to front seat passengers. The safety-mandated high-mounted stop light is mounted on the rear parcel shelf at the bottom of the windshield.

against the Lexus V-8 for refinement and the BMW V-8 for power delivery.

The square design of the AJ-V8 (86 mm bore x 86 mm stroke) was selected after considerable research with single-cylinder prototypes for its balance of power output with low emissions and high thermal efficiency.

While the 90-degree Vee angle is conventional and the all-aluminum construction is widespread, the die-cast block improves upon standard practice by employing a structural bedplate to establish a rigid, durable foundation for the engine. The bedplate is an intricate aluminum casting that forms the portion of the block below the crankshaft centerline, incorporating the five main bearing caps into a single ladder-type structure. Iron liners are cast in place at each bearing position to ensure that bearing clearance remains constant at all temperatures. Tying the bearing caps (which support the crankshaft) together with the bedplate results in a far stronger engine assembly that not only benefits long-term durability, but also helps to eliminate vibration at the source, improving refinement. It is a feature that is also employed in Cadillac's Northstar V-8 and the Oldsmobile Aurora V-8 that is derived from it and which, in highly modified form, will be one of two powerplants for Indy Racing League cars in 1997.

The working surface of the cylinder bores is formed by an electroplating process called Nikasil (for nickel/silicon carbide), which is applied directly to the aluminum parent material of the engine block. There are no separate iron cylinder liners. A precision casting of spheroidal graphite iron, the crankshaft has minimal bending and twisting under power.

With double overhead camshafts and four valves per cylinder, the AJ-V8 engine cylinder head continues a Jaguar tradition for advanced engine design. The head casting is produced through a proprietary technique developed by Cosworth. The engine's operating efficiency is aided by a narrow included valve angle of just 28 degrees between the intake and exhaust valves, which also contributes to the compact dimensions of the pent-roof combustion chamber.

Jaguar has designed variable cam phasing into the AJ-V8, which offers the midrange benefits of advanced cam timing and the high-speed advantage of retarded valve closing. The timing shift involves only the valve opening and closing points; it doesn't change the duration of the open period or the lift height to which the valve is opened.

Engine management electronics are supplied by Denso, formerly known as Nippondenso, and a company with considerable experience in the luxury market. Nippondenso supplied the management electronics for the 6.0-liter V-12.

Despite a considerable amount of available power, the XK8 does not have a gas guzzler penalty, as the V12 XJS it replaced did.

The all-aluminum AJ-V8 engine is coupled to Jaguar's first five-speed automatic transmission, manufactured by ZF. A unique feature is that the transmission fluid is installed at the factory and never needs to be checked by the owner.

There are two driver-selectable shift modes, Normal and Sport. Switching into Sport makes available a performance-oriented shift program, timing the gear changes for peak response. The transmission also carries a self-regulating "adaptive" feature, which enables it to compensate automatically for the effects of aging and to adjust shift quality based on slippage detected in actual use.

Jaguar's unique "J-gate" selector system is incorporated as well. The driver can operate the transmission in full automatic, or can manually shift between second, third and fourth gears, using the left side of the J-gate.

Front suspension of the XK8 incorporates a short- and long-arm double wishbone system. This style of suspension offers more vertical wheel travel and a greater potential for maximizing tire tread contact with the road. The front suspension is mounted to an aluminum cross-beam casting, which also supports the engine mounts. The use of a cross beam helps prevent noise and vibration generated at the road surface from being transmitted into the engine compartment.

Rear suspension is similar to that used in the XJR sedan. Like the front suspension, it uses a control arm design with coil springs and shock absorber mounted in a single unit. The spring is seated directly on the cast iron transverse lower wishbone, not the shock, which reduces friction to improve ride comfort and noise isolation.

Four-wheel disc brakes are used with a Teves Mk 20 anti-lock braking system. This Teves unit uses an Electronic Control Unit and four wheel-speed sensors. Brakes are 305 mm diameter at all four wheels and are also ventilated at all four wheels to improve resistance to fade and improve wet-weather performance.

The XK8 was designed at the Whitley Engineering Centre under Jaguar Styling Director Geoff Lawson. "One of the key factors in our choice of the coupe design was its ability to translate into a convertible," Lawson said. The fully lined and insulated convertible top retracts to a position slightly above the rear sheetmetal, and can be covered by an easily attached soft cover. Lawson added that, "A design that provides some soft material sitting proud of the sheetmetal is a cue of classic British coachwork. To stow the top under a hard panel would have required raising the rear sheetmetal, a measure not acceptable to us."

"With one-button operation and automatic latching, the XK8's top operation is among the

JAGUAR XK8 ROADSTER
In 1996, Jaguar introduced its first all-new sports car in 30 years, the XK8. The Roadster version exhibits clean aerodynamic lines combined with touches reminiscent of the E-type—wide oval grille, long nose and short tail, and striking performance. What the XK8 offers that the E-type didn't is greater attention to quality and the backing of the Ford Motor Company in the development of the car.

Like the classic British sports cars of the past, the XK8 Roadster's top does not retract completely into the rear deck when it is lowered. Rather, it is covered by a tonneau and is raised slightly above the body, lending a classic touch to this thoroughly modern sports car. Modern safety legislation also requires a high-mounted stop lamp, which is molded nicely into the rear deck lid just under the top. And unlike the classic sports cars of the past, the XK8 does not offer wire wheels as an option. The standard wheels are cast aluminum five-spoke units.

world's best," said chief program engineer Bob Dover. One of the salient features of the XK8 convertible is its fully lined top. Mohair lining and insulation give the XK8 the look and feel of a coupe with the top raised. On the highway at speeds up to 100 miles per hour, there is no wind noise. In fact, the XK8 convertible is in the same class as the famed Lexus LS400 as a quiet-running highway car.

Concept sketches for the XK8 began in 1991. Clay model construction began in January 1992. The final design theme was selected in October 1992.

Wood trim highlights the dash, as in Jaguars of old, and white-on-black analog instruments transmit information to the driver.

Jaguar is marketing the XK8 against the Mercedes-Benz SL500 and BMW 840Ci, and holds a price advantage of approximately $20,000 and $5,000 over those cars, respectively, based on 1997 pricing. The XK8 is still about $12,000 cheaper than the XJS it replaced, when you add in the XJS's $3,700 gas guzzler tax. Advertising debuted on October 3, 1996, with the theme, "A new breed of Jaguar."

As Jaguar cars have been modernized in construction and equipment, they have never lost their traditional looks and performance. Always built with the finest components and unsurpassed luxury, Jaguar products remain the equal of anything on the road in terms of speed, handling and safety. Through Ford's investments in manufacturing facilities and processes, the cars have reached a quality level which firmly ensures that Jaguar's reputation for value will carry on into the next century.

Bibliography

The literature about Jaguar is continually expanding. The books listed below were, in most cases, primary reference sources. Some are included because they are important general reference works for anyone interested in a more in-depth history of the company. Check your Motorbooks International catalog for any recent entries.

Essential Jaguar XK: XK120/140/150. Lawrence, Mike. Bay View Books, 1995.

Jaguar E-Type. Stone, Matthew L. Motorbooks International, 1995.

Jaguar E-Type: The definitive history. Porter, Philip. Automobile Quarterly, 1989.

Jaguar in America. Dugdale, John. Britbooks, 1993.

Jaguar Product Guide. CDI, 1995, 1996, 1997.

Jaguar, Fifth Edition. Lord Montagu of Beaulieu. Quiller Press, 1986.

Jaguar: Catalogue Raisonné 1922–1992. Automobilia, 1991.

Jaguar: History of a classic marque. Porter, Philip. Orion Books, 1988.

Jaguar: The history of a great British car. Whyte, Andrew. Patrick Stephens, Ltd., 1980.

PORSCHE 911

PATRICK PATERNIE

ACKNOWLEDGMENTS

First off, I need to thank the usual suspects for their patience and support during the "birthing process" of this book. Unfortunately, unlike mothers delivering real babies into this world, my moaning, whining, or whimpering is stretched out over the entire period of gestation. So hats off to my wife, Linda, my kids, friends, and associates for bearing with me.

My editor, John Adams-Graf of MBI Publishing Company, not only puts up with my whining and excuses but probably thinks up even better ones for me to stay in good graces with our collective boss at MBI, Zack Miller. John is also a hardcore 911 enthusiast, so he serves as good inspiration as well.

I can always count on Matt Stone for whatever I may need at any given time. And of course my "sponsor" who helped me tumble down the rabbit hole into the crazy world of automotive writing, the infamous Larry B., wherever he is today.

It is also an honor and a pleasure to have the photographic excellence of Randy Leffingwell and Les Bidrawn to accompany my words.

Thanks to all the wonderful people and places that you discover just hanging around Porsche 911s. People who lent their time and in many cases their cars so this book could come together include Bruce Sansone, Jim Edwards, Pete Lech, Richard Price, Gary Barnhill, Stewart Thomas, Hal Holleman, Randy Garell, and Ed Buliavac. Ted Mumm, Cris Huergas, Phil and Pat Van Buskirk, and Craig Stevenson also made contributions that are appreciated.

I am also grateful to Jens Torner at Porsche AG, who has always been generous with factory photos and information whenever I contact him. The same is true for Bob Carlson and Eleanor Smith at Porsche Cars North America.

Cris Huergas, Freeman Thomas, Kevin Beard, Pete Johnson, and all the others who make up the R Gruppe get a special thanks for being the quintessential 911 enthusiasts. They are "keepers of the flame" dedicated to keeping the original sports car concept of the 911 alive. Their old hot rod 911s are done the way that would make both Steve McQueen and Michael Delaney break into that little smirk and present a raised thumb salute.

INTRODUCTION

For the best introduction as to what it is about the 911 that transforms its drivers into enthusiasts, I must defer to Steve McQueen who captured the essence of the 911 in the opening scenes for his movie Le Mans. The racing film, which probably has the least human dialogue since 'talkies' were invented, lets a slate gray 911S coupe do the talking as the camera follows its clas-

sic silhouette through the French countryside to the town of Le Mans and then out on the 24 Hour race circuit. (I know it looks black, but you can't be a true Porschephile unless you study up on arcane details like this.) The only sound is the unique whirring, metallic cacophony of the air-cooled 911 flat six-cylinder as McQueen's character, Michael Delaney, puts it through its paces.

(More trivia: Delaney, in a later scene on one of the rare occasions he does speak, utters the immortal phrase: "Racing is life. Anything that happens before or after is just waiting." Owners of 911s can relate to this thinking in terms of time spent behind the wheel of other cars.)

Porsche, with 16 overall victories, is synonymous with Le Mans. And a big part of the spell cast by the 911 is that when your left hand twists the ignition key, no matter how mundane your actual commute, you feel like Michael Delaney at Le Mans. The view through the panoramic arch of the windshield, over the wipers parked at its base, and between the front fenders at the road disappearing under the sloping hood, even at 20 miles per hour, evokes fantasies of being in the cockpit of a legendary Porsche 917 as it gobbles up the tarmac of the Mulsanne Straight. Look down at the dashboard and, as in a race car, a big round tachometer stares back, the speedometer relegated to the side. The tach's needle acts as a baton leading a concert of raucous sounds from the rear that covers a scale from muted whine to guttural moan to high-pitched snarl. A breathtaking experience, or as in the case of Michael Delaney, one that leaves you speechless.

What other car approaches the level at which the 911 combines the sounds and sensations of a race car in a package that can be reasonably driven to work every day? In fact, until recently, when the firm's lawyers and accountants became as important as its engineers, Porsche prided itself in offering 911 models that could be driven directly to the racetrack from the showroom floor.

Another part of the 911 mystique is that, for most of its life, with one swift twitch of its engine-laden tail, it could separate the enthusiasts from the dilettantes and poseurs, usually by tossing the latter off into the trees. Once again, it's that race car attitude in a world where "user friendly" equates to the lowest common denominator. Be smooth, pay attention to the feedback through the steering wheel, and be sensitive to how weight transfers while braking, cornering, or accelerating, and driving a 911 is definately an exhilarating experience. Sure the engine is hanging out back, but the driver's butt sits centered between the front and rear wheels. An ideal spot for sensing what the car is doing. Developing a "feel" for what the 911 is communicating takes practice, preferably in a wide open area, but it forms a bond between driver and vehicle that transforms one from an owner to an enthusiast.

Ever the classic, the 911 never forgets its roots yet manages to be a trendsetter as well. Turbochargers, whale tails, biplane wings, and painted brake calipers all debuted on 911s through the years. The 911 was the only sports car to make the top five list of the greatest cars of the twentieth century, which, as Muhammad Ali would say, at this point in history also means for "all time." The 911 is the only car of the five that has continuously remained in production—a side benefit for all of its enthusiastic fans, because that means they can't be accused of being "old car freaks."

So much for the philosophical aspects of the 911's classification as an enthusiast's car. The following chapters will give you a short course in the car's history and development, which, and it should not come as a surprise, was carried out by a dedicated corps of 911 enthusiasts.

Of course, the best introduction to understanding a 911 is by driving one. That's what Michael Delaney would tell you.

The 1967 911S established Porsche as a manufacturer capable of making a world class high-performance GT. Many Porschephiles consider the 1967 911S to be the perfect example of a European version of a "muscle car" that offers quick quarter-mile acceleration times combined with outstanding handling and high top speed. The 1967 911S could deliver 15-second runs at the drag strip and 140 miles per hour on the autobahn. *Les Bidrawn*

THE EVOLUTION BEGINS
BUTZI DRAWS THE LINE

For 36 years and still counting, although the mechanicals underneath have undergone significant changes, the unmistakable profile of the 911 has remained essentially the same. So much so that Porsche has used the 911's outline as a logo. It ranks as one of the most recognizable silhouettes this side of a Coke bottle.

Ferdinand Porsche III, son of Dr. Ferry Porsche and nicknamed "Butzi," is the man responsible for composing this distinctive shape. It evolved from sketches he first drew in August 1959 and altered as the decision process regarding the car's dimensions, seating arrangements, and powertrain continued until 1963.

Butzi's inspiration began by borrowing the high-mounted headlights of the 356. He considered them to be an important part of the "face" that the world recognized as a Porsche. He accentuated them with a lower, flatter trunk lid. From there back he penned the curve that the world then, and well into the future, would recognize as

the 911—a steeply angled windshield topped by a roofline that gracefully spilled rearward down to the taillights and bumpers.

Butzi and his father had begun planning a successor to the 356 as far back as 1956. Remember that Porsche had been founded in 1930 as an engineering consulting firm and not an automobile company. Market demand for what began as a postwar sports car project propelled Porsche into the automobile business and the manufacture of the 356. Like many businesses before and after (Steve Jobs and the Apple computer being a textbook example), the Porsche family's dilemma was what to do for an encore after coming up with such a signature initial product. Ferry Porsche, as an engineer, realized that despite its sales success and loyal following, the 356 was really stretching the limit of engineering work and technology that traced its roots back to the prewar Volkswagen project. More importantly, Ferry Porsche, the marketeer, understood that the problem wasn't

Ferry Porsche and a 1968 911. Porsche passed away in 1998, but the design criteria he established for the successor to the 356 lives on, as the 911 moves into the twenty-first century. What Ferry Porsche decided was that Porsche should stick to what it did best, by making the 911 a bit roomier than the 356 but still a two-seater. He determined that the wheelbase for the new car would be 4.4 inches longer, for a total of 87.0 inches. He also specified that a six-cylinder power plant with overhead camshafts, as opposed to a pushrod-actuated valve train, be used. After he established these initial criteria he handed over the design to his Chief of Styling, and son, Butzi Porsche. *Porsche AG*

simply one of designing a more modern car, it was designing a more modern *Porsche*. The task was to take the sports car prowess melded to the sturdy and practical nature of the 356—what people had come to expect a Porsche to be—and carry it forward in a design that could stay ahead of the ever quickening pace of an automotive world that was approaching full stride as its war wounds healed.

After toying with a number of styling themes and engine combinations, including a full four-seat model, Ferry Porsche laid down two key stipulations that affected the ultimate form of the model that would be known initially as the Porsche 901. The first was that the wheelbase of the new car should be 87 inches, 4.4 inches longer than the 356, primarily to improve the ride. The other decision by Ferry Porsche was that the new car's six-cylinder engine would not have a pushrod-actuated valve train, but a modern overhead camshaft design. A six-cylinder was deemed necessary to keep up with the more powerful offerings of competitors like Jaguar. Company tradition, experience, and knowledge combined with what best fit in the 911's tail section to decide in favor of the engine being air-cooled. A key figure in working out the intricacies of the overhead camshaft valve train for the 901 engine was a young engineer named Ferdinand Piëch. Piëch would continue to play a major role in the development and success of the earlier 911s as well as being the driving force behind Porsche's rise to

Ferdinand Porsche (Butzi), Ferry's son and grandson of company founder Ferdinand Porsche, poses with a 1963 Porsche 901. He was only 28 years old in 1963 when the 911 made its debut. As Chief of Styling, Butzi had the task of designing a car that would link Porsche's past with its future. Today, the familiar profile Butzi created for the 911 is as recognizable as that of a Coca-Cola bottle. Butzi followed up the 911 with another timeless expression of the Porsche essence, the 1964 Porsche 904. *Porsche AG*

dominance in sports car and endurance racing during the late 1960s and 1970s.

The Porsche 911, then known as the 901, made its world debut on September 12, 1963, at the Frankfurt International Auto Show. At least part

WHO ARE ALL THESE GUYS NAMED FERDINAND?

A QUICK CLIMB UP THE PORSCHE FAMILY TREE

Professor Ferdinand Porsche, patriarch of the Porsche clan, was born in 1876. In 1930, he founded the eponymous consulting firm that would eventually become one of the world's most respected sports car manufacturers. It was officially registered by the German government in 1931. Among some of Professor Porsche's more notable automotive projects were the Mercedes-Benz SS and SSK supercharger-powered roadsters of the late 1920s, the rear-engined "Silver Arrow" Auto Union race cars of the 1930s, and the first Volkswagen.

Ferdinand Porsche and his wife, Aloisia Kaes, had two children. A daughter, Louise, born in 1904, and a son, Ferdinand Anton Ernst, nicknamed Ferry, who was born in 1909. Louise married Dr. Anton Piëch. Both Piëch and Ferry Porsche went to work in the senior Porsche's consulting firm. Piëch, an attorney, handled contract negotiations, while Ferry Porsche followed in his father's footsteps as a design engineer. Louise also followed in her father's footsteps, with an understanding of the technical aspects as well as a love of automobiles.

Following World War II, Ferdinand Sr., Ferry, and Anton Piëch were imprisoned by the French and for a time Louise Piëch was left to manage the company on her own. Ahead of her time, Louise was a skillful businessperson and an ardent automobile enthusiast, who continued to be involved in company affairs during her lifetime. After an active role as a race driver during the 1930s, in 1949 she began developing the company that would become the successful importer of Volkswagen and Porsche cars to Austria.

Ferry was released in July 1946 but it was a year later, in August 1947, that the elder Porsche and Anton Piëch were finally freed. Professor Ferdinand Porsche died in 1951, and Anton Piëch died of a heart attack the next year.

The next generation of the Porsche family tree entered the business during the 1960s. Ferry and his wife, Dorothea, had four children—Ferdinand III, Wolfgang, Gerd, and Hans-Peter. The eldest son, Ferdinand Porsche III, called Butzi, worked his way up to be the head of the styling department, and left his mark as the designer of both the 904 and the 911. His brother Hans-Peter Porsche joined the company in 1963. Louise Piëch had four children, and three went to work in the company—Michael, Ernst, and Ferdinand. Working in research and development, Ferdinand Piëch played a dynamic role in the development of the 911 and Porsche's racing efforts, before leaving the company in 1972 and ending up at Audi's R&D department. Today he is the chairman of the board of Volkswagen. Butzi also left in 1972 to set up his own firm, Porsche Design, which is best known for its Carrera Design eyewear and line of Porsche watches and chronographs.

The departure of Butzi and Ferdinand Piëch was the fallout from a decision made by Ferry Porsche in 1971 to take the business from a closely held family-run company to a corporate entity. He feared that family squabbles over management would hurt the company, and he encouraged all family members to assume passive roles. The Porsche and Piëch families retained all the shares of Porsche AG until it went public in 1984.

Ferry Porsche died in 1998, and his sister, Louise Piëch, died the following year.

Porsche tried a number of iterations before it decided on the eloquently simple shape of the 911. Best guess is that this split-window Batmobile was an attempt to camouflage the new design for public road testing, and not a desire to make the 911 the Cadillac of sports cars. *Porsche AG*

of it did, as the yellow car on display was a prototype (Chassis 13 325, Number 5 of 13 prototypes produced between 1962 and 1964), with a nonoperational mock-up of the six-cylinder engine in its engine compartment. This car continued to appear at auto shows until February 1964, when it was fitted with a working engine and used on sales tours to dealers throughout

Europe. In December 1965, a testing accident sent the car to the scrap heap, a fate met by all but one of the 13 prototype 901s. Only Number 7, Chassis 13 327, survives in the hands of a private U.S. Porsche collector.

Production of the 911 began a year after its unveiling in September 1964. Considered 1965 models, 235 cars were produced until production

shut down for the holidays in December 1964. Starting up again the following January and continuing through July 1965, Porsche turned out an additional 3,154 of the new 911s to complete the production run for the model year 1965. Subsequent model years all had production terms starting in August and ending the following July.

The first series of 911s are known as the "0" series cars and were made from 1964 to 1967. It was February 1965 when the 911 reached the United States bearing a sticker price of $6,500. A new 1965 356 SC cost $4,577. What you got for the extra two grand was a car that had almost twice the luggage capacity of the 356, a slipperier body (coefficient of drag was 0.380 for the 911 versus the 356's 0.398), and modern, for that time, touches like rack-and-pinion steering, MacPherson strut front suspension, and an independent rear suspension with semitrailing arms instead of archaic swing-axles. The 911 also had a five-speed synchromesh transmission and a 2.0-liter (1,991-cc) overhead cam six-cylinder engine (with a dry sump lubrication system like many race cars) that put out 130 horsepower versus the 356 SC overhead valve four-cylinder's 95 horsepower. Both

Top, left: Porsche was still deciding on final details for the 911 right up to the car's debut. This 1963 photo shows that the twin grilles of the 356 were first considered for the rear deck of the 901. *Porsche AG*

Center: Interim concept for air vent on 901 engine cover depicts an intermediate stage in the evolution of the twin grilles from the 356 coming together in a single vent as the 901 neared its final form in 1963. *Porsche AG*

Bottom: Final iteration of 901 rear deck lid had the air grille spread horizontally across the entire width, in what has become a design characteristic of the 911. *Porsche AG*

Ferry Porsche checks out the latest 1965 911s to roll out of Werk II at Zuffenhausen. Bodies for the 911 were initially supplied by Reutter, which had been building bodies for Porsche since 1951. In 1963, Porsche acquired the Zuffenhausen body plant from the Reutter family when the owners balked at making the investment necessary to begin production of the 911. *Porsche AG*

Go ahead. Drive it.　　　　You'll never forget it.

tic or overseas delivery, see your Porsche dealer or write Porsche of America Corporation, 107 Tryon Avenue West, Teaneck, New Jersey 07666.

This 1965 advertisement for the new Porsche stressed the aerodynamic efficiency, added room, and racing-bred development of the 911. Thirty-five years later, Porsche's ad copy for the 911 can boast the same attributes.

the 356 SC and the 911 had four-wheel disc brakes, similar 11.2-inch rear discs, and the 911 had slightly larger-diameter 11.1-inch front discs, versus 10.8-inch on the 356 SC. The two models shared 4.5Jx15-inch steel wheels with 165HRx15 radial tires. The 911 weighed almost 400 pounds more (2,376 pounds versus 1,980 pounds), but its average 0 to 60 time of 8 seconds was about 2.5 seconds quicker, and top speed was 15 miles per hour higher at 130 miles per hour. In 1966, the 912 replaced the 356 SC, mating the 911 body with the SC 1.6-liter four-cylinder engine. At $113 more and 154 pounds heavier, it took 11.7 seconds to go from 0 to 60 miles per hour. Customers didn't seem to miss the 356, because that year Porsche built a record 12,820 cars, of which 9,090 were

912s. About half of the cars produced went to the United States, quickly establishing the popularity of the 900-series cars in this country.

A key ingredient in maintaining the 911's popularity during its long lifespan has been that, starting with the earliest production versions, evolution has been a key part of the manufacturing process. The spin-off of the four-cylinder 912 is an obvious example, but other running changes and design tweaks—from improved external door handles, to changes of the interior trim and storage pockets, to mounting Weber carburetors— were common practice, as the factory approached the 911's early years as a work in progress. Part of the charm of crawling around a 900-series car that has retained its original condition is discovering

Business was booming for Porsche's 900-series cars, thanks to the American market's acceptance of the four-cylinder 912 variant of the 911. This 1967 photo shows production lines building 911s and four-cylinder 912s side-by-side. Production of the 912 began in April 1965, but 2 of the 13 prototype 901s were four-cylinder models, indicating that Porsche had been studying the feasibility of this model for a few years. *Porsche AG*

Butzi Porsche wanted to add a Cabriolet version to the 911 but was forced by the company's desire to keep production costs as low as possible to come up with a more creative alternative for open air motoring. The rollbar added occupant protection along with structural rigidity to the Targa. *Porsche AG*

built to be driven and enjoyed by their enthusiast owners, not to serve as sacred relics handed down from the heavens. And it was something other than divine inspiration that prompted Butzi's next iteration of the 911, which was unveiled two years after the coupe at the 1965 Frankfurt Auto Show. Well ahead of his time in addressing the issues of rollover safety and security for open-top cars, Butzi conceived the Targa (Italian for shield) version of the 911. A folding, rubberized removable center top section, brushed stainless steel roll bar, and a zippered, plastic rear window gave drivers the option of *al fresco* motoring without sacrificing the rigidity of the unibody or their protection if the car turned over. Butzi had to stray a bit from the elegant roofline he laid down for the coupe, although the result was no less sensational.

First put into production in December, 1966, the Targa became a big hit with customers, but given his choice, Butzi would have preferred to have drawn up a cabriolet version of the 911. Production issues forced him to come up with the alternative that would

an anomalous bit of trim or equipment fitted at the factory, say a Talbot racing mirror in lieu of the round Durant style, that shows the human touch of cars built by hand in a small family-run company. Of course, such discoveries can wreak havoc in the perfectly ordered universe created by some of the more anal retentive Porsche experts who sometimes forget that these cars were originally

not require as many changes to the body structure. The Targa took one more step farther from being a cabriolet in 1968, when a fixed glass rear window was offered as an option. This was in response to complaints that the plastic rear window was prone to scratch and crack, in addition to being hard to zip in place. The glass rear window became standard in 1969 models, although the

The 1967 911S shows off the classic curves of the 911 shape as penned by Butzi Porsche. Weighing only 2,272 pounds in street trim with a 2.0-liter engine that can be modified to make over 200 horsepower, the 1967–68 911S is a favorite of vintage racers. The 1968 models, which never were imported to the United States, do have a slight weight advantage for racing, as their chrome trim pieces were made of a lighter material than the prior year. *P. C. Paternie*

The 1968 911S engine was the same as the 1967. The 1,991-cc, single overhead cam flat six featured a 9.8:1 compression ratio, Weber 40 IDS carburetors, forged light alloy pistons, and a three-into-one heat exchanger exhaust system. It made 160 horsepower at 6,600 rpm.

Interior of 1967 911S shows leather-wrapped steering wheel, roomy flat floor, and five-gauge instrument panel that placed tachometer squarely in front of driver's view. Like the exterior, this would remain essentially unchanged until the 996. *Les Bidrawn*

Next Page: The 1967 911S (Super) featured a 160-horsepower 2.0-liter engine, 4.5Jx15-inch Fuchs alloy wheels, Koni shocks, ventilated disc brakes, a 15-millimeter front antiroll bar, and a 16-millimeter rear antiroll bar. The Fuchs alloys became legends in their own right, appearing on 911s until the late 1980s. A new 1967 911S cost $6,990. A little over 2,000 were built. *Les Bidrawn*

The 1969 911S had a 170-horsepower engine and wider, 6Jx15, Fuchs alloys. It also had mechanical fuel injection replacing the Weber carburetors of the earlier 911S. This was the last year for the 2.0-liter engine. New for 1969 was the 911E (*Einspritzung* is German for fuel injection), which had a 140-horsepower fuel-injected engine and a self-leveling, hydropneumatic front suspension. The 911T, which was not available as a U.S. model in 1968, became the base model 911 in all markets. U.S. prices were: 911T coupe, $5,795; E coupe, $6,995; S coupe, $7,695. Going with a Targa added $620 to the price of each model.

"soft window" remained as an option for that model year.

An interesting footnote to Porsche history is that one of the first Targa models built, on December 21, 1966, was also the 100,000th Porsche. This particular car was a "police special" equipped with a flashing signal light on the driver's side of the roll bar and an air raid shelter-sized siren mounted below the rear window. The hood said "POLIZEI" in bold letters. Much to the chagrin of European speeders, Porsche would build more of these specially equipped Targa patrol cars over the years.

As startling and trendsetting as the new Targa was, it was the introduction, also in 1967, of another 911 version that would become the stuff

The first year for 911s with a longer wheelbase (by 2.4 inches) to improve handling was 1969. This is the 911S. Rear trailing arms were lengthened to move rear wheels back without relocating engine. Dual batteries were installed in front fenders to further enhance the car's balance.

of legends and establish the Porsche as a world-class sports car. The 911S was powered by a high-revving version of the 2.0-liter that had bigger valves, larger Weber carburetors, forged light alloy pistons, soft nitrided forged steel connecting rods, and a 9.8:1 compression ratio (the base engine compression ratio was 9:1) to put out 160 horsepower at 6,600 rpm as opposed to 130 horsepower at 6,100 rpm. The hotter engine stretched the torque curve by 1,000 rpm over the base version, to develop 132 ft-lbs at 5,200 rpm.

Other items that set the S (for Super) above the garden variety 911 were Koni shock absorbers, a larger (15-millimeter) front antiroll bar, a

leather-rimmed steering wheel, basket-weave trim on the lower dash, and, despite the sporty extras, a weight saving of 154 pounds, to tip the scales at 2,272 pounds. The S also carried a number of "firsts." It was the first European car to have ventilated front brake discs, oddly enough, trailing what Porsche enthusiasts consider to be the less-sophisticated Corvette in pioneering this technology. (In 1965, the Corvette became the world's first car to be so equipped). The 911S was equipped with a 16-millimeter rear antiroll bar, the first one fitted to a Porsche road car. And last, but leaving the longest impression, were the five-spoke, forged alloy Fuchs wheels. These were 5 pounds lighter than the stock steel wheels but still measured a skinny 4.5Jx15 inches. It wasn't until the 1968 911S, which was never offered as a U.S. model, that 1-inch wider Fuchs wheels were fitted.

Original Targa models in 1967 had plastic (soft) rear windows that could be unzipped for more airflow. Owner complaints about scratches and recalcitrant zippers led to a fixed glass rear window option. In 1969, the glass window became standard, but this 1969 911S was special ordered with soft rear window.

Those skinny tires, a relatively short wheelbase, and about 406 pounds of engine hanging behind the rear wheels, when combined with the 160 horsepower, limited exploring the handling prowess of the 911S to a small group of very skilled drivers. But anyone who could stomp on the accelerator and shift gears could enjoy the giant sucking sound of a

Air vents were added to the Targa bar in 1969. Green tinted glass also became standard that year. When the original buyer of this 1969 911S opted for the plastic rear window instead of fixed glass, he was probably more concerned with maximum ventilation than what a rarity his car would be 30 years later.

In addition to the plastic rear window on this 1969 911S, the car features special order lipstick-red checked seats. The interior of all 1969 911s featured a new ventilation system with a three-speed fan and storage compartments under the armrests of both doors.

pair of triple-choke Webers with their throats wide open plus the shriek of the timing chains and all those other internal forged bits of steel and alloy furiously pumping their way toward 7,000 rpm. This was a decade before the Turbo appeared, but the thrill factor was very close. Everything seems under control approaching 5,000 rpm, about when a normal engine reached its peak, then—*Wham!*—the 911S leaps to life, rushing forward with a high-pitched wail.

Car and Driver magazine's test driver did a 0 to 60 time of 6.5 seconds. The 911S would reach 90 miles per hour in third gear on its way to a top speed of 140. *Road & Track* reported that the 911S was "everything a Porsche should be—and more." More than 30 years later, you will find that after driving a 1967 911S, or one of its immediate successors through the 1973 model year, many Porsche enthusiasts still agree with *Road & Track*'s assessment.

The endearing charm of the 911 is that despite being over 30 years old, the early cars can be driven as hard, or harder, than they were when they were new. Many parts from later models can be easily retrofitted for added durability, handling, and speed. Surprisingly, relatively limited production and exotic performance has not boosted market values of the early cars beyond the reach of the average enthusiast.

The last of what the Porsche connoisseurs called the "early 911s" (before so-called safety bumpers altered the front and rear appearance) was the limited edition Carrera RS. This rare silver model was actually yellow the first time it left the factory. One year later, its owner brought it back for a color change. Also rare are the factory installed road lights mounted on the hood. The lights were an option that was ordered primarily for cars used in rallies or night racing.

THE 1970s
PEAKS AND VALLEYS ON THE EVOLUTIONARY CURVE

The introduction of the S model in 1967 established the 911 as one of the world's top GT cars. Good news for most of the world, but the big island known as the United States has always had its own ideas about what automobiles should and shouldn't be. And just one year after the S revved its way into the hearts of enthusiasts, growing concern over automotive emissions and safety in the United States, Porsche's biggest market, made the S an illegal alien.

For 1968, all U.S. buyers could get was a basic 911 and a neutered version of the 911S known as the 911L. The L (Lux) had all the optional S goodies but with the base 130-horsepower engine in the tail. Tacked on cars bound for the United States were safety side marker lights and an air pump to control emissions. Things improved in 1969, when the S returned along with the new 911T and 911E, all on a longer wheelbase. But 1968 was a harbinger of the low point for U.S. 911

enthusiasts, from 1975 to 1978, when performance and reliability suffered while various methods were tried to control emissions, before catalytic converters and oxygen sensors came on the scene. Until the world decided that cleaner air and safer cars were not such bad ideas after all, U.S. Porsche enthusiasts, especially in California, had to accept compromises to the 911's performance. Starting in 1975, even the handling of U.S. 911s was compromised by the "5-mile per hour bumper" law that raised the ride height to conform. This lasted until the 1983 model year.

But going back to 1969, before the bureaucrats became involved with suspension settings, the emphasis was on improving the handling of the 911. To take some of the twitchiness out of the handling, beginning with the 1969 models, the wheelbase of the 911 was stretched by 2.4 inches to bring it up to 89.4 inches overall. This was done by increasing the length of the rear trailing arms to move the rear wheels back without relocating the

During the late 1960s, Porsche developed special performance packages that could be fitted to the 911 for racing and rallying. For 1967, a run of 22 lightweight (1,800-pound) cars called the 911R became the first in a long line of 911s that took basically stock cars and modified them for racing by using lightweight body parts and high-performance engines. In 1970, as the stock 911 engine grew to 2.2 liters, Porsche was well within the GT racing rules to further increase cylinder bore from 84 to 85 millimeters for a slightly increased displacement of 2,245 cc. Dual ignition, aggressive cam timing, bigger valves, and a 10.3:1 compression ratio produced 240 horsepower at 7,800 rpm. This engine, in a lightweight body, propelled the 1970 911 driven by Bjorn Waldegard to his second win in a row at the prestigious Monte Carlo Rally. It was the third win in a row for a 911, and made Porsche the first manufacturer to have such a win streak in the event's 39-year history. *Porsche AG*

Special lightweight 911S models, referred to as the S/T, were prepared by the factory for racing. Plexiglas side and rear windows, fiberglass trunk lids, front fenders, and bumpers, plus aluminum-skinned doors got weighted down to under 2,000 pounds. The 2.4-liter production engine was increased to 2,494 cc, and with fuel injection put out 275 horsepower at 7,900 rpm. Note the location of the oil filler door on the right rear fender of this 1972 model. *Porsche AG*

The lightweight 911S also had big fender flares to clear 7-inch wheels up front and even bigger 9-inch wheels used at the rear. The best part about these rocketships was that anyone with $15,574 in 1972 could walk into the factory at Zuffenhausen and drive one away. *Porsche AG*

The stock 1972 911S engine displaced 2.4 liters (2,341 cc). It had mechanical fuel injection and an 8.5:1 compression ratio, and made 190 horsepower at 6,500 rpm. The red fiberglass fan shroud is an easy way to spot the S engine. The 911E engines had green shrouds, while the T models were either black or yellow. *Matt Stone*

While the 2.4-liter 911S with its 190 horsepower was making a lot of noise at the upper end of the scale, the bread-and-butter portion of the 911 line-up, the 911T, starting midway through the 1973 model year, became the first Porsche to use the new Bosch K-Jetronic (CIS) fuel injection system. This would become standard on all 911s in 1974. It produced 140 horsepower versus 130 for the carbureted version used in Europe.

The infamous flap for external oil filler that caught unwary fuel attendants off guard during the 1972 model year. Porsche engineers had relocated the tank in front of the right rear wheel for additional handling balance. After problems with people assuming it was a gas tank filler, the tank was moved back to its original location, and the flap removed, for the 1973 cars. This is the most obvious visual difference between the otherwise mechanically identical 1972 and 1973 911 models.

The 1973 911T could be ordered with all S options except, of course, the engine. Steel spoiler was part of the package. Only U.S. models for 1973 had large rubber front bumper guards.

engine. The front and rear wheel openings were flared slightly to accept larger wheels and tires, which on the 911S were now 6Jx15-inchers with 185/70VR15 tires. Another move to improve handling was the installation of twin 12-volt batteries mounted in the fenders ahead of the front wheels. The thought was to improve weight distribution toward the front of the car and achieve balance between the left and right sides of the car.

Joining the 1969 911S (now with mechanical fuel injection that raised horsepower to 170) in its return to the United States, were two other 911 variants. The 911T (Touring) was the basic model equipped with a carbureted 110-horsepower engine and 5.5Jx15-inch wheels. The 911E (Einspritzung is the German word for fuel injection) had a 140-horsepower fuel-injected engine and the same wheels and tires as the S. The distinguishing

At the rear, the unique rubber bumpers of 1973 cannot detract from the elegant classical lines penned by Butzi Porsche. The large rubber protuberances only appeared, front and rear, on 1973 911s sold in the United States. They were Porsche's quick-fix attempt at meeting the impact safety requirements that came into effect for that model year. In 1974, to better meet the 5-mile per hour impact requirements of U.S. bumper laws, Porsche would reshape both the front and rear ends of the 911.

feature of the 911E was its front suspension, which consisted of self-leveling hydropneumatic struts in lieu of torsion bars. This was a joint effort by Boge and Porsche that was continued as standard equipment on the E until 1972. Unfortunately, the system was prone to leaks and in some cases total collapse. Most of the 911Es on the road today have been converted back to the tried-and-true 911 setup of shock absorbers and torsion bars.

Porsche effectively increased the cylinder bore of the flat six to 84 millimeters, also enlarging the engine size to 2.2 liters for the 1970 and 1971 models. Power increased across the board

Timeless beauty, the early 911 silhouette in the form of a 1973 T. A coupe like this would set you back $7,960 in 1973, plus the cost of the S options. Equipped with the CIS K-Jetronic fuel injection, the 1973 T still makes a great daily driver that does not require the constant attention of carbureted or mechanically injected models.

Unique two-tone interior (most cars were ordered with solid color interiors) sets off the Light Ivory exterior of a 1973 911T with the S option package. The car also has the optional air conditioning featuring underdash vents. Note the dual storage pockets mounted on door panels that were on 1969 to 1973 cars. These were changed in 1974, along with the use of high-back bucket seats to replace the more traditional low-back models that are reminiscent of the 356.

with the T now having 125 horsepower, the E up to 155 horsepower, and the S motor making 180 horsepower.

The zenith for the early models of the 911, and for the 911 overall according to the purists who feel later models traded some of the raw edginess of a sports car for the cushiness of a luxury GT, came with the introduction of the 1972/73 cars. Engine size went up to 2.4 liters, thanks to an increase in stroke to 70.4 millimeters, and all models got a forged crankshaft. Compression ratios were lowered on U.S. cars to meet the requirement for unleaded fuel, but the U.S. T received mechanical fuel injection. Fuel injection gave the U.S. T a 10-horsepower advantage, 140 horsepower versus 130 horsepower, over the T models in the rest of the world. The E now made 165 horsepower and the 911S a whopping 190 horsepower. The S also sported a steel front spoiler.

In January 1973, U.S.-spec T models became the first 911s to use Bosch K-Jetronic (CIS) fuel injection. Horsepower stayed at 140,

continued on page 40

SHIFTLESS IN STUTTGART:
THE SPORTOMATIC TRANSMISSION

It seems odd that a car representing the mechanical incarnation of Steve McQueen's bad boy racer attitude should provide for clutchless shifting, but the 911 has offered some form of automatic transmission throughout most of its production life. The Tiptronic has been available since January 1990 and has even made the option list of Porsche's latest Turbo. Thanks to microprocessors and other assorted bits and bytes, the Tiptronic gives up little, if any, discernible performance to a manually shifted car. In the new Turbo, for example, the five-speed Tiptronic is just 0.7 seconds slower from 0 to 60 miles per hour and tops out at 185 miles per hour as opposed to the six-speed manual's top speed of 189 miles per hour. That's with a factory test driver working the clutch. Depending on the quantity of left feet you possess and how adept you are at using them to shift gears, your times, as the small print says, may vary to a point of negligible difference.

Long before sophisticated electronics made the automatic transmission a close competitor to a manual stick shift, Porsche engineers had devised the Sportomatic transmission, which was a capable, if not comparable, alternative. Porsche had begun experimenting with automatic transmissions on the 1961–1962 356B. Having the United States as its biggest market, Porsche felt that offering some form of automatic transmission was a marketing necessity.

The Sportomatic was first offered as a $280 option on the 1968 911, including the 911S. It continued as an option, although a lack of interest dropped it from S models in 1970, until it was canceled after the 1980 model year. Part of its demise could be blamed on the change made in 1975 that eliminated a

forward gear to make it a three-speed. Porsche made the change, which resulted in slower acceleration times, to decrease engine sounds in order to meet stricter drive-by-noise standards for various countries. In the early years, as proof that Porsche did understand its customers in America, it was installed on almost 25 percent of the cars delivered to the United States.

Technically, the Sportomatic was a semiautomatic transmission. It consisted of a conventional four-speed synchromesh gearbox (the synchromesh, shift collars, and shaft bearings are identical to the manual Type 901 transmission), a hydraulic torque converter made by Fichtel & Sachs, and a single-disc clutch. The clutch was operated by vacuum-controlled linkage that was set into motion by an electric switch at the base of the shift lever. According to road testers of the day, this switch was extremely sensitive, so the driver had to be mindful of only touching the gear lever when he or she intended to shift gears.

The shift knob bore the legend of P (Park) and R (Reverse) to the left of a conventional H marked with L, D, D3, and D4. Porsche suggested that L was only for "ascending or descending steep grades, or for driving on sand or ice." D was selected for normal starts with D3 and D4 as "driving gears" depending on traffic, terrain, and road conditions. Depending on how much shifting you were willing to do, you could start in any one of the four gears.

When *Motor Trend* tested a 1968 Sportomatic 911L the testers recorded acceleration times from 0 to 60 miles per hour starting in D only, D3 only, D4, and L, then shifting through the remaining gears. The results were times of 13.3 seconds, 16.1

seconds, 19.7 seconds, and 10.7 seconds respectively. Road & Track recorded 0 to 60 miles per hour in 10.3 seconds for the 1968 911L as compared to a similar car equipped with a five-speed manual that did it in 9.0 seconds flat. The bigger difference, due to gear ratios and torque converter slippage, was in top speed, which maxed out at 117 miles per hour for the two-pedal car, versus 132 miles per hour for its manually shifted counterpart. The Sportomatic was able to post closer comparative numbers when it came time to measure fuel economy. Surprisingly, fuel mileage was similar for both cars, the Sportomatic returning 16–19 miles per gallon against the manual's 15–20 miles per gallon.

The Sportomatic triggered a disparity of opinion among journalists. The road testers at the European magazines were generally more open-minded about the Sportomatic than their American counterparts. British magazine Motor said getting the most out of driving the Sportomatic required a "Porsche mentality" versus an "automatic mentality." Auto Italiana found in track testing a 130-horsepower Sportomatic versus a manual shift 160-horsepower 911S that on certain sections the automatic was a second faster due to less time lost shifting gears.

The finding came as no surprise to Porsche, as the Sportomatic's debut was at the 1967 Marathon de la Route. This consisted of 84 hours of racing around both the North and South loops (17.58 miles per lap) of the Nurburgring. The Sportomatic was fitted to a lightweight 911 with a 175-horsepower engine, essentially one of the first 911R models. The car covered 6,148 miles at an average speed of 73.15 miles per hour over the tight and twisty circuit, to capture overall honors based on a handicap system.

Even a tough guy like Steve McQueen could appreciate a gutsy performance like that.

Presenting a Porsche 911 without a clutch pedal that shifts as well as a Porsche 911 with a clutch pedal.

The 1973 Porsche Sportomatic: A Porsche you can take up and down through all four gears and never have to worry about a clutch pedal. Because there isn't any.

A Porsche you can actually shift as fast as a Porsche with a clutch pedal.

A Porsche that can do zero to 60 in 8.0 seconds (like our S Model, for example).

A Porsche so responsive, so rugged that when it first ran in competition, it won an international endurance race. The 84-hour Marathon de la Route.

And finally, a Porsche you can put in "D" and just cruise around and not shift at all.

The 1973 Porsche Sportomatic, designed for the person who has always wanted to own a Porsche but never wanted to own a clutch pedal.

This 1973 advertisement for the Sportomatic transmission stressed its winning debut in the 84-hour-long Marathon de la Route run over the entire old Nurburgring circuit. A complete lap included both the North and South loops for a total of 17.58 miles. Three 175-horsepower 911s equipped with Sportomatic transmissions were entered in the 1967 running of the Marathon. The winning 911 completed a distance of 6,148 miles with Vic Elford, Hans Herrmann, and Jochen Neerpasch all taking turns behind the wheel.

The 1973 Carrera RS debuted the 2.7-liter version of the flat six. Mechanical fuel injection and an 8.5:1 compression ratio were good for 210 horsepower at 6,300 rpm. The engine's increased capacity was achieved by changing the bore of the 2.4-liter 911S engine from 84 millimeters to 90 millimeters. Otherwise the two engines were essentially the same. *Autocar* magazine tested a Carrera RS Touring in 1973 and got a 0-to-60-mile per hour time of 5.5 seconds. The quarter-mile time was 14.1 seconds, and top speed was 149 miles per hour.

Porsche began listing its options with an "M" prefix in 1970. One of the most famous was the 1973 M471 code, which stood for the Carrera RS Sport, a lightweight version of the 911S, intended for club racers. Thinner gauge steel was used in the body panels along with thinner window glass; insulation, carpeting, rear seats, and other interior trim were all deleted. Recaro sports seats, a ducktail rear spoiler, and larger wheels and tires (6x15 with 195/60 front, 7x15 with 215/60 rear). Only 200 of the sport versions were made, and they sold for $10,200. Option M 472 was the Carrera RS Touring, a more deluxe version that was equipped similarly to the standard 911S; 1,308 of the Touring version were made. U.S. price was $11,000.

The fiberglass over an aluminum frame deck lid with ducktail spoiler is the most distinguishing characteristic of the 1973 Carrera RS. On later production cars, the aluminum was replaced with steel framing. Larger rear wheel flares and 7-inch-wide rear wheels also differentiate its exterior from a 1973 911S. The "1st RS" on the license plate of the car pictured represents that this particular car (Serial Number 911 360 0016) made the first public appearance for the Carrera RS on the stand at the Paris Salon in October, 1972, when Porsche debuted the RS model. The car also went on to be displayed at auto shows in Geneva and London. Its first owner purchased the car directly off the floor of the London show.

Continued from page 35

but the improved operation and low maintenance (versus tinkering with carburetors or the mechanical injection) of this system, along with excellent fuel economy, make these cars excellent drivers even today.

One change Porsche made to the 911 for 1972 was not as well received and disappeared on the 1973 cars. The dry sump oil tank was relocated from a position behind the right rear wheel to a spot ahead of it. In conjunction with this move, an external filler door was placed on the right rear fender to allow oil to be added without going into the engine compartment. Porsche engineers moved the oil tank to further enhance the handling balance of the 911. Unfortunately, unwary filling station attendants mistook the outside oil filler for the fuel door. This happened often enough to prompt Porsche to move the oil tank

For 1974, the Carrera RS 3.0 and RSR models carried the Carrera RS theme to further extremes. Whale tail rear wings replaced the smaller ducktail for increased stability at high speeds. There was also a big change under the rear spoiler, as the RS 3.0 had a 3.0-liter engine replacing the 2.7-liter unit for a 105-horsepower increase.

in the Carrera RS was now fitted with Bosch K-Jetronic (CIS) fuel injection and installed in all 911s, but the bad news was that its power was significantly reduced. The T and E models were replaced by the base 911 with 150 horsepower and the 911S, which had 175 horsepower. The Carrera was no longer a special model but a regular production car assuming the top-of-the-line role of the S. Emissions controls limited its power to 175 horsepower. The rest of the world still enjoyed Carreras with 210-horsepower mechanically injected engines.

Fitting new safety bumpers not only affected the exterior of the 911, it reduced trunk space, which led to the elimination of the twin batteries. A larger, single battery now resided at the rear of the trunk.

There were some improvements. Revisions were made to the suspension. Forged aluminum trailing arms, 7.7 pounds lighter, were used in the rear while up front, a simpler method of mounting the antiroll bar was used. It no longer passed through the inner fender walls, but beneath the body pan.

Inside, high-back seats with integral headrests added a more modern look to the 1974 911, which also benefited from an improved interior ventilation system.

By 1975, ever tightening emissions laws had created California and 49-state cars, both versions suffering from diminished horsepower ratings. The U.S. Carrera was more bark than bite. European versions of the Carrera still produced 210 horsepower at 6,300 rpm, while the U.S. cars put out a puny 165 horsepower at 5,800 rpm. *Porsche Cars North America*

This 1974 factory photo shows workers installing the Sportomatic on 911s. It was a $425 option. Close to 25 percent of early 911s delivered to the United States were equipped with the transmission but its popularity dwindled, along with its gearing, which went from four forward speeds to three, through the 1970s until it was dropped from the option list in the 1980 model year. *Porsche AG*

In 1975, U.S. 911s were divided into 49-state cars and California cars depending on the emissions controls fitted. In addition to an air pump, California cars had thermal reactors and exhaust gas recirculation (EGR) systems. As stated above, the next three years, with the exception of the 1976 debut of the 260-horsepower Turbo, was a dismal period for U.S. 911 enthusiasts.

Things began to brighten when the 3.0-liter 911SC came on the scene in 1978. Horsepower increased to 180 for all markets, including California—good news after 1976 models in the state had been choked down to 160 horses. Wider rear fender flares on the SC allowed Porsche to upgrade the standard wheel and tire package. Fitted up front were 6Jx15 wheels with 185/70VR15 tires, while 7Jx15 wheels with 215/60VR15 tires were slipped under the larger rear fender openings. Power brakes became standard on all 911s. First time options included 16-inch wheels, 6J in front and 7J at the rear.

Having survived the last half of the 1970s, the 911 was poised to make a strong comeback in the 1980s.

From special order to a special production model in 1987, factory Slant-nose Turbos (referred to as the 930S in the U.S.) were a status symbol of the 1980s until a rash of cheap knock-offs eroded their unique appeal.

THE 1980s
THE SURVIVAL AND REVIVAL
OF THE SPECIES

By 1980, the 911 had adapted fairly well to the ever increasing safety and emissions regulations that had threatened to strangle its performance in the latter half of the 1970s. The larger 3.0-liter engine of the SC, though limited to 180 horsepower in the United States, was good for 0 to 60 times of 6.3 seconds, according to a 1978 Road & Track test. It was also more reliable than the previous 2.7-liter, which was never designed to accommodate the heat and stress associated with the U.S. emissions controls that had been adapted to it. With the 3.0-liter powerplant and a body made of galvanized steel, introduced on the 1976 models, the 911SC held the promise of a long and healthy future.

Unfortunately, that was a promise that could have been broken if Porsche's CEO at the time, Ernst Fuhrmann, had had his druthers. Fuhrmann believed that the 911 had run its course and that it should be phased out. He wanted marketing and development efforts concentrated on cars like the 924 and 928. Fuhrmann, who in his early days as

an R&D engineer had designed the legendary four-cam Carrera racing engine used in the RS Spyders, had been appointed to top management in 1971. Ferry Porsche decided that to avoid family squabbles over who should run the business, it would be better if the limited partnership (consisting of Porsche and Piëch family members) that controlled the company was changed to a public corporation. Family members were to give up significant management roles, a decision that precipitated both Butzi Porsche and Ferdinand Piëch to leave the company to successfully pursue their goals elsewhere. One would be foolish to find fault with Ferry Porsche's reasoning at the time. It was an ironic twist of fate that in doing what he believed to be the best move for the company's future, he set in motion a plan that would eliminate from that future the two men who had inherited the vision and enthusiasm that he shared with his father. Porsche went public in 1973.

Fuhrmann had been a big supporter of the 911 in the factory GT racing programs of the 1970s, but

THE SLANT-NOSE TURBO:
PORSCHE'S STYLE SETTER FOR THE
DISCO ROLLER CROWD WAS, LIKE, SO 1980S

The Slant-nose Turbo exemplifies the best and worst extremes of the 911's evolutionary path through the 1980s. These cars are some of the most easily recognizable of any 911 variant, distinguished by their flat, front fenders, with louvers punched into their top surfaces, which slope down to the bumper line. At the sides, box-shaped lower doorsills taper back into wide rear fenders that are accented with gaping air intakes. Later models have pop-up headlamps. Under all this flashy bodywork sit the basic ingredients that make up a 930 Turbo with horsepower ratings stretching as high as 330 horsepower.

The first Slant-nose conversion was built in Porsche's restoration shop as a special order in 1981. From 1982 through 1987, when it then became a limited production option (M506, also known as the 930S in the United States), 235 more were turned out. In 1987, 200 930S cars came to the United States, followed by 278 in 1988, and 147 in 1989. There were an additional 50 of these production versions delivered to other parts of the world.

Looking like street versions of the 935 race cars, the Slant-nose models built by Porsche were exciting cars, whether you were outside or inside one. Riding in one, even at low speeds, feels like being strapped into the front seat of a runaway roller coaster. The illusion is of being perched on the nose of the car as the road rolls under you and the rest of the world hurtles over and around you. Check out the side view mirrors and the tips of the large rear wing look like miniature alien spacecraft pacing your progress. A very impressionable experience, even as 911 Turbos go.

Unfortunately, the swoopy looks of the Slant-nose also made a huge impression on the gold chain crowd, who felt more comfortable driving them to discos than on the racetrack. Soon, cars that began as plastic imitations of the factory's handiwork escalated into gross exaggerations. It did not take long before, in shops and garages and a few backyards all over the country, there emerged a cottage industry in which innocent 911s, and quite a few 912s, were being hacked up and "converted" into Slant-noses. Some people used metal fenders,

like the factory, but usually fiberglass was the medium of choice. Imitation may be the sincerest form of flattery but when it came to Slant-nose replicas, it was a case of adding insult to the badly injured 911s and 912s used in the process.

A special Porsche model that took its cue from what Porsche does best—racing—soon became symbolic of drug dealers and other nefarious characters. Fortunately, like any fad, the Slant-nose look faded away. One rarely sees these cars today. The nonfactory cars have either been converted back to conventional looking 911s or presumably are stashed away as confiscated evidence in a large DEA warehouse in Florida.

The factory cars can now enjoy the respect that they deserve as unique 911 variants.

The major difference between the factory-produced Slant-nose and its imitators was the use of hot-dip galvanized steel fenders by the factory. The original concept for the car was the dropped nose of the 935 factory race cars that took advantage of a loophole in FIA racing regulations to gain an aerodynamic edge over the competition. Other components used by the factory Slant-nose conversion option were retractable headlights, air vents along the top of the front fenders, rocker panel fairings, air scoops with horizontal ridges (strakes) in the rear fenders, an oil cooler with a cooling fan mounted in the rear air scoop, and, on European models, an increase of 30 horsepower over the standard 300-horsepower Turbo engine. Randy Leffingwell

In 1986, 959s finished first and second in the Paris-Dakar 8,000-mile-plus rally. A special four-wheel drive version 911, with a 230-horsepower engine, had won the event in 1984. For the 1985 attempt, Porsche used a hybrid that mated the 959 chassis to a nonturbocharged powerplant similar to that used in 1984, but with less than successful results. For 1986, the cars entered were true 959s with twin-turbo engines that put out 390 horsepower and the four-position drive selection system of the road model. Rene Metge, who had driven the 1984 winner, repeated the feat in 1986. Jacky Ickx, more famous for his winning Porsche drives at Le Mans, was second. Porsche engineer Roland Kussmaul, who served as the team manager and chief mechanic, drove a third 959 to sixth overall. *Randy Leffingwell*

This communications breakdown between car and driver may explain why amplifiers and other bits of stereo gear suddenly began populating the trunks of 911s during the 1980s.

Another example of the sybaritic path chosen by the 911s of this decade was the Weissach Edition of 1980. In the 1960s and 1970s, limited editions, like the 911R or Carrera RS, usually deleted comfort items to pare down weight while adding a combination of larger wheels and tires with more powerful engines to raise the performance level. The 408 Weissach models produced for the United States in 1980 took a different tack. They were distinguished by a choice of either Black Metallic or Platinum Metallic paint, full leather interiors, Fuchs alloys painted to match the body color, power antenna, power sunroof, fog lights, and a passenger side exterior mirror. The only addition that could be considered as a performance improvement was the mounting of the whale tail rear spoiler from the Turbo.

239

A popular option on Carrera 3.2 models was the Turbo Look. You actually got more than just the look. Besides the bulging flares and front and rear spoilers, Porsche also included the big brakes, big wheels (7- and 9-inch widths, front and rear), rear torsion bars, and antiroll bar of the Turbo.

In 1983, for its final year of production, the SC did add a distinguished accomplishment to its resume before bowing out to the Carrera 3.2. The first factory edition of the 911 Cabriolet, essentially a Targa with the roll bar removed and replaced by a folding alloy frame covered with a three-layered convertible top, made its debut as a 911SC. In the United States, a 1983 Cabriolet, with manual top, was priced at $34,450 while the Targa listed at $31,450.

The Carrera 3.2, while continuing to add more comfort and convenience touches during its production run, reenergized the performance side of the 911 as well. The 3.2-liter engine was essentially the same in all markets except for the compression ratio and emissions equipment, which was determined by whether a market used leaded or unleaded fuel. In the United States, Canada, and Japan this meant using pistons that gave a compression ratio of 9.5:1, while what Porsche

Turbo Look was only available on coupes until 1986, when it became available also for Targas and Cabriolets. Cars looked fast and handled better than a "narrow" body car, but 110 pounds of Turbo fat hurt acceleration a bit.

Porsche brought another name out of the past to boost sales in 1989. A limited production run of Cabriolets with cut down windshields, humpbacked fiberglass rear seat tonneau covers, and low-slung convertible tops were called Speedsters. Here a couple of the 2,065 built go through final assembly. *Porsche AG*

Reflections of the past made the Carrera Speedster a "must have" for collectors when it first came out. The sticker price for a 1989 Speedster was $65,480 but the cars have not become the sought-after collector's car that many who paid that or more when the car came out had anticipated. Neither faster nor better looking than the regular production Cabriolet, the 911 Speedster lacks the cult appeal of the original 356 Speedster. As a no-frills roadster, the seats, windows, and top all operate manually. The 911 Speedster top

was not as well fitted or insulated as on the Cabriolet. Porsche advised customers not to run the car through an automatic car wash. Customers were also asked to sign a statement accepting increased wind noise and the possibility of water leaks when the top was in place. The top's most endearing feature was that, when raised, it covered the hunchback rear seat cover. There were 823 Speedsters made to U.S. specs. Of the 2,065 total cars produced, 1,894 were fitted with the Turbo Look body.

THE 959: PORSCHE'S EXOTIC 911

Porsche engineers and enthusiasts have always taken pride in what can be achieved by taking a production-based 911 and turning it into a race car. In 1983, at the Frankfurt Auto Show, Porsche took the wraps off the 959 to let the world take a peek at what could be accomplished with a 911-based race car turned into a street machine. It also offered a glimpse up the road that future 911s would travel, as many of the 959's technical and styling traits have evolved into the regular production versions from the 964 to 993 to 996.

Powering the 959 was a twin-plug, 24-valve, double overhead cam, 2.85-liter (2,849-cc), flat six-cylinder with sequential twin turbos, Bosch Motronic fuel injection, and water-cooled heads that were derived from the 956 engine. This combination was good for 450 horsepower at 6,500 rpm. With a drag coefficient of 0.32 and weighing around 3,200 pounds in street trim, the 959 could go from 0 to 60 miles per hour in about 3.6 seconds and top out around the magic 200-mile per hour mark.

The 959 featured a six-speed manual transmission, an electronically adjustable suspension, ABS brakes, and 17-inch hollow wheels (8-inches wide in front and 9-inches wide at the back) equipped with sensors to detect low tire pressure. The main attraction, of course, was the electronically controlled four-wheel drive system that could vary power distribution from front to rear, based on road conditions. The driver could select from four automatic drive programs including: dry road, wet road, ice and snow, and full traction.

Although it served as a dramatic engineering showcase, Porsche's decision to build the 959 was not to serve as a concept car, but as a race car. Building 200 road-going customer versions of the car not only meet the Federation Internationale de l'Automobile (FIA) regulations for the Group B rally class it was designed to compete in, but also defrayed some of the development costs.

Following the lead of the all-wheel drive Audi Quattro in 1981, a car developed by ex-Porsche R&D chief Ferdinand Piëch, the Group B rally cars had earned the nickname of "Killer Bees" for their extremely high-speed capabilities on dirt trails and forest roads. Speeds and danger to spectators and drivers increased as

Although the 959 spent very little time on the race track compared to other high-performance variations of the 911 theme, it is considered by many to be the ultimate 911. At the time of its introduction, the 959 pioneered such innovations as sequential turbochargers, electronic fuel injection and turbo boost control, six-speed transmission, all-wheel drive, and speed-dependent ride height adjustment. Its 450 horsepower and top speed of 196 miles per hour are still high water marks for production 911s. Randy Leffingwell

other manufacturers followed Audi's lead in all-wheel drive. Unfortunately, the Killer Bees would live up to their nickname in tragic accidents that led to changes in the rules before the 959 was ready to compete.

Helmut Bott, Piëch's successor at Porsche, had been experimenting with four-wheel drive 911s starting in 1975. In 1984, he entered a three-car team made up of four-wheel drive variants of the 911SC rally car, with normally aspirated 3.3-liter engines, in the grueling Paris-Dakar raid, the event so named because it resembled desert warfare more than a rally. Finishing 1st, 6th, and 26th, Porsche decided to return in 1985 with cars decked out in 959 bodywork and an early version of the 959 drivetrain, again excluding the turbo motor. A lack of horsepower prevented the Porsches from winning. For 1986, Bott entered three full-on 959s, which resulted in a 1-2-6 victory that proved to be the 959's competition high point. The road racing version of the 959, known as the 961, did race at Le Mans twice in 1986 and 1987. It won its class in 1986, finishing 7th overall. The 1987 effort had a more dismal ending, as the car caught fire after blowing its engine.

Ironically, as things turned out, at a price close to $200,000 a copy when the car was ready for market in 1986, the sold-out production run of 959s proved to be a bigger commercial than racing success for Porsche. The exotic car market was booming during the 1980s, trying to satisfy the needs of the serious hardcore enthusiasts as well as the self-indulgent appetites of the "Me Generation" and its attendant speculators. The limited availability and 200-mile per hour capabilities of the 959 played right into this market. A good example was the on-again, off-again delivery plans for Environmental Protection Agency- and Department of Transportation-approved versions of the 959, which drove sticker prices to at least $300,000 for cars that could not legally be driven in the United States. Porsche lore says that at least four of these cars were imported, but no definitive answer is available. More than a decade later, the legal issues of owning and operating a 959 in America have not been resolved.

Despite its limited competition success and the circumstances surrounding its commercial success, the 959 stands tall as a technical tour de force. Almost 20 years later, its performance is still state of the art and its mechanical attributes, allowing for the dramatic progress made in computer controls, still qualify as world class.

referred to as the Rest of the World (RoW) engines had a compression ratio of 10.3:1. Both numbers were up from the 3.0-liter SC engine, which in 1978 had a compression ratio as low as 8.5:1 across the board. From those of the 3.0-liter SC engines, horsepower numbers took a dramatic leap upward, as RoW engines soared to 231 from 204 horsepower. U.S.-spec cars broke the 200-horsepower barrier for the first time ever, if you exclude the 210 horses that powered the limited edition 1973 Carrera RS. The performance leap over the SC by the U.S. Carrera 3.2 cars because of the jump from 180 to 204 horsepower was a dramatic one in spite of an added 110 pounds that brought their weight to 2,670 pounds.

A big part of the 3.2-liter engine's performance advantage could be attributed to having the first application of the Bosch Motronic 2 DME (Digital Motor Electronics) engine management system combined with LE-Jetronic fuel injection. Improved oil-fed chain tensioners, henceforth known as "Carrera tensioners," were also a major feature of the 3.2-liter engine.

Other performance enhancements on the new Carreras included larger and thicker brake discs front and rear (11.8-inch diameter and 12.1-inch diameter, respectively) and, in 1986, thicker antiroll bars, measuring 22 millimeters (front) and 21 millimeters (rear) were added, along with rear torsion bars that increased in size from 24 millimeters to 25 millimeters.

Bodywork was essentially the same as the SC with a new front spoiler that incorporated fog lights. Sixteen-inch wheels (7J front, 8J rear) were optional. A popular option was the Turbo Look that essentially added the fender flares and spoilers from the Turbo along with its suspension, brakes, tires, and wheels.

On the luxury side, the Carrera 3.2 had its radio antenna integrated into the windshield, vanity mirrors in the sun visors, leather seats as standard on U.S. cars, and central locking as standard starting in 1986. Power seats and mirrors became standard equipment in 1988. In 1987, Cabriolet models all came equipped with power-operated tops.

The 959 combined all-wheel drive, ride height adjustment, and turbocharging to become a super 911. It was not built for off-road superiority as an FIA Group B rally car, but for what Porsche had hoped would become a sports car road racing series based on Group B regulations. Porsche, required to make at least 200 road versions of the 959 to meet the FIA homologation requirements for a production car, produced a total of 284. Two versions of the road car were offered. The standard 959 came complete with power windows, air conditioning, and rear seats, while the lighter-weight 959 Sport, intended for club racing, deleted those items. Lightweight construction involved using a number of materials, including galvanized steel for the basic body structure, aluminum for doors and trunk lid, reinforced fiberglass for the front fascia, and an aramid composite for rocker panels, roof, and fenders. Despite these efforts, the fully equipped road version of the 959 weighed 3,194 pounds, considerably more than its 2,423-pound minimum weight for racing. *Randy Leffingwell*

Basic philosophy and outline of the 911 changed very little from 1965 to 1984. However, safety and emissions regulations, and consumers who demanded more comfort and luxury in their performance cars, resulted in big changes during the first 20 years of production. A 300-pound weight gain was off-set by 101 more horsepower. Evolution can be costly as price also increased—from $6,500 to $31,960. *Porsche AG*

Another big change occurred in 1987 when the Type 915 transmission was replaced by the Getrag-built G50 five-speed with Borg-Warner synchromesh. The 915 had reached its torque limit and required its own oil cooling system. The G50 was a cheaper alternative. With the new transmission, 911 drivers seeking reverse had to get used to moving the lever to the left and up as opposed to going right and down. With the G50 also came a larger (240-millimeter, like the Turbo) clutch, which was now hydraulically operated.

In 1989, 16-inch wheels were standard along with an alarm system. But prices had risen from $31,960 in 1984 to $51,205 for a 1989 coupe. By then U.S. sales had plummeted from a high of 7,801 cars in 1987 to 3,377 in 1989. A special run of 1989 Speedster Cabriolets accounted for 823 more U.S. cars, along with 7 lightweight Club Sport limited edition models, but an economic downturn had curbed the spending appetites of yuppies. And those who still could afford a Porsche were ready to trade in their sports cars and join the trendsetters driving SUVs.

Speaking of trends, an interesting one had developed regarding U.S. Cabriolet sales. In 1984, Cabriolet sales were roughly half that of the Targa model which, in turn, sold in equal amounts to the Coupe. By 1987, the Cabriolet moved ahead of the Targa in sales. For that year, Coupe sales were 2,916; Targas 2,232; and Cabriolets 2,653. In 1989, Porsche sold 1,361 Cabriolets in the United States, compared to only 860 Targas. At the time a Cabriolet listed for $59,200 while a Targa cost $52,435. In addition, 823 more convertibles were sold as limited edition Speedsters, with a price tag of $65,480.

The Speedster was a marketing effort by Porsche to boost sales by reviving the memory of one of its most famous models. What was really needed was a model that looked to the future, not the past. Porsche felt it had such a model in its first attempt at a "new 911," the Type 964. Following the example of Porsche's limited production supercar, the exotic 959, the 964 series had the four-wheel drive Carrera 4 as its flagship to lead Porsche and the 911 into the 1990s.

The 2000 Carrera coupe carries a slicked-back version of Butzi Porsche's 911 silhouette into the twenty-first century. Propelling the new Carrera into the future is something that Butzi didn't imagine, a liquid-cooled 3.4-liter flat six with direct coil-over-plug ignition and self-adjusting hydraulic valve lifters. It still sits behind the rear axle as Butzi intended. *Porsche Cars North America*

THE 1990s
EVOLUTION OR REVOLUTION?

Type 964, 993, then 996. Could any of these numbers equal 911? During the last decade of the century, Porsche was hard at work on finding the right equation for making a 911 that would appeal to the past, present, and, most importantly for the company's profitability and survival, future owners. One of the big discoveries the company made was that it is hard work to keep a living legend alive. Butzi Porsche grappled with the same problem when he started doodling designs for the original 911 to pick up the torch from the 356. A good measure of how difficult such a task can be is that Porsche went into the 1990s with the Type 964, which was billed as a "new 911" and came out of the 1990s with the New 911 (Type 996). In between came the 993, which, largely because it is the last air-cooled engine model, many Porsche purists consider the ultimate evolution of the 911 design as conceived by Ferry and Butzi Porsche. So Porsche made three tries in a little over 10 years to settle on how

much history they had to lug down the road to the future.

Let's examine the first of the "new" 911s. Internally it was called the Type 964, but it came to be more commonly known as either the Carrera 2 or Carrera 4 models depending on which drivetrain was used. The 964 qualified for distinction as a "new 911" because, even though it looked similar to the 911s that had been coming out of Zuffenhausen since 1963, Porsche claimed that 87 percent of its parts were new. The roof, front fenders, trunk lid, doors, and seats were all carried over from the previous model so the 964 still bore a strong resemblance to the old 911. Underneath the old 911 look, however, the engine, suspension, brakes, and drivetrain were all "new 911" technology. The Carrera 4, which went into production in January, 1989, could also be called an evolution of the 959 because Porsche's all-wheel drive supercar, and its Paris-Dakar rally-winning 961 siblings, served as the

Porsche revived the Carrera RS name in 1992 with special lightweight club racer specials for European customers. The United States and Canada got the RS America instead. The U.S. cars weighed 2,955 pounds, as opposed to the European Carrera 2 RS, which tipped the scales at 2,712 pounds. Deleted to save weight were air conditioning, power steering, power sunroof, sound insulation, and rear seats. The sunroof and air conditioning could be ordered as options.

inspiration for building a regular production model with four-wheel drive. Porsche had been experimenting with four-wheel drive systems for the 911 since 1975 and displayed a four-wheel drive 911 at the 1981 Frankfurt Auto Show. The system that went into the 964 was a new system and not the same as that of the 959. The four-wheel drive Type 964 Carrera 4 hit the market as a 1989 model with Carrera 2, the rear-wheel drive only version, joining it for the 1990 model year.

The four-wheel drive system of the Carrera 4 comprised a five-speed gearbox, based on the G50, that transferred power to a front differential via a rigid torque tube that carried a central driveshaft. A transfer case split engine torque, with 31 percent directed to the front wheels and 69 percent to the rear. ABS wheel sensors were used to detect wheel spin and redirect torque (up to 100 percent) from front to rear or vice versa as needed. The gearbox of the 964 carried the designation G64/00.

Driving all those wheels was more new and exciting technology. Increasing the bore and the stroke of the previous 911's 3.2-liter six, Porsche engineers came up with a 3.6-liter engine that produced 250 horsepower for all of the markets, including the United States. The last time U.S. cars were on equal horsepower footing with the Rest of the World was in 1978, and that came about by decreasing RoW horsepower. With the new 3.6-liter, everybody shared in the power gain. RoW horsepower ratings went up from 231

The RS America was powered by the stock Type M64/01 3.6-liter 250-horsepower engine, which ran on 95 RON unleaded fuel. The Carrera 2 RS had the Euro-spec M64/03 motor, which ran on 98 RON unleaded fuel to make 260 horsepower. The factory claimed a 0–62-mile per hour (100-kilometer per hour) time for the RS America of 5.4 seconds and a top speed of 162 miles per hour, the same as for the Carrera 2 RS. The Type M64/01 engine was the same as in the regular production Carrera 2/4, with a 100-millimeter bore and a 76.4-millimeter stroke, for an even 3,600-cc capacity. Other features were a twin-spark ignition system with dual distributors, antiknock sensors, a 12-blade cooling fan, and cylinder heads with ceramic port liners for cooling efficiency.

horsepower while U.S. customers gained a whopping 33 hp!

A twin-spark ignition system, knock sensors, and a new Motronic engine management system with sequential fuel injection were the major components responsible for the across-the-board power increase, catalytic converters installed or

Andial converted 25 of these cars to full Carrera Cup specs; they had to be reconverted once the series was canceled. All of the cars were Grand Prix White with black interiors, except one that was painted Guards Red.

The RS America came with sport seats, while the Carrera Cup car had stock seats. RS America weighed 2,955 pounds, thanks to deletion of air conditioning, power steering, sunroof, sound insulation, and rear seats. However, for RS America buyers, air conditioning, stereos, and sunroofs were popular options, which negated much of the weight saving over a Carrera 2.

The RS America in these photos is fitted with aftermarket racing wheels. Standard wheels on RS America were 17-inch Cup Design alloys measuring 7 inches wide in front and 8 inches wide in the rear. Carrera Cup car has wider 17-inch Cup Design alloys that are 7.5 inches wide up front and 9 inches wide in the rear. Most notable visual difference between the RS America and U.S. Carrera Cup car is the large rear spoiler on the RS America, in lieu of the moveable stock unit retained on the Cup car.

not. A 12-blade cooling fan, ceramic port liners, and a revised cylinder wall design kept things cool enough to make the 964 the first 911 without an engine oil cooler. And starting with 1993 models, Porsche also switched to the use of synthetic motor oil.

An even bigger departure from Porsche's past was the suspension of the new Carrera 2/4.

Gone were the torsion bars, victims of the space requirements of the four-wheel drive system. MacPherson struts were retained up front with new cast-aluminum lower arms. The rear was suspended by cast-aluminum trailing arms with coil-over shocks. More bad news for the purists, the increased forward weight of the new drive system necessitated

Porsche claimed that the 993 had 80 percent new parts, compared to the Type 964 that it replaced. The exterior only carried over the roof and hood of the previous model. Underneath the altered body panels were major changes to the suspension and drivetrain. Gone were the traditional semi-trailing arms at the rear. The LSA (Light, Stable, Agile) multi-link suspension that replaced them was more driver friendly through turns, decreasing susceptibility to drop-throttle oversteer. This was a good idea, since out back was a more powerful 3.6-liter engine putting 272 horsepower through an equally new six-speed transaxle.

Narrow waist and bulging fenders along with revised bumpers gave the 993 more visual appeal than the model it replaced. As the last air-cooled 911, many consider it the highest evolution of Butzi Porsche's initial concept.

The taillights and bumpers of the 993 evoke more of the classic 911 look than the bulky rear end styling of its predecessor the 964. The moveable rear wing, which was first introduced on the 964, carried over to the newer model. The wing pops up at speeds over 50 miles per hour to improve high speed handling and as the car slows to around 6 miles per hour, the wing lowers itself back into place on the rear deck lid. Depending on the whim of the driver, the rear wing can also be raised or lowered when the car is standing still by a switch on the console.

Modern interior look of this 993 is enhanced by gray-and-blue leather with titanium-colored gauge faces. Driver and passenger airbags became standard in all markets, which prompted Porsche to update the interior's appearance and improve heating and air conditioning systems. Traditional five-gauge setup was retained but a rainbow of colored information screens lurked behind them, ready to educate or warn the driver as necessary.

the installation of power-assist to the rack-and-pinion steering.

It was too little, too late to save his job, but Ernst Fuhrmann had to be delighted to know that at least part of the 928 progressed into Porsche's future product line. The brakes fitted to the Carrera 2/4 were derived from the 928 S4 and featured all-wheel ABS. The five-spoke Fuchs alloy wheels that had so long been associated with the 911, since their debut on the 1967 911S, were retired in favor of modern 16-inch alloys. Called Club Sport wheels, they have seven short spokes

and large, convex centers that may be more aerodynamic but are certainly less visually exciting than the Fuchs wheels. In 1992, a more attractive option, the five-spoke Carrera Cup wheels, became available.

Speaking of good looks, the appearance of the 964 reverses the axiom that "beauty is only skin deep." With all of its advanced technology, it looks better below the skin. The thermoplastic body-colored front and rear bumpers and lower side sills may have been more aerodynamically efficient but gave the 964 a lumpy, unfinished

The 1999 Carrera 4 brought all-wheel drive to the 996 model line-up, in coupe or cabriolet body styles. The new system incorporated a viscous clutch, which moved from the gearbox location of the 993 to the front differential housing for better weight distribution. Power, anywhere from 5 to 40 percent depending on conditions, is transmitted to the front wheels via drive shaft in the frame tunnel. Porsche Stability Management (PSM), which uses a combination of traction control, braking, and engine management to reduce oversteer, was also part of the Carrera 4 package. Externally, the only way to spot the 1999 Carrera 4 is by its unique 17-inch wheels and the titanium color of the name badges and brake calipers. *Porsche AG*

The 996 has all the amenities of a contemporary luxury car, including the navigation system. Five-speed Tiptronic S and all-wheel drive of the Carrera 4 add a sophisticated level of high performance without disrupting the luxury image. *Porsche Cars North America*

look. One could be extremely unkind and say that these pieces looked more like the plastic cladding one would expect from Pontiac, not Porsche.

The evolution of 911 styling has always been a good example of form following function, and, despite the bumpers and side trim, the 964 did make a significant evolutionary contribution. In a concession to retaining the elegant slope that Butzi had penned for the rear of the 911 while improving high-speed stability, the rear wing of the 964 was designed to raise and lower itself into the engine lid depending on the car's speed. The wing would pop up as speeds exceeded 50 miles per hour and drop out of sight when the car decelerated below 6 miles per hour. No one can say if the engineers involved with its development considered the possibility of it being used as incriminating evidence in traffic court.

Another part of the 911's past was recalled in January 1990 when the Carrera 2 offered the option of a four-speed automatic transmission. The Tiptronic, like the old Sportomatic, could either be shifted manually or used in a full automatic mode. A Tiptronic-equipped Carrera 2 was about 1.0 second slower from 0 to 60 miles per hour than a manual shift model.

Establishing itself as leading edge in safety as well as performance, the 1990 United States version Carrera 2/4 was one of the first cars to come with dual air-bags as standard equipment. In 1991, all left-hand drive 964s were so equipped.

All this technology had its price. At $58,500 for a C2 coupe, the 964 cost over $7,000 more than the car it replaced. The four-wheel drive added another $11,000 to the sticker and well over 200 pounds to the vehicle's weight. At 2,970 pounds, the Carrera 2 was already 300 pounds heavier than the previous Carrera 3.2. Despite the added weight, thanks to the big increase in horsepower, the C2 managed to shave about a half second off its predecessor's 0 to 60-mile per hour time, clocking in at 5.6 seconds.

Porsche may have billed the Carrera 2/4 as the "new 911," but no one was buying it, literally. Hitting U.S. showrooms just as the country was heading for a major economic downturn, sales of the car were dismal. In the 1993 model year, the last full year the car was produced, there were about 1,700 cars sold in the UnitedStates and a quarter of that total was a special 450-car run of lightweight RS America models. Besides having a slight performance advantage, the RS America listed at $53,900, a substantial price advantage over the regular production coupe. Another special edition, the Carrera 2 Speedster in 1993, was not as well received. Porsche planned to make 3,000 of the Cabriolets with cut-down windshields and humpbacked fiberglass covers over the rear seats, but only 936 were ever built. Just 427 of these were U.S.-spec cars.

At this point in time, it not only looked again as if the 911 might become extinct, but

THE TARGA
TAKES COVER

As pointed out in Chapter 3, by 1989, Cabriolet sales were outpacing those of the Targa by almost two to one. This trend increased with the Type 964. In 1991, Porsche sold 2,207 Cabriolets and only 746 Targas. Worldwide sales figures had a similar ratio, with 3,886 Cabriolets being produced versus 1,196 Targas. Sales of all the 964 models fell drastically until production stopped at the end of 1993, but Cabriolets continued to outpace Targas by more than three to one.

When the 993 took over from the 964, the Targa version was conspicuous by its absence. In 1996, Porsche brought back the Targa, but it was much changed from the concept Butzi had unveiled in 1966. Built on a Cabriolet chassis, the new Targa had the appearance of a coupe with a huge, tinted skylight. The skylight was actually a glass panel that could, at the push of a button, slide back and under the rear window. The panel was insulated and coated to filter out ultraviolet rays to avoid creating a greenhouse effect in the cockpit. For added protection, a screen could be rolled out to further cut down on sunlight.

While the rest of the world was intrigued enough by this concept to cause Targa sales that first year to give the Cabriolet a run for the money, 1,980 Targas to 2,066 Cabriolets, U.S. customers still bought 2,152 Cabriolets versus only 462 Targas. In 1997, U.S. sales had similar results while in the rest of the world, Cabriolets outpaced Targas by 400 units. There were reports of leakage and some people complained about the view out the rear when the top glass was lowered next to the rear window.

The Targa was not part of the original 996 line-up but is expected to return, possibly as soon as the 2001 model year.

Watching the 996 convertible top going through its paces can be a crowd-pleasing experience. Operated by a push button on the dash, the top raises or lowers itself in 20 seconds. Part of the show includes the deck behind the rear seats, which raises itself up as the top folds back into a recess behind the seats. This area is covered up as the deck drops back into place. An aluminum alloy hardtop, weighing just 73 pounds is easily installed for extreme winter weather conditions.

In 2000, the 996 engine got a performance bump to an even 300 horsepower, thanks to new exhaust system. Other changes include a soft-touch grain dashboard and interior trim. Aluminum accents on the shift knob, handbrake handle, and inside door handles are a nice touch that also livens up the interior. *Porsche Cars North America*

Porsche, at least as an independent company, might also disappear. The next 911, the 993, did turn out to be the last air-cooled 911, but as such it successfully bridged the gap between the original 911 concept and what was needed for Porsche and the 911 to be viable entities in the twenty-first century. The muscular styling of the 993, almost a macho caricature of Butzi's original design, won back the purists put off by the bulkiness of the 964. Only the roof and trunk lid were carried over from the 964.

The 993 retained the 3.6-liter engine, but lighter pistons and connecting rods with an upgraded engine management system raised the power level to 272 horsepower. Hydraulic lifters were added for quieter running and to reduce maintenance. The 993 chopped 0.3 seconds off the 0 to 60 miles per hour of the 964, stopping the clock at 5.4 seconds.

A new rear suspension marked the most radical departure of the 993 from past 911s. A multi-link system replaced the semitrailing arms used on previous models. Called LSA—Lightweight, Stable, Agile—the suspension consisted of a two-piece cast-aluminum transverse-mounted arch to which were attached dual wishbones, also of cast-aluminum. The main advantage of LSA was a decrease in the 911's long-familiar propensity for

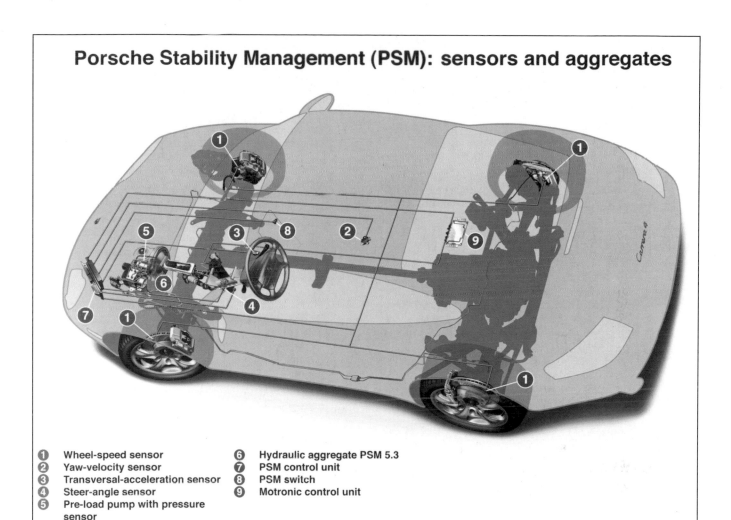

Porsche Stability Management (PSM): sensors and aggregates

1. Wheel-speed sensor
2. Yaw-velocity sensor
3. Transversal-acceleration sensor
4. Steer-angle sensor
5. Pre-load pump with pressure sensor
6. Hydraulic aggregate PSM 5.3
7. PSM control unit
8. PSM switch
9. Motronic control unit

Optional for 2000 on rear-drive models is the Porsche Stability Management System (PSM), which can detect a loss of grip at either end of the car and compensate by braking the appropriate wheel, or, if needed, by altering engine power. *Porsche Cars North America*

Next page: In 1999 and 2000, Porsche declined to field a factory-based effort to race at Le Mans for the overall win. The company wanted to devote all of its engineering talent and budget to developing a Sport Utility Vehicle. It relied on its customers to represent the Porsche name using the 996-derived 911 GT3R. The normally aspirated water-cooled 3.6-liter six-cylinder puts out 420 horsepower. The GT3R did win its class at Le Mans 2000, a class in which all of the entries were Porsches.

PORSCHE 911 GT1:
THE ULTIMATE RACING 911

When a Porsche 935 won the 1979 24 Hours of Le Mans, it seemed a pretty safe bet that this would be the last 911-derived car to ever win the classic endurance race. At the time, even the production 911's future looked bleak. Twenty years later, the 911 is still going strong and has added a 1998 victory in France by the 911 GT1 98LM to its family album.

After years of domination by sports prototype racers that bore little resemblance to road-going cars, the overall victory at Le Mans in 1995 by the racing version of a McLaren F1 exotic road car created interest among other manufactur-

ers to build similar cars. According to Le Mans rules, these cars competed in the GT-1 category for limited production sports cars, which, although they were race cars, could theoretically be offered in street versions. Porsche decided that it would build such a car, based on the 911, for the 1996 Le Mans race.

The carbon fiber constructed exterior silhouette of the GT1 was unmistakably that of the 911, but it was also part 911 under the skin. The front end of a 993, back to the B pillar was used as part of the chassis. The 3.2-liter, twin turbo, liquid-cooled engine was derived from the 911 flat six. Power

in Le Mans trim was rated at 600 horsepower at 7,200 rpm. A six-speed gearbox, ABS, and power steering were also part of the package. From the rear, above the twin air diffusers were a familiar-looking pair of 911 taillights.

The GT1 was a success in winning the GT-1 class at Le Mans in 1996. In 1997, the GT1 was leading overall at the 22-hour mark when the car caught fire and burned. For 1998, Porsche upped the ante of its GT1 by building the entire body and chassis of carbon fiber, to shave about 250 pounds off the car's weight. A longer tail and swoopy new fender lines added 7 inches in length while the car also became wider and an inch lower, to improve speed and handling down the Mulsanne Straight. The 3.2-liter, twin turbo, four-valve engine with TAG 3.8 engine management system looked the same on paper as its predecessor, but benefited from tuning tweaks derived from the 996 program.

Whatever Porsche did, it worked, as a pair of GT1 98LMs finished one-two in an exciting race that featured a duel with the favored Toyota GT-One, which was not decided until the final hour. Besides the victorious driving team of Allan McNish, Stephane Ortelli, and Laurent Aiello, 911 fans around the world had reason to celebrate. The 911 had won Le Mans again and fittingly, as Porsche's most successful model, in the company's 50th anniversary year.

Porsche's GT1 was introduced in 1996 after the FIA instituted rules for a GT class based on production-based sports cars, of which only one road-going example needed to be made. Porsche had to move quickly in order to enter such a car for Le Mans that year, so it used the front end of a 993 attached to a conventional racing chassis. It also used the water-cooled version of the flat six engine, producing 600 horsepower, mounted ahead of the rear wheels for optimum handling balance. The GT1 project was completed in eight months. The two cars entered at Le Mans in 1996 finished first and second in class, and second and third overall to a Porsche prototype car. Similar cars ran less successfully at Le Mans in 1997 and in the FIA GT world championship series.

snap oversteer when the driver lifted abruptly off the throttle while cornering. LSA also controlled rear end squat during acceleration.

The 993 featured larger ventilated and cross-drilled brake discs up front, 12.0 inches in diameter, while the ventilated and cross-drilled rear rotors remained at 11.8 inches in diameter. Four-piston calipers were used at all four wheels. An improved ABS system was part of the package. The ABS sensors also functioned as part of the Automatic Brake Differential (ABD) option, available on cars with manual transmission, to detect wheelspin at the rear wheels upon acceleration. Selective braking was then applied performing a function similar to a limited-slip differential.

A new six-speed manual transmission was part of the new 993 package, or buyers could choose an optional improved version of Tiptronic.

To complement its more aggressively styled body, Cup Design 93 wheels, with spokes designed to draw hot air off the brakes at speed, were standard equipment. Wheel sizes were 7Jx16 inches up front and a wider 9Jx16 inches in the rear.

The Type 964 remained in production through December 1993. Production of the 993 began in January 1994 as part of the 1994 model year. Porsche sold nearly 15,000 993s that year, and nearly 18,000 the next year. That was 1995, which saw the debut of the 993 Carrera 4 with a redesigned all-wheel drive system. The new system used a viscous coupling and central shaft to send power to the front wheels and weighed about half as much (111 pounds) as the computer-controlled system of the 964. ABD traction control was standard on the new Carrera 4.

Also beginning in 1995, Tiptronic customers could order the Tiptronic S version, which included thumb switches on the steering wheel in addition to the console-mounted lever for selecting gears in the manual mode.

For 1996, a variable length (via sliding runners) intake system, called Varioram, was added to the 3.6-liter engine. Horsepower increased to 282 horsepower, most notable in midrange performance, while fuel consumption and emissions were reduced. A distinctive siren sound above 5,000 rpm let the world know that Varioram was at work.

As good as the 993 was, and it is still highly regarded by 911 fans some of whom prefer it to the latest model, only so much can be done to improve on a design that stretches back to the late 1950s. It was time for a New 911. And Porsche was able to deliver it in the form of the 996.

Though its appearance has been criticized as being a bit too bland, especially following the Rubenesque lines of the 993, the shape of the 996 brings the evolution of Butzi's classic 911 curve to a state-of-the-art, aerodynamically efficient conclusion. Porsche did make the mistake of grafting the 996 nose on the Boxster, which preceded the 996 to showrooms, a move that opened the door for complaints that the shape of the latest 911 is not distinctive enough. Critics also argued that the 911 should not share body and mechanical components with a lower priced "entry level" Porsche.

What established the 996 as the New 911 as opposed to a "new 911" was the change from an air-cooled engine to one that is liquid-cooled. In order to keep up performance, and keep engine heat under control, while meeting stricter noise and emissions requirements around the world, Porsche was forced to make the switch. Making 296 horsepower at 6,800 rpm, the latest flat six develops more horsepower than the 993's air-cooled unit, despite moving down in displacement from 3.6 to 3.4 liters. Dual overhead cams operate four valves per cylinder. VarioCam (variable valve timing) adjusts intake valve timing for maximum breathing efficiency whether at high or low rpm. Also on board is the latest iteration of Varioram, Porsche's two-stage induction system. Previous systems relied on sliding intake runners while the latest version uses a butterfly valve to match intake pressure to rpm. Fuel economy is up, and 0 to 60 times are down, to 5.2 seconds, compared to the 993.

The new engine required a stronger six-speed gearbox, which has a cable-actuated shift mechanism and is worked by pedals that are hinged from the top, not from the floor as on all previous 911s and 356s. A reworked five-speed Tiptronic S now has five computer maps that adapt the automatic shift points to match the driving style of whoever is behind the wheel.

The front and rear suspensions have been modified to take full advantage of a chassis that has been stiffened by 50 percent, yet weighs 154 pounds less. The wheelbase has also been extended by 3.2 inches to measure 92.8 inches overall. Larger brakes have also been fitted front and rear. Seventeen-inch wheels, 7 inches wide in front and 9-inches wide at the rear, are standard equipment, with 205/50ZR and 265/35ZR tires fitted, respectively. Optional wheels are 7.5Jx18 and 10Jx18.

Harm Lagaay, Porsche's chief designer, said his goal was to design "a car that would have the clear lines distinguishing all Porsches of the 356 and 911 ancestral line." He had aerodynamic goals, as well as ancestral ones, to meet. As a result, the windshield rake of the 996 has been laid back from the 60-degree slant of its predecessors to a more airflow-efficient 55 degrees. Better integrated bumpers, repositioned side mirrors, and a slipperier underbelly have given the 996 a drag coefficient of 0.30. The retractable rear spoiler now pops up at 75 miles per hour and assists the 996 to a top speed of 174 miles per hour.

The longer, wider body and more efficiently packaged engine have also made the 996 roomier inside.

Is the 996, then, the perfect 911? The highest peak on the 911 evolutionary curve, it is clearly the best engineered and designed 911 so far. If it has a failing, subjective views on styling aside, it is that it is too good of a 911. The handling limits are so high and the car performs so well that it is almost too easy to drive at the speeds one can reach outside of a racetrack. At least to those to whom the 911 experience includes the constant tugging on the steering wheel to offset the feedback

A 1998 family group photo. Boxster roadster behind 996 coupe could easily be mistaken as a slightly downsized 996 Cabriolet. Note the distinctive glass roof of 993 Targa on the right. The sliding glass roof version of the Targa debuted in the 1996 model year. Lower wind noise and better rollover protection than the traditional soft-top Targa were the driving forces behind the electrically operated glass panel that was also treated to filter the ultraviolet rays of the sun. The roof added 66 pounds over the weight of a 993 coupe. The Targas were built on Cabriolet bodies. *Porsche AG*

from the changing road surface and the challenge of making throttle adjustments to keep the rear tires in line. Also missing is the raspy exhaust note accompanied by a mechanical symphony of timing chains and fan blades. The original 911 was a very visceral piece of machinery, and mastering its complexities and eccentricities was part of the experience. The 996 is comfortable and a delight to drive. But it may be a little too sophisticated and aloof to command the devotion and enthusiasm of the earlier, less perfect, examples of the 911.

Deciding which is the best 911 comes down to personal preference. Porsche has done its job of following the evolutionary curve laid down by Butzi. It is up to the enthusiast to decide how far along the curve he or she wants to go before getting off.

The Porsche Turbo once again raises the bar for rear wing style and function. The Turbo also raises the upper part of its two-piece rear stabilizer when speeds above 75 miles per hour are reached, and the wing lowers as speed decreases to 50 miles per hour. The wing aids in the flow of intake air. Rear fenders are also 2.6 inches wider on the Turbo to accommodate 18-inch alloy wheels with 295/30ZR18 tires. Air scoops in the fenders direct air to intercoolers. *Porsche Cars North America*

THE 911 TURBO
EXCELLENCE
EXCEEDS EXPECTATIONS

Ernst Fuhrmann, the man who a decade later would lose the top spot at Porsche for feeling that the 911 had reached its evolutionary peak, was the driving force behind the original 911 Turbo, or 930 in reference to its internal project number. Coming up through the development engineering side of the company, Fuhrmann was a strong advocate of racing as a means to improve the breed.

Author Karl Ludvigsen in his history of Porsche, *Porsche, Excellence Was Expected*, has a quote from Fuhrmann regarding the special relationship that made racing an integral part in the design process of Porsche's road cars. It is especially poignant considering the company's recent decision to cut back on its racing program in order to use those funds to diversify its product line.

"It belongs to us, this racing business," Fuhrmann said. "We are often asked why we spend so much on it. If you design a production car, you know in five or six years what you've done. In racing, you know in a year."

What Fuhrmann knew from racing the 917 in the Can-Am series was that turbocharging an engine could extract gobs of horsepower with what he felt were very little trade-offs. That convinced him to have his engineers develop a turbocharged 911 for his personal use. The results from experimenting with a 2.7-liter engine using Bosch K-Jetronic fuel injection were encouraging enough to create a show car in this configuration for the Paris auto show in September, 1973. Ten years after the debut of the original 911 that was destined to become an automotive icon, the introduction of the Turbo heralded a version of the 911 that was to transcend being an automotive icon to become a cultural icon. Whether it was the outrageous styling or the promises of 280 horsepower and speeds of 160 miles per hour, more likely the

combination of the two, the Porsche Turbo created such a powerful image in the public eye that soon everything from laundry detergents to vacuum cleaners were being advertised as delivering "turbo- charged'"performance.

Starting in 1974, Porsche would apply turbocharged performance to its 911 racing efforts in cars like the 934 RSR and the mighty 935 that would rule world sports car racing for the rest of the decade.

The first production model of the Turbo came out in October 1974 as a 1975 model. Unlike the Paris show car, the engine was a 3.0-liter (2,994-cc) variation of that used in the Carrera 3.0. This engine was chosen over the 2.7-liter primarily because of its better low-end throttle response, which reduced some of the "lag" felt during acceleration before sufficient turbo boost built up. The Turbo engine had thicker cylinder heads than the normally aspirated

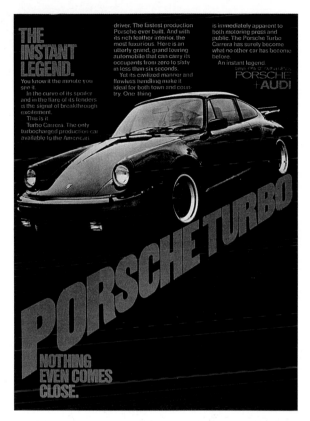

The Porsche Turbo Carrera not only was an "instant legend," with a top speed of over 155 miles per hour and 0 to 60 in 5.5 seconds, it became a cultural icon for anything outrageously fast or powerful. But it was the sudden surge of power that came on like a rocket booster around the 2,500-rpm mark and just kept going to 5,500 rpm, that created the Turbo legend.

Left: Bulging fender flares and large rear wing have been a Turbo trademark since the first ones entered the United States as 1976 models.

3.0-liter engine. The compression ratio was lowered to 6.5:1. The KKK turbocharger was mounted at the left rear of the engine. A unique feature that had come down from the racing cars was a blow-off valve controlled by manifold vacuum pressure that kept the turbo rotors spinning even if the throttle was closed momentarily. This was another way Porsche had sought to overcome turbo lag. The Turbo engine package weighed 456 pounds, tipping the scales

Sold as Turbo Carreras, the first year Turbos featured blacked-out chrome, body-colored headlight rings, headlight washers, fog lights, and power sunroof.

about 70 pounds heavier than a normally aspi-rated 2.7-liter unit.

Debuting in Europe, the 1975 Turbo was the first street Porsche to feature a breakerless igni-tion system. To handle the added torque of the turbo motor, a new transmission was designed. Dubbed the 930/30, it was a four-speed with a wider ratio set of gears that were also beefier than the ones used in the 915. A larger (240-mil-limeter) clutch was also part of the 930 package. Suspension changes included revisions to both the components and suspension geometry. The 15-inch Fuchs alloys of the first 930 were 7 inches wide in front and 8 inches wide in

the rear. The 930 was the first production car to make use of the new Pirelli P7 low-profile high-performance radial tires. These measured 205/50 and 225/50, front to rear. They were optional in 1975 but became stan-dard in 1976.

While European versions of the Turbo boasted 260 horsepower at 5,500 rpm, U.S. emissions equipment, including thermal reac-tors, limited the power to 245 horsepower at 5,500 rpm. Good enough for Car and Driver magazine to set a clutch-searing, tire-scorching 0 to 60-mile per hour time of 4.9 seconds! The European magazines that had tested the more

The 3.0-liter engine had one KKK exhaust-driven turbocharger. When 0.8 bar boost came on, the compression ratio of 6.5:1 effectively became 11.7:1, to squeeze out 245 horsepower on U.S.-spec cars.

powerful versions had more conservative times (and launches), hovering around the 6-second range. U.S. cars were introduced in August 1975 as the 1976 Turbo Carrera. Equipped as luxury models, the Turbo Carrera's $25,850 sticker included a stereo, fog lights, air conditioning, and leather interior.

In 1978 a new 3.3-liter engine with intercooler boosted horsepower to 300 for RoW cars while the U.S. cars went to 265 horsepower.

The Turbo disappeared from the U.S. line-up in 1980 as rumors of the demise of the entire 911 range began to spread. The car continued to be sold everywhere else, averaging sales of well over 1,000 units per year.

In 1986, thanks to the magic of Bosch's Motronic DME (Digital Motor Electronics) and oxygen sensors in the exhaust which allowed the use of catalytic converters and unleaded

The Turbo interior had standard leather trim and a three-spoke steering wheel but was basically the same as the 1976 911. No boost gauge was fitted.

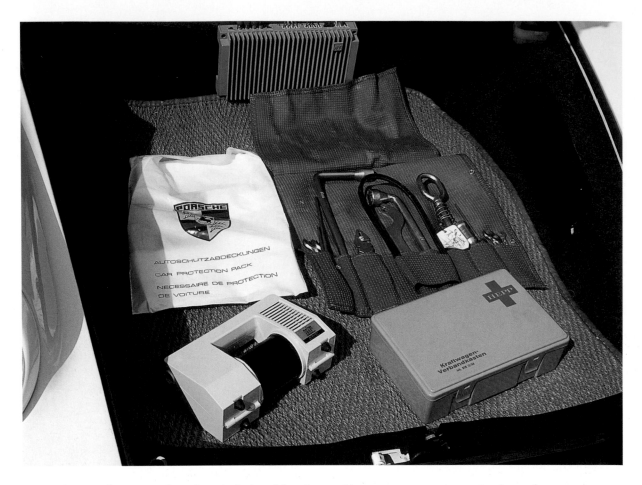

The Turbo's well-equipped trunk included tool kit, first aid kit, air compressor, and a box of protective covers to avoid scratching the car while maintenance was carried out.

fuel, the Turbo was again deemed to be worthy of reentry into the United States. For $48,000, you got 282 horsepower and 16-inch wheels that were 7 inches wide in front and a whopping 9 inches at the rear. In 1988, the Turbo became available for the first time as a Targa or Cabriolet. The good news for 1989 was that the five-speed G50 with hydraulic-actuated clutch became available. The bad news was that the change to the Type 964 in 1990 eliminated the Turbo model.

The Turbo's absence lasted only a year and it reappeared in the new 964 body style wearing a large flat rear wing. A revised exhaust system, larger turbo charger, and a larger intercooler had raised the horsepower to 320 at 5,750 rpm. U.S. models were now equal in power to the RoW cars. New 17-inch Cup Design wheels were part of the package.

The changeover from the 964 to the 993 took the Turbo model off the market again for the 1994 model year. It was back better than ever in 1995 wearing the 993 bodywork with a sleeker rear wing. Under that wing things looked even better, thanks to a new 3.6-liter engine sporting twin turbos and two intercoolers. Power was up to 408

continued on page 92

The 360-horsepower 3.6-liter engine that debuted in January 1993 retained the Turbo's role as Porsche's image model. A five-speed manual, limited-slip differential, and three-piece Cup Design 18-inch wheels were all part of the package. *Matt Stone*

The 3.6-liter Turbo engine had a 7.5:1 compression ratio and made 360 horsepower at 5,500 rpm. Space restrictions limited this engine to one spark plug per cylinder. *Matt Stone*

Below: The racecar evolution of the 911 progressed from the 1967 911R to the Carrera RS and RSR of 1973 and 1974 to the turbocharged 934 which was built to 1976 FIA Group 4 regulations. The 934 had a 3.0-liter (2994 cc) turbocharged engine that put out about 530 hp. *Randy Leffingwell*

Porsche's GT2 race car made 430 horsepower, but for $150,000 you could buy a limited edition Turbo S that had 424 horsepower and the luxury of a custom leather interior. *Matt Stone*

PORSCHE 911 TURBO RACE CARS: WHALE TALES, THE MOBY DICK, AND MORE

Porsche's notoriety for producing powerful turbocharged 911s is not limited to road cars. Some of the most powerful, and creatively engineered, 911s ever produced were turbocharged racing models that ruled GT racing from 1976 to the early 1980s. Like many successful Porsche race cars, they were built by taking advantage of rules that were intended to level the playing field among Porsche and its competitors. Thanks to the engineering and interpretive genius of Porsche racing boss Norbert Singer, and much to the chagrin of sanctioning bodies and competitors, these rules had the opposite effect. For Porsche fans, Singer's talents not only provided winning celebrations but also

memorable cars like the outrageous Type 935/78 Moby Dick 1978 Le Mans car.

The Group 4 Turbo RSR was designed to meet the regulations for the 1976 international GT racing season as specified by the Federation Internationale de l'Automobile (FIA), the sport's governing body. They were called Type 934 to indicate that they were 930 (Turbo) models built to Group 4 Grand Touring Specifications. Because the 934 had a turbocharged 3.0-liter engine, it was classified by the FIA as the equivalent (1.4 times more powerful than a normally aspirated 3.0-liter engine) of a 4.2-liter car. The minimum weight for a 4.0–4.5-liter car was 2,470 pounds, or slightly less than a fully loaded 930 street car. As a result, very little weight was taken out of the 934 and of the 31 cars built, some ran with their electric windows still in place. The biggest difference that the 934 had over the stock Turbo was the use of 16-inch wheels and an air-to-water intercooler that allowed boost pressures capable of producing 500 horsepower or more. Porsche chose to limit the 934 to 485 horsepower at 7,000 rpm. The 934 was highly successful in various European GT championships as well as Trans-Am and eventually IMSA racing in the United States.

Left: The 935 started out as a leaner, meaner 2.8-liter 590-horsepower version of the 934 to conform to the less restrictive 1976 Group 5 GT class rules. By the 1978 season, Porsche racing boss Norbert Singer had read deeply between the lines of the FIA rule book to produce a GT race car that still retained the production roofline of a 911 but had otherwise become an 800-horsepower aerodynamic device. The long, sweeping rear fenders designed primarily for stability on the Mulsanne Straight, gave rise to the car's nickname of Moby Dick. They also let it reach a top speed at Le Mans of over 227 miles per hour. Unfortunately, Moby Dick failed to win the 24 Hours, but it did inspire similar efforts from privateers like the Kremer brothers, who built a 935 that won in 1979. Randy Leffingwell

As formidable a competitor as the 934 was, the 935 version, built to conform to the looser rules of the Group 5 or Special Production Car category, was even more intimidating. Because of a sliding weight scale tied to engine displacement and freer rules regarding tire sizes and suspension components, there were cars that competed as either a 934 or a 935, but Porsche did build two specific 935 cars for the 1976 season. Using a 2.8-liter engine and an air-to-air intercooler tucked into a huge rear wing, coil suspension, and 19-inch tall by 15-inch wide rear wheels, these cars were rated by the factory at 600 horsepower with available bursts of up to 630 horsepower if necessary. Testing at Paul Ricard, the 935 had had a higher top speed than a six-wheel Tyrell Grand Prix car also using the circuit. A Road & Track magazine comparison test of a 1976 935 versus a 934 had the 935 going from 0 to 60 miles per hour in 3.3 seconds while the 934 was clocked in 5.8 seconds. More impressive were quarter-mile times of 8.9 seconds against 14.2 seconds and the 935's reaching 0 to 150 miles per hour in 11 seconds flat, almost twice as fast as the 934's 21.4 second reading.

But Singer wasn't done with the 935 or the rules regarding it. For the 1978 season, he read into the regulations that defined the "body" in reference to what had to be left stock on the race car. What he ended up with was the 935/78 that had a 911 roofline and doors sitting between sloping front fenders devoid of headlights, exaggerated box-like fender flares, and a swoopy tail extension that earned the car its nickname of Moby Dick. The low-slung racer also had a 3.2-liter engine with water-cooled heads that produced 740 horsepower at 8,200 rpm. With full boost, the car produced close to 900 horsepower. At Le Mans, the Moby Dick reached 227.5 miles per hour on the Mulsanne Straight. Unfortunately, various problems kept the 935/78 from being more than an artistic success. It finished 8th at Le Mans. It did serve as the basis for future refinement by private teams. In 1979, the Kremer Brothers modified 935 won the 24 Hours of Le Mans.

Continued from page 86

horsepower, with improved low-end torque that brought acceleration times down near 4.0 seconds to travel from 0 to 60 miles per hour. Other niceties included a six-speed transmission and four-wheel drive. Wheels and tires measured 8Jx18 with 225/40ZR radials up front and 10Jx18 with 285/30ZR radials at the rear. Huge brakes (12.7-inch rotors) led to epic stopping potential. The Turbo could travel from 0 to 60 miles per hour and back to 0 in less than 6.5 seconds.

Released as a 2001 model, the 996 version of the Turbo takes this performance icon to even greater levels with a top speed of 189 miles per hour and a 0 to 60-mile per hour time of 4.0 seconds flat. Power is up to 420 horsepower at 6,000 rpm. For the first time ever, the Turbo is available with a five-speed Tiptronic as an option. It is only 0.7 seconds slower to 60 than the six-speed manual transmission. Larger brakes are also fitted, similar to the ones found on the current GT3 race car.

Not a bad way to celebrate the Turbo's twenty-fifth birthday.

Twin turbos and two intercoolers filled up all the available room in the Turbo S engine compartment. *Matt Stone*

Air scoops in the rear fenders and a sculpted rear wing make the Turbo S a visual treat from the outside, but a look inside at the yellow accents of this example is by no means a letdown. Custom leather interior trim was part of the Turbo S package. *Matt Stone*

APPENDIX

TALE OF THE TAPE:
WEIGHTS AND MEASUREMENTS THROUGH THE YEARS

Dimensions

1965–68

Wheelbase	87.0 inches
Height	52.0 inches
Width	63.4 inches
Weight	2,380 pounds
Fuel tank capacity	16.4 gallons

1969–73

Wheelbase	89.4 inches
Height	52.0 inches
Width	63.4 inches
Weight	2,250 pounds
Fuel tank capacity	16.4 gallons

1974–77

Wheelbase	89.4 inches
Height	52.8 inches
Width	65.0 inches
Weight: 911	2,370–2,470 pounds
Turbo	2,630 pounds
Fuel tank capacity	21.0 gallons

1978–83

Wheelbase	89.4 inches
Height	52.8 inches
Width	65.0 inches
Weight: 911	2,560 pounds
Turbo	2,870 pounds
Fuel tank capacity	21.0 gallons

1984–89

Wheelbase	89.4 inches
Height	52.8 inches
Width	65.0 inches
Weight: 911	2,670 pounds
Turbo	2,940 pounds
Fuel tank capacity	21.0 gallons

1990–94 C2

Wheelbase	89.4 inches
Height	51.9 inches
Width	65.0 inches
Weight: 911	2,970 pounds
Turbo	3,234 pounds
Fuel tank capacity	20.0 gallons

1995–98 993

Wheelbase	89.4 inches
Height	51.8 inches
Width	68.3 inches
Weight: 993 C2	3,014 pounds
Turbo	3,465 pounds
Fuel tank capacity	19.4 gallons

1999 996

Wheelbase	92.6 inches
Height	51.4 inches
Width	69.5 inches
Weight	2,910 pounds
Fuel tank capacity	16.9 gallons

911 PERFORMANCE CHART

Model	Engine	0–60 mph (seconds)	1/4-mile (seconds)	Top Speed (mph)	Source
1965 Coupe	2.0-liter	9.0	16.5	132	*Road & Track*
1967 911S	2.0-liter	8.1	15.7	141	*Road & Track*
1968 911L/Sportomatic	2.0-liter	10.3	17.3	117	*Road & Track*
1970 911S	2.2-liter	7.3	14.9	144	*Road & Track*
1972 911T	2.4-liter	6.9	15.1	N/A	*Car and Driver*
1972 911S	2.4-liter	6.0	14.4	N/A	*Car and Driver*
1973 Carrera RSR	2.7-liter	5.6	13.2	N/A	*Road & Track*
1974 911	2.7-liter	7.9	15.5	130	*Road & Track*
1975 Calif. Carrera	2.7-liter	8.2	16.5	134	*Road & Track*
1975 Turbo	3.0-liter	5.5[2]	24.21[1]	152.9	*Automobil Revue* (Swiss)
1976 935 Turbo	2.8-liter	3.3	8.9	150	*Road & Track*
1978 911SC	3.0-liter	6.3	15.3	N/A	*Road & Track*
1979 930 Turbo	3.3-liter	5.3	13.4	160	*Motor*
1980 911SC	3.0-liter	7.0	N/A	141	*Porsche*
1984 Carrera	3.2-liter	5.6	N/A	159	*Autocar*
1990 Carrera 2	3.6-liter	5.7	N/A	162	*Porsche*
1990 Carrera Tiptronic	3.6-liter	6.2	N/A	157	*Porsche*
1991 Turbo	3.3-liter	5.0[2]	N/A	168	*Porsche*
1993 RS America	3.6-liter	5.4	N/A	162	*Porsche*
1995 Turbo	3.6-liter	3.9	12.5	180	*Road & Track*
1998 993	3.6-liter	5.4	N/A	171	*Porsche*
1999 996	3.4-liter	5.2	N/A	174	*Porsche*

[1] One kilometer distance from standing start.
[2] 0 to 62 miles per hour (100 kilometers per hour)

NOTE: Information for this chart has been compiled from various sources and does not necessarily represent the definitive performance of any of the models listed. Its purpose is to entertain 911 aficionados as much as enlighten them.

BIBLIOGRAPHY

Adler, Dennis. *Porsche 911 Road Cars*. Osceola,
    Wisconsin: MBI Publishing Company, 1998.

Aichele, Tobias. *Porsche 911, Forever Young*.
    Stuttgart, Germany: Motorbuch-Verlag, 1993.

Anderson, Bruce. *Porsche 911 Performance
    Handbook*. Osceola, Wisconsin: MBI Publishing
    Company, 1996.

Boschen, Lothar and Jurgen Barth. *The Porsche Book*.
    New York City: Arco Publishing, Inc., 1977.

Flammang, James M. *Standard Catalog of Imported
    Cars 1946–1990*. Iola, Wisconsin: Krause
    Publications, Inc., 1994.

Frere, Paul. *Porsche 911 Story*, 6th edition. Somerset,
    England: Patrick Stephens, Limited, 1997.

Harvey, Chris. *The Porsche 911*. Somerset,
    England: The Oxford Illustrated Press, 1983.

James, Drayton, Editor. *The Porsche Family Tree*.
    Vienna, VA: Porsche Club of America, PEA,
    Porsche Club of America, 1995.

Leffingwell, Randy. *Legendary Porsche*. Osceola,
    Wisconsin: MBI Publishing Company, 1996.

Ludvigsen, Karl. *Porsche, Excellence Was
    Expected*. Princeton, NJ: Princeton
    Publishing, Inc., 1977.

Morgan, Peter. *Original Porsche 911*. Osceola,
    Wisconsin: MBI Publishing Company, 1998.

Starkey, John. *Porsche 911 R-RS-RSR*. Dorchester,
    England: Veloce Publishing Plc., 1998.

CLUBS AND SOURCES FOR THE PORSCHE 911

The Early 911S Registry
P.O. Box 16001
Newport Beach, CA   92659-6001
www.911sregistry.org
Fax 949-642-9543

R Gruppe (early 911 performance and
    vintage race cars)
Crio Huergas
1530 Court Street
Alameda, CA   94501
e-mail: crispin_d_huergas@ffic.com

Porsche Owners Club
Hotline: 310-784-5653
www.porscheclub.com

*PML, The Market Letter for Porsche
    Automobiles*
P.O. Box 6010
Oceanside, CA   92058
888-928-9111
www.pmletter.com
e-mail: pmletter@aol.com

Porsche Club of America
PCA National Office
P.O. Box 30100
Alexandria, VA 22310
703-922-9300
www.pca.org

VIPER

MATT STONE

FOREWORD

I n the late 1980s, a group of dedicated car enthusiasts dreamed of creating the Ultimate American Sports Car. Not long after—on January 4, 1989, at the North American International Auto Show in Detroit—a one-of-a-kind Dodge Viper RT/10 show car appeared before the public for the first time, with the goal of testing public reaction to the concept of a back-to-basics high-performance limited-production extreme sports car. The reaction was stunning, as "orders" began to flow in before the show was over. Little more than a year later, the decision was made: Viper was a "go." The dream was quickly evolving into reality.

Reality hit like a ton of bricks. Loud, wickedly fast, hair-raising, outrageous, and exhibiting an unmatched road presence, the Dodge Viper RT/10 Roadster was the Ultimate American Sports Car. Automotive enthusiasts flocked to it.

A few years later, in 1993, the Dodge Viper GTS Coupe was displayed at the North American Auto Show in Detroit and the Greater Los Angeles Auto Show, where enthusiasts' senses were exhilarated in only a slightly more refined manner. More than just adding a roof to the Roadster, over 90 percent of the Coupe was new, and it boasted more power and less weight. The goal was to cast the GTS in the mold of the world's premier Grand Touring cars—and cater to a broader customer base than the Roadster. The Viper GTS Coupe hit Dodge showrooms in 1996.

Viper enthusiast Matt Stone expertly conveyed Chapter One of the Dodge Viper legacy (the RT/10 Roadster) and most of Chapter Two (the GTS Coupe) in the first edition of *Viper*. In this, his latest

edition, he wraps up the GTS story—with the Viper GTS-R's unprecedented string of international racing triumphs that included three FIA GT2 world championships, three class victories at Le Mans, and the overall win at the 2000 Rolex 24 at Daytona—before taking readers through the evolution of Chapter Three: the Dodge Viper SRT-10.

In January 2002 Performance Vehicle Operations—or PVO—was formed, combining Chrysler Group's specialty and performance vehicle production

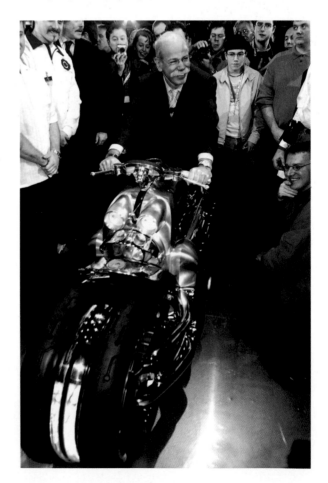

Dr. Dieter Zetsche president and CEO, Chrysler Group, aboard the Viper V10-powered Tomahawk concept at the 2003 Detroit auto show. *Chrysler*

engineering expertise with its motorsports and Mopar Performance Parts engineering know-how. Fittingly, the icon of the Dodge brand was PVO's first endeavor. Branded "SRT" for "Street and Racing Technology," the Viper SRT-10 brings Viper owners exactly what they were looking for: a true convertible with even more power, even lighter weight, and even better brakes, in a refined package that still exudes outrageous design and road presence. With its three 500s (500 horsepower and 525 ft-lb of torque from its 505 cubic inch V-10 engine), arguably the world's best brakes, and virtually unbeatable 0-100-0 mph times, there simply is no other car on the road like it.

And . . . there never will be.

Why? First, no vehicle has the history—or the ongoing ability to turn heads and drop jaws—that the icon of the Dodge brand does. Second, our vision at PVO is to continue to raise the bar, and to never rest on our laurels. And finally, our loyal Viper owners will continue to wave the flag of the car they love like no other owner group ever has or ever will. About 18,000 Vipers now cruise the world's roads and racetracks, and, remarkably, some 5,000 Viper owners are members of the Viper Club of America. They—and "a group of dedicated car enthusiasts" here at the Chrysler Group and PVO—will ensure that the Viper continues to retain its "Viperness," and remains true to our original mission: creating the Ultimate American Sports Car.

—Dr. Dieter Zetsche
President and CEO, Chrysler Group

ACKNOWLEDGMENTS

My sincere thanks first and foremost to the Viper's "Fourfathers": Bob Lutz, former Chrysler president and chief operating officer; Tom Gale, former Chrysler executive vice president of product design and international operations; Francois Castaing, former vice president of vehicle engineering and international operations and former general manager of powertrain operations; and the legendary Carroll Shelby, performance consultant to the Viper Project. Each has done well in their post-Viper careers: Bob Lutz has worked wonders in his capacity as Vice Chairman of General Motors of North America; Francois Castaing and Tom Gale have retired from Chrysler, though remain consultants to the company; and Carroll Shelby—at age 81—has just announced his re-association with Ford (expect new Shelby Mustangs and Cobras to follow). Special thanks to Mr. Gale, Mr. Lutz, and Mr. Shelby, who set time aside from their furious schedules to chat with me about the Viper, as did Roy Sjoberg, former executive engineer of the Viper Project; Ron Smith, former vice president of Dodge marketing; Pete Gladysz, former Team Viper chassis manager; John Fernandez, former Director of Performance Vehicle Operations and current head of the Chrysler Group's Motorsport programs; Dan Knott, Director of Performance Vehicle Operations; and the Viper's own "Grailkeeper", PVO Vehicle Synthesis Manager Herb Helbig.

A special thanks to Chrysler Group President Dieter Zetsche for contributing the Forward that opens this book. He, Chief Operating Officer Wolfgang Bernhard, Director of Design Trevor Creed, Dodge General Manager Darryl Jackson, and so many other Chrysler Group executives clearly committed to keeping the Viper not only alive and in production but at the top of the domestic performance heap.

Assembling the background information and archival artwork, arranging the shooting of new photography, and access to Viper cars for this project were all made possible by many current and former members of Chrysler's Public Relations staff, including Tom Kowaleski, Chrysler's former director of product PR, and Terri Houtman, manager of corporate image and brand PR. Major kudos to today's Viper PR guru, Todd Goyer, who helpfully provided a ton of information, made several interviews possible, did it all on short notice, and made it look easy. Others who helped along the way include Lisa Barrow, Lindsay Brooke, Juli Butkus, Dave Elshoff, Stephanie Harris, Jeff Leestma, Pamela Mahoney, Brian Zvible-

man, Art Ponter of the Chrysler Archives, and others who no doubt contributed behind the scenes. The copyrighted materials and trademarks contained herein are reprinted and used with permission from DaimlerChrysler Corporation.

Several of the profession's best photographers fixed their lenses on Vipers for this project: the incomparable John Lamm and racer/designer/legend/friend Peter Brock, plus John Kiewicz, David Newhardt, Bill Delaney, and Wes Allison. I appreciate the editorial contributions made by writer types John Kiewicz, Steven Cole Smith, and Viperabilia whiz—and the Viper Club of America's first president—Maurice Liang. Our thanks as well to those folks whose cars were "snapped" along the way, but whose names are unknown to us.

Others who helped in one way or another: Rick Roso, marketing manager for Skip Barber Driving School; John Hennessey of Hennessey Motorsports; John Thompson, Mark Giannotta, Kim Vogt, and everyone at J.R. Thompson Company; Lee Corsack of visual Graphics of New England; and Tom Lindamood and his crew at A&M Specialists West. Thanks again to Tim Parker, Peter Bodensteiner, Zack Miller, Christine Hunter, LeAnn Kuhlmann, and all the other professionals at Motorbooks International.

Deepest appreciation to my family and friends for putting up with all this car nonsense, which continues to be one of my great passions in life.

—*Matt Stone*

The Fourfathers' autographs grace the rear trunk panel of this RT/10. From Left: Carroll Shelby, Bob Lutz, Tom Gale, and Francois Castaing.

INTRODUCTION

The mere fact that the Viper exists today as a production vehicle is nothing short of amazing. Building cars is tough business these days: Society demands they be recyclable, biodegradable, nonpolluting, economical, safe-as-armor, and politically correct (whatever that means). Automakers need to satisfy a million government regulations and agencies, their own accountants and stockholders, and (somehow) the people who buy their product. This environment has helped create many supremely competent but hopelessly boring cars. Yet in the midst of this sea of seemingly red-tape-bound mediocrity, Dodge brought forth a 488-cubic-inch, two-seat roadster that will break most speed limits in any of its six gears. In the beginning, it had no door handles, roll-up windows, airbags, or air conditioning. Even though it has since acquired all these accoutrements, anyone who's driven a Viper knows it remains a visceral experience. Credit Chrysler Corporation's vision and guts in producing a vehicle designed and single-mindedly focused on performance, individuality, and driving pleasure—at a price tag not even approaching six figures.

The Viper served as the pilot within Chrysler for the cross-functional "team" approach to developing and producing cars, a philosophy that has proliferated throughout the company (and other auto makers) as a better way to get the job done. The significance of Team Viper cannot be overemphasized as a *major* element in the car's aura and success. Even though the players have changed over the years, and this group is now under the auspices of Chrysler's Performance Vehicle Operations group (PVO), the Viper still represents the company's performance flagship and Dodge's brand poster child.

Some of you may own or have read the previous edition of this book, first published by Motorbooks in 1996. The GTS concept had just been introduced, and we knew an updated RT/10 would come along with it for the 1997 model year. The GTS-R was

beginning its assault on international sports car racing, and it was a pleasure watching it kick major butt all over the world, including back-to-back-to-back class wins at my favorite endurance race, the 24 Hours of Le Mans, in the years that followed. I knew it wouldn't be long before I'd be at work on an updated version of that original *Viper*, as there was little doubt in my mind that the car's story would continue, and that its popularity could only increase over time. The introduction of the new-for-'03 Viper SRT-10 was all the excuse we needed to give that original book a freshening, and a few more chapters.

I am not at this time a Viper owner, but I have put in many a mile at the wheel, and I have enjoyed them immensely. I also enjoy the infectious enthusiasm shared by Viper owners. Don't bother them with talk of the 1960s or any other era: For them, *these* are the Good Old Days. And even though the Viper is as masculine as a car can get, I'm pleasantly impressed with how many of them are owned, and truly driven, by women.

This is certainly not an all-encompassing volume on the Viper, as our space here is limited; future books will be written, and the car will continue to evolve. I hope you enjoy this look at the Viper's beginnings, its first 10 years as a production car, its impressive success on the world's racetracks, and the ripple effect it has had on other Chrysler products.

Thank you for purchasing *Viper*.

Author Matt Stone. *David Newhardt*

O N E

Viper Genesis

Chrysler might have been the last American company you would expect to set out and build an elemental, high-performance roadster such as the Viper. Both Ford and General Motors have an extensive history of producing high-performance sports cars. Ford has won Le Mans and has powered Indy 500 winners; Chevrolet has built what was (at the time) rightly called "America's only true sports car," the Corvette. But the smolderings at Chrysler were there and were probably first recognizable after World War II. At least two factors set the stage for its postwar performance awakening: the Hemi V-8 and chief stylist Virgil Exner.

History on display: VM02, foreground, and VM01 make a public appearance at the Pebble Beach introduction of the GTS-R racer at a 1995 press conference.

The fire power Hemi V-8, first introduced in 1951, gave Chrysler a modern, overhead-valve V-8 with exceptional performance potential; its basic architecture is still found in today's supercharged, nitro-burning NHRA top fuel and funny car drag racers, with outputs exceeding 6,000 horsepower. It was called "Hemi," owing to its hemispheric combustion chambers, which placed the spark plug in the center of the combustion chamber for more efficient burning and better performance. The engine grew to 392 cubic inches by the end of the 1950s. Virgil Exner, a talented and flamboyant stylist, came to Chrysler from Studebaker in 1950. He admired the design talent and coachbuilding ability of the Italian styling houses, or *carrozzeria*, particularly that of Ghia. Ghia had designed and constructed a number of styling exercises, or "idea cars," as they were often referred to at the time, for Chrysler. The cars had sporty flavor, and included the Plymouth Explorer, the Chrysler K-310 and C-200, the Chrysler Falcon, and a series of machines dubbed Firearrow. Several of these machines featured Hemi V-8 power. Though none made production per se, they had some influence on Chrysler design throughout the 1950s and into the early 1960s.

The Hemi's first real foray into a production sports car was not a Chrysler product but was a very American effort nonetheless at the hands of race

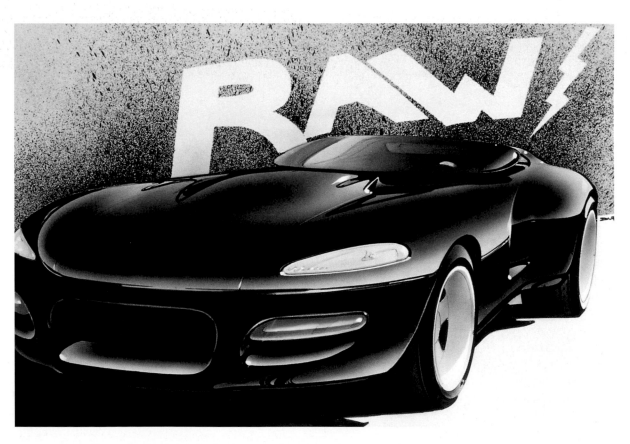

This styling concept drawing shows that the makings of the overall shape, rear sport bar, and hood-mounted exhaust vents were already in place in late 1988. *DaimlerChrysler*

No top, no side windows, no door handles, but Chrysler-powered and made in the USA: the Cunningham formula certainly provided inspiration for the Viper-to-be. This photograph was taken in August 1951, about 40 years prior to the first production Viper RT/10s.

driver, team owner, yachtsman, and car constructor Briggs Swift Cunningham. Cunningham had done reasonably well at the 1950 24 Hours of Le Mans endurance race in France with two Cadillac-powered entries; he once commented that "the French welcomed us to come back, but said to bring smaller cars." He began building his own Cunningham racers and limited-production street cars in Palm Beach, Florida, and turned to Chrysler's Hemi for power. Cunningham's racing creations were mostly taut roadsters, bodied by Italy's Vignale; they were truly the American Ferraris of their day. In the case of the C-4R, for example, the Hemi was tuned to deliver more than 300 horsepower, and C-4Rs were often clocked at well over 150 miles per hour.

Cunningham also produced handsome coupes and roadsters for the street, in an effort to help support

This early rendering testifies that many of the Viper's styling elements were cast early on, such as bulging rear fenders, low-cut windshield, hood vents, and an early idea for the RT/10s "sport bar." *DaimlerChrysler*

293

The shape is different from the final version, though note that one important cue is already in place: a V-10 engine. *DaimlerChrysler*

the racing venture. The first C-2s were constructed in 1952, and the final C-6 models in 1955, with most being Chrysler powered. Although Cunningham never did achieve his goal of building and driving the first American car to win Le Mans, he had racing successes at other venues. Cunningham would continue to compete successfully in Jaguars, OSCAs, Maseratis, and Corvettes. Still, when searching for the Viper's earliest roots, you need only look as far as, say, a Cunningham C-4R competition roadster, drifting through a corner, tires clawing for grip, Hemi V-8 barking all the way.

Throughout the 1960s, Chrysler performance went mostly in a straight line—and about a quarter mile at a time. Drag racing had matured considerably, the horsepower wars were raging between American manufacturers, and the muscle-car era was in bloom. A second-generation Hemi came from the factory packing four-barrel carburetors and 426 cubic inches. Other notable Mopar performance motors included the 413 and 426 Wedges and the 440 Six-Pack, running three two-barrel carbs. The nameplates these engines powered have all become significant pieces of

The Original Snake: Carroll Shelby

As one of the Fourfathers, Carroll Shelby played an integral and inspirational role in the Viper's development. The ancestral connection to the Shelby 427 Cobra comes through loud and clear. I spoke with Carroll in July 1995 to gain some insight on how this legendary race driver and car constructor feels about his relationship with Chrysler and about the Viper itself. Here are some excerpts:

Author: You are awaiting a heart transplant during the planning and development states of the Viper. Please describe your involvement with the car.

Carroll Shelby in 1993, at the introduction of the Viper GTS Coupe, which was inspired by Shelby's Daytona Cobra Coupe of the mid-1960s.

Shelby: I went to all the Viper meetings for about the first year and a half, and then it got so that I couldn't go anymore, waiting for a heart. All I ever did was keep preaching, "let's keep the weight down, keep the weight down," 'cause when you start building something like that inside of a big corporation, weight is always a problem. . . . My main input into the thing is that I sat down with Lutz and he said, "Let's build us a sport-car." He wanted to put the V-10 in it; I wanted to put the V-8 in it, and he won. The main contribution I made, besides the Cobra, you know, it being a modern Cobra, was working with Iacocca and meeting with him about every two weeks . . . we were moving into a recession, and to keep him OK and writing checks every two weeks [for the Viper program]. . . .

Author: Considering the environment in large automotive corporations, I think it's impressive the Viper ever got built.

Shelby: When people ask me about the Viper, when they say, "Oh, it has no roll-up windows," or when they're critical of the Viper, I say "If you knew what we had to go through, what Bob Lutz and I had to go through with Iacocca, just to get him to let us build it, then you [would] realize how badly we need to change the image of Chrysler, [and] you'd never say a critical word about it. . . ."

Author: What about the Viper would you change?

Shelby: Oh, I'd whack 500 pounds off of it, but I'm not going to say that in a critical sort of way, because I don't think that if the corporation sat down and started to build the car again, with all the givens that they have, all they have to put in the car, I don't think they could save over 300 pounds. . . .

Author: The Cobra had an approximate six-model-year production life. How long would you envision the Viper to be a viable, marketable piece?

Shelby: It's just according to how greedy they get! If they would build 250 cars a year, it would last for 15 years, but they aren't going to do that. They're going to saturate the market; the bean counters will take the place of common sense every time.

muscle-car history: Road Runner, Barracuda, 300, Super Bee, Charger, Challenger.

Beginning about 1973, big-inch performance went on hiatus at Chrysler—and everywhere else. Government safety and emissions regulations, unleaded fuel, the boondoggles that were called "gas crunches," and other factors all conspired to quiet the voice of factory performance machines. By the end of the decade, Chrysler had to contend with all of the above, plus crippling financial woes that nearly put it out of business. Then along came Lee Iacocca.

Iacocca was among the senior managers who contributed to Ford's success in the 1960s. After being fired by Henry Ford II, he took over the top spot at Chrysler in 1978 and was tagged as the man who could save the car maker from looming bankruptcy in the late 1970s. With tax concessions and a $1.5 billion loan guarantee from the U.S. government, a new management team, and some new products—including more fuel efficient cars, front-wheel-drive, and the modestly priced K-Car line—Chrysler turned itself around and stayed in business. It was also during

RENKERT 6-25-90

Shelby Cobra influences are clearly demonstrated in this mid-1990 rendering: wheel designs, paint scheme, and Daytona Cobra Coupe grille and headlight shapes. Team Viper also rendered this same concept in Ferrari red with wire wheels. Any wonder who their targets were? *DaimlerChrysler*

Iacocca's term as chairman that one of the Viper's key creators joined Chrysler: Robert A. Lutz.

Bob Lutz is a "car guy" of the first order, having been with General Motors, Opel, BMW, and Ford of Europe. He joined Chrysler in 1986 and in January 1991 was appointed president of Chrysler Corporation, which he held until 1998. You'll read much more about Mr. Lutz in later chapters.

Among the many things Bob Lutz, and more particularly Chrysler design chief Tom Gale, accomplished at Chrysler was to modernize and reinvigorate the notion of the "concept car" or dream machine as an instrument to let designers stretch their creative legs. They also helped a carmaker gauge potential customer interest and media reaction to a future design theme before committing to production. The Izod concept car of 1985 may even be seen as a link between the Cunninghams of the 1950s and the Vipers of the 1990s, since it was conceived as a front-engined, V-8 powered roadster. It never got beyond the mockup stage, however, and shows virtually no resemblance to the Viper in appearance.

Besides the Cunningham, the Viper's two most obvious progenitors would have to be the Corvette and Shelby's 427 cobra. The fiberglass Chevy two-seater had been making sales—and image—hay for GM for the better part of 40 years, a fact not lost on Chrysler management. While the 'Vette can be packaged for brute force or reasonable comfort, no such thing can be said of the Cobra: its performance ability and legend need no introduction here: Its brute force would prove to be a key to the design philosophy of the Viper.

When Bob Lutz assembled the Viper's Four-fathers, he chose a group of men— Carroll Shelby,

The final version of the RT/10 had taken shape in this late 1990 rendering. Very few details differ; this car has 5-spoke wheels, while the RT/10 was launched with 3-spokers, and the dual, external gas fillers didn't make the mix. *DaimlerChrysler*

Tom Gale, Francois Castaing, and himself—whom he felt had the skills and the mind-set required to deliver the Viper. The car had to be conceived, designed, engineered, built, and marketed in a unique fashion. For conceptual inspiration, he tapped on the shoulder of Carroll Shelby himself. What better way to ensure the Cobra vibe made it to Chrysler's no-nonsense roadster? The Shelby-Chrysler connection already existed, due to Carroll's role as a performance consultant to the company. The goal of Chrysler's design director Tom Gale was to create eye-searing looks and packaging. Bringing the Viper from the drawing board to the showroom required the drive of Chrysler's top engineering executive, Francois Castaing. Besides

being savvy businessmen, these individuals were all serious automobile enthusiasts. Shelby's racing success needs no further explanation, and Castaing was involved with Renault's Formula 1 engine program Gale and Lutz each have a stable of performance-oriented machinery.

According to both Shelby and Gale, Bob Lutz was really the "spark plug" behind the Viper concept: build a modern-day Cobra using 1990s technology and design, with emphasis on performance above all else, yet make it producible by a large corporation and deliverable for a well-below-six-figure price. No technology-laden gimmicks were envisioned, not even ABS—just an elementally designed roadster with a

The Viper show car on display at the Detroit auto show in 1989. Crowd—and media—reaction was overwhelming, confirming what Chrysler was no doubt hoping to hear: the demand and the market was there. Though this original concept vehicle shares no body panels with a production Viper, it's little short of amazing that so much of the look made the translation from show car to customer's garage; often by the time a dazzling concept car sees production, its impact is watered down considerably. *DaimlerChrysler*

The interior of the show concept car shares no detail with the production version, though a considerable amount of the shape and flavor did carry over. This car carries a five-speed transmission.

huge naturally aspirated engine putting the power down to the rear wheels, a pure connection between machine, driver, and the road. Driving for the pure pleasure of it. As a marketing tool, such a machine could do wonders for Chrysler's performance image, which was flagging in 1988.

Based on little more than a few conversations in early 1997, Gale's Highland Park Advance Design staff began sketching the shape that would become the Viper. Even the earliest renderings put all the right cues in the mix: an open roadster form, long hood, short deck, arching fenders, and wheelwells over huge rolling stock. Windows? Door handles? A top? Forget 'em. This was to be a serious performance roadster. The Cobra cues may have been there, but the Viper was not then, and is not now, just a restyled or updated version of the Cobra.

The heart and soul of any such automobile is the engine. While it would have been understandable

if the design team just spec'd out an updated version of the 426 Hemi, they ultimately found their power plant under the hood of an upcoming *pickup truck*. According to Francois Castaing, "One of the first major projects we got going was to put a new big V-10 on its way. Jokingly, we said 'That's the kind of engine that back in the sixties, [Giotto] Bizzarrini and [Alejandro] De Tomaso would have bought to create the great sports car of back then. You know, very powerful, torque, big gas American engine, put into a nice body.'"

Dodge's new 8.0-liter (488-ci) V-10 was to be an all-iron unit, too heavy for the roadster project, but if it could be cast in aluminum alloy and tuned for more horsepower . . . Shelby would later say that he initially favored the use of a large V-8, but according to commentary from the other three Fourfathers, it was "V-10 all the way."

When the major design elements were in place,

Roy H. Sjoberg,
Former Executive Engineer, Team Viper

"It's really the basic foundation: teamwork. The Viper was truly Chrysler's pilot for the cross-functional team. I believe the key to the Viper product is the Viper Team, not any one individual, other than our sponsor, Bob Lutz. It's been the team functioning together, coming to understand each other. Not always agreeing, and it's not always been happy times; there have been frustrating times. The evolution of that has brought what I believe is an excellent sports car, and an American sports car.

"There are five keys to good teamwork that Viper has.

"Number one is vision, and . . . Bob Lutz, Tom Gale, and Francois Castaing gave us that vision. Number two is product passion . . . everyone on the team has that product passion, and it can overcome a lot of roadblocks. Third is that it's a Team that's *hands-on*. Nobody steers the car from behind the desk. We are all hands-on, working on the product, understanding the product, from the craftsperson to the executive of the project, which is me. Fourth, which has been really key . . . is the empowerment and the acceptance of risk. In a large company, bureaucracy can overrun a small skunk works like we are. Management that empowers and accepts risk is paramount to success. Last is management by coaching. Those are the five keys to 'How did Chrysler do it?' and why the car is what it is."

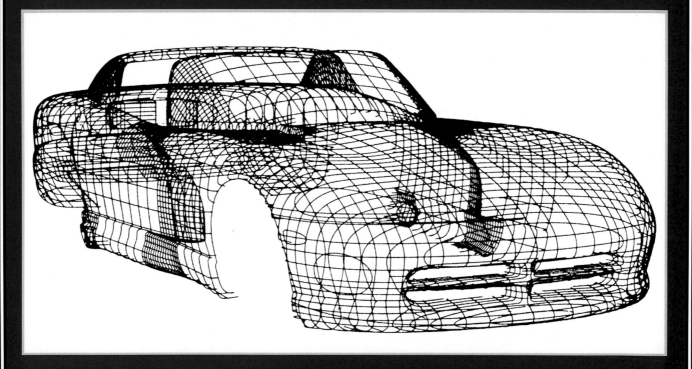

This CAD/CAM outline represents the shape of the original RT/10. *DaimlerChrysler*

Lutz authorized construction of show and test vehicles in May 1988, with an eye toward the 1989 auto-show circuit. When the brilliant-red Viper show prototype was debuted at the 1989 North American International Auto Show in Detroit, the Chrysler managers could not have anticipated the response. The car appeared in newspapers and in every enthusiast magazine. Mail, phone calls, and even deposit checks deluged the managers. It was immediately apparent that Chrysler had a potential hit on its hands, and had to at least study the factors involved in actually producing it.

Less than three months after the red roadster's Detroit appearance and a bit of discussion about hiring outside entities to build it, Chrysler announced the birth of Team Viper. This would be no everyday product, so there could be no ordinary way of

The interior of VM01 is business only, at best, as this vehicle's primary purpose was chassis and running-gear engineering.

Rear view of VM01 demonstrates lack of sports bar, so the high-mounted stoplight was affixed to the rear deck, as was the gas filler.

designing and building it. Castaing chose Roy H. Sjoberg, who had joined Chrysler in 1985 after more than 20 years with GM, to assemble the team that would transform the show concept to production reality.

Cross-functional teams are not new to the industry, but the Viper would be the first Chrysler project designed and produced in this format (see sidebar). Instead of passing the project from department to department, design, production, purchasing, and even suppliers would all be involved and empowered from the beginning. It was hoped this would result in less waste, less time spent, and a more unified vision of the final product. The concept has proven highly successful, and Chrysler and many other auto manufacturers have now developed products in this fashion.

Space limitations do not allow coverage of every aspect of the Viper's pre-production development, and more details about hardware and performance will come in Chapter 2. But suffice it to say that in May 1990, 15 months after that first auto show appearance, Chrysler announced that the Viper would be produced in limited quantity, with the first cars to be 1992 models. Viper was on the road to being on the road, so to speak.

And how did the car get its name? With the Cobra as its spiritual predecessor, a snake moniker was obvious. According to a quote from Bob Lutz in *Viper: Pure Performance by Dodge*, it came to him on an airplane trip. He toyed with the names Python and Sidewinder, but none had the right ring. "So 'Viper' seemed to be [the one]...it rolls off of the tongue easily."

So it does.

The interior of VM02 shows the wear and tear that comes from a hard life of engineering tests.

Left: The VM02 prototype. Much more of the Viper's final form is evident here than compared to the VM01.

303

TWO

On the Road
1992–1996

Clearly the Viper would be no ordinary vehicle, even among performance cars, so special development and construction methods, and a particular group of people, would be necessary to build it. Roy Sjoberg and other Chrysler managers interviewed hundreds of potential Team Viper members before selecting what they felt would be the most enthusiastic and qualified group. Its structure was much like that of a small entrepreneurial business, or perhaps a racing team, where problems are addressed immediately and solved quickly. An increased level of interaction would occur between management and the people who actually assembled the product.

An imposing sight in anyone's rear view mirror, the Viper crossbar grille theme has now been translated throughout Dodge's product line, even to the Ram trucks and vans; a successful effort on Dodge's part to unify the appearance of its product line-up and enjoy a bit of the performance-image rubbed off from the Viper. *DaimlerChrysler*

This cutaway of a 1992 Viper RT/10 shows the car's modern design and complexity. *David Kimball, courtesy DaimlerChrysler*

Each craftsperson would have a much higher level of responsibility for a car's assembly than in the past. They would often be involved in the build-up and installation of entire systems, rather than just attaching one component to each car as it rolled down a fast moving assembly line. Unlike many production-line environments, Team Viper would have direct communication with the designers and engineers, so process improvement could be effected quickly. Using a "custom-built" approach, groups of approximately five people would assemble one Viper at a time.

Chrysler selected its New Mack Avenue assembly plant in Detroit to be the home of Viper production. Beginning in 1990, the plant was remodeled into a modern facility, yet one that would not be focused on high-speed car production, but rather hand assembly and the craftsmanship required to build low-production, niche-market vehicles.

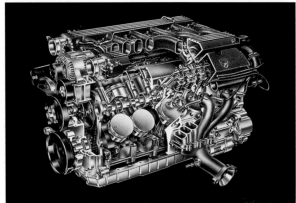

No multiple camshafts, four valves per cylinder, or other "exotica" for the Viper powerplant, just conventional V-8 technology brought up to modern standards . . . with two more cylinders, of course. *David Kimball, courtesy DaimlerChrysler*

Bob Lutz,
Former President, Chrysler Corporation

Bob Lutz is a rabid automotive enthusiast who just happens to be the president and chief operating officer of Chrysler. He spent time with BMW and Ford of Europe prior to joining the company in 1986. Among his other passions are aircraft, motorcycles, and fine cigars! Bob is a Viper owner and spoke candidly about what the car means to the company and customers.

Author: Chrysler has proven its ability to address enthusiast-market niches with Viper and concepts such as Prowler. How do you see Viper's success spilling over to other niches in the marketplace?

Lutz: Obviously, Viper has sent a strong signal [within] the corporation that it is a good thing to go with strong hunches, and if you have a clear vision on something that a small group of enthusiasts within the company would gladly and eagerly build for themselves, then you know that unless you're on a completely different planet, you know that if you do that vehicle, you're going to find a few thousand like-minded people per year [to purchase them]. That's really the philosophy that the Viper is all about, which is, dare to do something really terrific; not only despite the fact that nobody has tried it before, but because of the fact that nobody has tried it before.

Author: The GTS-R says a lot about Chrysler's enthusiasm for performance. In addition to producing the customer cars, do you envision a "works" GTS-R?

Lutz: None yet.... It's not currently planned, but I wouldn't categorically say we would never do it.

Author: How different will the Viper of say, 2001 or 2005, be from today's?

Lutz: It will be evolutionary. The car will get better and better. By the 2001 it will be highly likely that the shape will not be changed at all, but we'll unquestionably go for ever more performance enhancements. We want to keep it the ultimate affordable sports car.

Author: What would you change?

Lutz: I don't think I would change anything.... I suppose if we could wave the magic wand—and were not dealing with such onerous noise restrictions, which pretty much dictate what you do about exhaust sound—we are always enthralled with the way they sound when we use low-restriction mufflers ... you wish you had more sound and better sound, but it's hard to get there working around the ever-more-severe noise restrictions.

Bob Lutz with the Viper GTS Coupe he drove to pace the 1996 Indianapolis 500.

Like the Model T, the Viper was initially offered in only one color combination: red with gray/black interior. More colors would soon follow. *DaimlerChrysler*

The development of mainstream products often involves dozens, or even hundreds, of engineering mockups, prototypes, chassis "mules," and test vehicles. Team Viper, operating on both a strict budget and fairly short time constraints, did the job with only a few. Besides the original show vehicle, there were only a handful of engineering prototypes, plus a minimum of pre-production pilot vehicles.

The first prototype, chassis number VM01, was completed in December 1989 at a shop facility borrowed ("commandeered" would probably be a more accurate term) from Jeep. After the takeover, the shop became lovingly known as the Snake Pit. Painted white, the prototype carried hand laid-up fiberglass panels that were pinned to the frame; the rear "sport bar" was not yet present. Visually, VM01 resembled the ultimate production Viper only in terms of overall shape and proportion. For power, it

used a hopped-up Chrysler 360 V-8 and a German-made Getrag six-speed transmission.

The second prototype, chassis number VM02, was completed in April 1990. Painted red, this was the first Viper test mule to carry a V-10 engine, though it was an all-cast-iron unit, rated at 380 horsepower. A Borg-Warner six-speed transmission replaced the Getrag unit, and a good deal of the Viper's production development was done on this vehicle. It had side exhaust, a windshield, and an interior that were a step closer to what the production Viper would carry. Still hand-built of fiberglass, it was also tested heavily by the media, as it appeared in many magazine articles.

The original steel-bodied show car was also a steel-bodied prototype built outside of Team Viper's Snake Pit, by Metalcrafters in Southern California. Metalcrafters was a European-style *carrozzeria* that had developed numerous special projects and concept cars for Chrysler and other manufacturers.

The Viper's design and construction methods are a unique blend of time-tested, traditional elements, combined with modern componentry and materials. The philosophy was tightly focused on a brute of a roadster, but everyone at Chrysler knew they would be heavily criticized if they ended up with a throw-back car or anything that could be written off as merely a factory-built "kit car."

Team Viper engineers chose tubular steel as the base material for the chassis. The steel space frame included a center spine structure with tubular outriggers to support the body panels. This method of construction was selected over a unitized, monocoque chassis for two reasons: it had a shorter development time than the more complex stamped-steel, stressed-panel design, and monocoque designs rely on the roof structure to stiffen the overall chassis—but the Viper had no roof. The required structural rigidity was easier to obtain using a more conventional frame. In the end, the Viper's chassis stiffness was exceptional for an open car, at approximately 5,000 pounds per degree of twist.

The suspension was fully independent, with unequal-length upper and lower control arms at each corner. With the exception of the front upper control arms, these pieces were fabricated from tubular steel. Two stabilizing toe links were used with the rear lower control arms, and gas-charged Koni coil-over shock/spring units with front and rear anti-roll bars summarized the underpinnings. A car that was designed to hit well over 160 miles per hour needs powerful, fade resistant brakes, and the Viper had them: 13-inch ventilated discs with Brembo calipers at all four corners. ABS? Never was a part of the mix.

A unique three-spoke wheel design would carry Viper through its first four model years. Cast in aluminum alloy, the wheels measured 17x10 inches in front and 17x13 inches in the rear. Michelin developed special XGTZ uni-directional radials just for the Viper, size P275/40ZR17 and P335/35ZR17,

Although the Viper's V-10 shares its displacement and basic architecture with the 300-horsepower, iron-block engine used in Ram trucks, it's really an altogether different piece. Lamborghini, owned by Chrysler and competing as a Formula One engine supplier at the time, consulted with Team Viper on the V-10's design and metallurgy. *DaimlerChrysler*

respectively—the same steamroller-like sizes found on the $250,000 Lamborghini Diablo. The rolling stock was controlled via power-assisted rack-and-pinion steering designed to provide maximum driver feedback and road feel, yet the car was easy to maneuver at very low speeds.

As mentioned, Team Viper had to get the car to production quickly and on budget. This all but ruled out full steel body panels. Instead, a body and interior structure of several different resin transfer molding (RTM) composites was employed. Only the floorpan enclosure was formed of molded sheet steel. Besides the cost and time savings, the RTM panels yielded weight savings. "There's roughly about one-third weight reduction of sheet metal," according to Roy Sjoberg.

In the RTM process, glass fibers are placed inside a mold, the mold is closed, and resin is then injected to mix with the fiberglass, forming a finished panel. According to Russell Spencer, Viper technology development executive, "We...control the panel-forming process so precisely that when each piece comes out of the mold, it will require only 10 to 15 minutes of hand finishing before reaching a 'Class A' level appearance." This construction method also aided the ease of future appearance updates.

What could be a more important part of a performance sports car than its engine? Chrysler decided on a mix of pure big-block tradition and modern technology. Though there must have been some temptation to power the Viper with a modern-day rendition of the 426 Hemi or 440 Six Pack, in truth the car was virtually destined for the V-10

from the beginning. The earliest designs were built around it, and it is one of the features that gives the Viper its own identity, rather than simply copying the Cobra or Cunningham.

As mentioned earlier, the basis for the 8.0-liter "Copperhead" V-10 was the power plant being developed for the new 1994 Dodge trucks. But the truck engine's power characteristics would be all wrong for a sports car and the all-iron construction too heavy. "I guess you could say we took a straight-forward approach in developing this engine," recalls Jim Royer, Team Viper engine manager. "We didn't want to risk getting into exotic technology in so short a span . . . of development time."

Team Viper tapped the expertise of Lamborghini Engineering, which certainly had experience with high-performance street engines and would later

Original spec RT/10 interior spared the details, including air bags, and even air conditioning in the first 200 cars. *DaimlerChrysler*

Performance Comparison
Source: *Car and Driver, July 1995*

Model	0-60 (sec)	0-100 (sec)	1/4-Mile (ET@speed)	Top Speed (mph)	Price (as tested)
Viper RT/10	4.3	10.5	12.8 @ 109	168	$61,975
Ferrari F355	4.5	10.9	13.0 @ 110	179	$128,800
Acura NSX-T	5.2	13.0	13.8 @ 103	162	$86,642
Lotus Esprit S4S	4.4	10.9	13.0 @ 108	162	$87,904
Porsche 911 Turbo	3.7	9.4	12.3 @ 114	175	$106,465

Black-on-white gauges add a bit of a retro touch. Instrument visibility is excellent overall, as is performance from the heating and air conditioning system. Though it may seem a bit odd, one of the most pleasurable Viper driving modes is on a hot day with no top . . . and the A/C on full blast. *DaimlerChrysler*

develop V-10 engines for use in Formula One racing, although those engines were completely different units from those that would end in the Viper. It probably also helped that Lamborghini was a Chrysler-owned concern at the time.

The first goal was to reduce the engine's weight by at least 100 pounds. This was accomplished by casting both block and heads in aluminum. In keep-ing with the muscle car tradition, the V-10 would retain its overhead-valve configuration, with a single block-mounted camshaft. The block, with six crankshaft main bearings, employed an interesting cooling strategy. An external water manifold run-ning along the side of the block provided coolant to individual cylinders, which then flowed into the heads and back to the radiator. In the best race-car

All four colors available in 1995 take a bow; it's difficult to tell, but the second Viper from left is the dark green one, with a black car just to its right.

tradition, the alloy cylinders contained iron liners and forged alloy pistons; compression was a relatively low 9.0:1.

Though dual Carter AFB four-barrel carbs would not seem out of place atop the Viper engine, it's hard to beat modern hardware when it comes to intake systems and engine management. An aluminum ram-tuned manifold system with dual plenums works in concert with multipoint fuel injection to deliver a docile idle and the low emission numbers that the old Hemi could only dream of. Thin-wall, cast exhaust manifolds each expel the spent gases via a one-piece stainless-steel catalytic converter/muffler combination housed in what may be one of the Viper's most interesting performance statements: dual rocker-panel sidepipes, replete with labels warning "Hot Exhaust Pipe Below Door Opening" on the door sills. A fully electronic, distributorless ignition system works as part of a sophisticated engine-management computer system for maximum efficiency.

Every capacity of the Viper V-10 was "super-sized": At 488 cubic inches, it had the largest

mainstream production performance power plant in the world. Its official power rating (through 1995) was an even 400 horsepower at 4,600 rpm, with 450 ft-lb of torque at 3,600 rpm. (And the Viper's power output would climb steadily over the years.) Oil capacity? Not 5 quarts . . . how 'bout 11! Nearly 4 gallons of coolant! The 6,000-rpm redline may sound conservative when compared to high-winding Ferrari and Porsche power plants, but it's plenty high for an engine this large, and with so much torque on tap, more revs would serve little purpose. As a friend of mine, who is a big-block engine fanatic to an extreme, said of the Viper V-10: "Now that's a *motor*."

Backing the husky power plant was a Borg-Warn-er Model T-56 six-speed manual transmission, simply one of the best manual transmissions available. Its quick shifting action and capable synchromesh complemented the engine perfectly. The transmission case was also cast in aluminum and connected to the V-10 via a 12-inch single-dry-disc clutch. The 3.07:1 final drive incorporated a limited-slip differential.

The cockpit was quite traditional, focusing on driver input and performance: luxury seekers should look elsewhere. Comfortable, well-bolstered leather seats were separated by a fairly wide console. As the driver gripped the three-spoke, leather-wrapped steering wheel, the speedometer/odometer, tachometer, and warning-light cluster were in plain

The Viper logo pops up everywhere. Here it's embossed on the hood liner—in a *big* way. *David Newhardt*

view. Ancillary gauges (oil pressure, voltage, coolant temp, and fuel level) were in a binnacle at the top of the console, which also housed the Chrysler/Alpine sound system and heating, ventilation, and air conditioning (HVAC) controls. A security system was standard.

If anything spoke to the Viper's true purpose, yet seemed to draw criticism, it was the first roadster's weather protection system . . . or lack of same. Roll-up windows? None. Exterior handles? *Nada*. Hardtop? Zip. In their place, Chrysler designed a cloth top with zip-in side-curtain windows that did enclose the car but had to be considered vestigial at best. They're not particularly handsome and made the Viper feel a bit claustrophobic inside. When stowed, these pieces ate up a majority of the none-too-commodious trunk space. But hey, if you wanted to drive in a cocoon, you're looking at the wrong car.

The press, and the buying public, went bonkers for the Viper. Dodge had generated an overwhelming amount of PR, brand identity, and showroom traffic with the car. Every major automotive magazine had a Viper on its cover; some several times in the same year! Even today, a Viper on the road turns heads; one parked at the side of the road instantaneously draws a crowd.

It's also interesting that this most American of roadsters would be sold abroad. Export Vipers (branded as Chryslers, not Dodges) have metric gauges, revised lighting systems, tow hooks, wider license-plate brackets, an exhaust system that exits out the back of the car through the large dual pipes, and numerous other changes required by the varying regulations of European countries. One thing did not change: Vipers were as much of a hit in Paris or Frankfurt as they were in Los Angles or Cleveland, and they continue to be so.

It would be impossible to summarize the considerable media reaction, but a sampling of the commentary is worth note. *Car and Driver*'s Kevin Smith wrote, "Viper is one of the most exciting rides since Ben Hur discovered the chariot . . . It's intended to go fast, stop hard, hang onto corners, and give everyone in sight—driver, passenger, and bystanders—a thrill that will make their day." I particularly enjoyed *Sports Car International* editor Jay Lamm's thoughts: "The Viper is about having fun, playing games, and reliving a great childhood—maybe even somebody else's—and it's almost cheap enough for people to believe they could have one themselves someday, given a lot of hard work or a little good luck, it's an inclusionary sort of dream machine."

Ron Sessions of *Road & Track* reveled in his first Viper driving experience: "A driving route that included freeway cruising, delicious cut-and-thrust twisty bits, wicked mountain switchbacks, wide-open stretches of high desert, and some apex clipping hot laps at Willow Springs Raceway has afforded me a full measure of quality man-meets-machines bonding time. And with a tangled nest of split ends that passes for hair, I have the Viper-do to prove it." It would be hard to gather the impact of Viper's first four model years into one short paragraph, but *Motor Trend* came close when it said, "Nothing you can drive packs the personality, makes the statement, or snaps your neck like the Dodge Viper RT/10. Nothing at all."

Team Viper did not wait for model-year changeover to imbue the car with the latest improved hardware. Though collectors and historians, who track every little part change, may be driven a bit batty, the buyer gets the benefit of having the most improved version available at the time. Still, the 1992–1995 RT/10s stood quite markedly as the first-generation Viper. Beginning in 1996, the pace picked up considerably, with an updated RT/10, production of the GTS coupe, and the announcement of the GTS-R factory racer. The chronology is a bit interwoven; the initial GTS Coupe development began in 1992, the same year the RT/10 entered series production.

A Viper Coupe, called GTS

As surely as cars like the Cunningham and 427 Cobra were the spiritual predecessors of the Viper RT/10, progenitors of the same eras—such as the Ferrari 250 GTO, the Shelby Daytona Cobra Coupe, and of course coupe versions of the Chrysler-powered Cunningham racers—appear to have inspired the Viper GTS Coupe.

The first GTS Coupes were shown at the North American Auto Show in Detroit and the Greater Los Angeles Auto Show in January 1993. Though billed as "An Automotive Concept" at the time, the car was clearly designed with production intent, and crowd reaction was much the same as it had been to the original Viper show car just a few years before: Build it!

Shown in an arresting shade of metallic blue, sporting an exceptionally handsome chrome five-spoke alloy wheel design, and race-inspired white "Cunningham stripes" down the middle of the hood, top, and deck, the GTS looked for all the world to be an updated, streetable version of the aforementioned Daytona Cobra Coupe or Cunningham C4R-K. Only six Daytonas were built, all race cars, and they carried the Shelby team to the World Championship for Makes title in 1965.

I was with Peter Brock, Shelby American team member and designer of the Daytona Coupe, when the GTS was first unveiled at that 1993 LA auto show. Brock commented, "Tom Gale came to me with some of the original drawings of the GTS Coupe the previous August at the Pebble Beach Concours d'Elegance and asked my opinion of the new car. He wanted to make sure that I had no problem with the resemblance to the Daytona, especially the blue and white paint scheme. I was flattered that they would even consider asking my permission . . . Overall, it just pointed out what a class act Tom Gale was running with the Viper program."

Prototype GTS Coupes made the rounds among the automotive enthusiast magazines, and in 1994 Chrysler made the announcement that the Viper GTS Coupe would become a production reality for the middle of the 1996 model year (see Chapter 3). But making the GTS production-ready would take more work than just creating new fastback bodywork, so its development was done in concert with a substantially updated roadster.

Part of the tooling-up process for the Coupe would involve a new home for all Viper production. In April 1995, Chrysler announced that its New Mack Avenue assembly plant would be remodeled for the production of a new generation of truck engine. By midyear, a 345,000-square foot facility on Conner Avenue in Detroit had been acquired and established as the new Viper production facility for 1996 models and beyond.

RT/10 for 1996

The 1996 roadster is a unique piece of Viper history, a bridge between the 1992-to-1995 cars and the 1997-and-beyond models. This scenario is somewhat reminiscent of the 1968 Jaguar "Series 1 $1/2$" E-Type, which shared componentry with the multiyear run of cars before and after it. Because of the plant move and the completion of GTS Coupe tooling, Dodge only made plans to produce about 600 to 700 1996 RT/10s.

Immediately noticeable was the switch from rocker-mounted sidepipes to a rear-exit exhaust system, with two large chrome pipes just below the license plate. This was seen on the first GTS concept car, and was very similar to the system on European-delivery Vipers. The exhaust pipes still followed along

Dodge got racy in terms of color combinations for the 1996 "transition year" Vipers. They added contrasting stripes, and for the first time, offered wheels painted in colors other than silver. Note the new 5-spoke wheel design, shared with the GTS Coupe. Was the yellow and red "Mustard and Ketchup" paint scheme a jab at Ferrari, who used the same color combo on race cars in the 1960s? *DaimlerChrysler*

the sills, but now turned inboard forward of the rear wheels. The pipes then passed over the rear suspension and entered a tandem muffler. Some felt that the "five-per-side" exhaust sound of the original pipes left something to be desired; to this writer's ears, the new system was a vast improvement, even though they gave up a bit of the sidepipes' charm.

Three 1996-only color schemes were introduced; no more emerald green or yellow Vipers. The choices were black exterior with silver accents and a black interior, white with blue accents (more Shelby cues), or a combination quickly nicknamed "ketchup and mustard": red with bright yellow wheels and a yellow Viper logo just ahead of the front doors. Squint hard and this little yellow snake could just as easily have

been a little yellow prancing horse on the fender of a red Ferrari endurance racer. The white cars also had blue leather accenting the steering wheel, shifter, and handbrake lever; the red/yellow combo included red leather on the same interior pieces.

The five-spoke wheels that were such a hit on the GTS show cars became standard production pieces for 1996 RT/10s. They were silver on black cars, white for white models, and the aforementioned yellow on the red ones. All roadsters (and the GTS) got new rolling stock as well. Though the sizes remained the same, Michelin designed its new Pilot SX MXX3 tires for improved performance, wet or dry. They were also a bit lighter than the previous XGT Z tires.

If there's one thing the Viper needed, even for a

hard-core roadster, it was improved weather protection and a real top for when *al fresco* was not the preferred method of travel. Though several aftermarket companies offered hardtops almost immediately after introduction, Team Viper chose to offer a factory optional unit for 1996. It also fit the previous models. The previous zip-out plastic side curtains gave way to sliding glass units, which could be used with the hardtop or the soft top. Much better.

Many of the 1996-model improvements were found beneath the skin, such as a reviewed chassis that is even torsionally stiffer than the original. The new exhaust also reduced back pressure, so the power and torque ratings increased to 415 horsepower and 488 ft-lb, respectively. A power-steering cooler was added. Other driveline revisions included a new windage tray for the engine, a stronger differential that is more stiffly mounted to the chassis, and uprated drive shafts.

The big change to the suspension system involved cast-aluminum control arms and knuckles to replace the previous steel and cast-iron pieces. The change of material yielded a weight

reduction of approximately 60 pounds. The rear roll center was lowered slightly and the suspension geometry was revised to reduce changes during suspension travel; the rear caster angle was also revised. Pickup points for the suspension were relocated to increase the effective shock-absorber travel; higher-rate springs (18 percent rear, 12 percent front) and revised shock-absorber valving were also specified. A recalibrated power-brake booster provided easier pedal modulation, as some owners and media road testers complained that the brakes were a bit too touchy.

All of the above worked together to not only increase overall handling limits, but also to improve control as the Viper neared its handling limits. The car had often been criticized as being too quick to "break away" at the limit of adhesion. Having driven a 1996 with the new suspension hardware and calibration, I can say it felt more progressive, communicative, and controllable than did the earlier Vipers—an improvement to what was already a fine handling sports car.

1996 represented a year of important change for the Viper, as it melded design cues from both the 1992 to 1995 cars, and the 1997 to 2002 machines that were on the horizon. Here you'll notice that the sidepipes have given way to rear-exiting dual exhausts. A factory-engineered hardtop is offered for the first time, though the removable side curtains remained for one more year. *DaimlerChrysler*

THREE

The GTS Coupe, and an Updated RT/10 1997–2002

GTS Coupe

As noted, the Viper GTS Coupe was far more than just a quick, hardtopped re-skin of the RT/10 roadster. Though the look was certainly Viper, there were numerous detail changes to the exterior—so many that it's really a different car. Also, Chrysler's marketing position for the GTS Coupe was more luxury-oriented than with the roadster, in keeping with the *gran turismo* notion represented by the GT portion of its name.

This dashing RT/10 Viper is complete with the new color combinations that were added in 1996. While some traditionalists prefer the single color scheme, the race-inspired stripes became a distinct GST Coupe feature. *Wes Allison*

The front fascia was a different unit, as were the driving lights, and of course the entire rear treatment was designed for the coupe. A race-inspired aluminum quick-fill cap sprouted from the passenger-side sail panel, and the top itself had two gentle bulges to improve head (or helmet?) room. Louvers sprouted along the crest of the front fenderline, just above the wheels. The wheel design made it from prototype to production virtually unchanged and was offered in a polished-only finish. A particularly neat touch was the Viper-logo-shaped, center-mounted stoplight. All glass was tinted, and the rear window opened hatch-style.

Did we say glass? There's more of it on the GTS: a closed coupe body meant side windows, power-actuated no less. With this evolution came door handles; lock/unlock was handled electronically via the key fob. The GTS cockpit received Viper's first interior remodeling. The dash was of a different instrument and control layout, and featured dual air bags. Credit Chrysler's interior designs for an exceptionally handsome integration of these safety devices. Even the air bag–equipped steering wheel still retained a

proper sporty look. Revised leather seats included a pump-up lumbar-support feature, and a more powerful stereo system included a CD player.

GTSs also had big news under the hood: a virtually complete redesign of the Viper V-10, which was about 80 pounds lighter than the original, and was rated at 450 horsepower and 490 ft-lb of torque. Head and block castings were new, and eliminated the aforementioned coolant delivery tubes outside the engine. A lighter forged crankshaft rode in cross-bolted main bearings.

The NACA duct in the hood was part of a cold-air intake system, which comprised new manifolding, a redesigned air-filter package, and even a water separator to avoid water getting up the GTS's nose. All of the suspension changes made to the 1996 RT/10 carried over to the GTS. The only color combination offered at launch was metallic blue with white stripes.

Almost from its 1993 concept car premier, the Dodge Viper GTS Coupe has been stealing attention from its open-topped brother, the RT/10 roadster. With its Daytona Cobra Coupe shape, and

Prepare for launch: the new GTS Coupe entered the lineup in mid-1996, joining the revised-for-1997 RT/10 roadster. *DaimlerChrysler*

the possibility of it having more power than the original Viper, the wait for the GTS seemed agonizingly long. GTS production began in May 1996, with about 1,700 coupes built that year.

The RT/10 had not exactly been sitting still, either literally or figuratively. A refresher: the 1992 to 1995 cars may be considered first series Vipers, the ones with three spoke wheels, sidepipes, and the original 400 horsepower V-10. 1996 was a crossover model, as the Viper picked up the GTS's revised fully-independent suspension, frame, 5-spoke wheels, and rear exiting exhaust system. The engine was rated at 415 horsepower, the increase courtesy of the new pipes. 1996 was a limited-build year, as Viper production moved to a new facility as part of the tool-up for GTS.

For 1997, the RT/10 got the rest of the GTS's benefits package, and it made the car both faster and

An early 1992 photograph of a Viper GTS Coupe styling study. This clay mockup used standard RT/10 sidepipes, which were not used on GTS prototypes, and standard Viper wheels. The "double-bubble" roofline was already part of the mix. *DaimlerChrysler*

Above and opposite: It doesn't take a long look at the Peter Brock-designed Shelby Cobra Daytona Cobra Coupe to understand the inspiration for the GTS. Although the Viper was first developed as a street machine, the Cobra was first and foremost a racecar.
Opposite bottom: Carroll Shelby joins former Chrysler VP of Engineering Francois Castaing at the Los Angeles auto show introduction of the GTS Coupe concept. *Above: DaimlerChrysler, opposite top: Wes Allison*

easier to live with. The RT's new 8.0-liter aluminum V-10 shared much of the architecture and design with the original 400/415 horsepower version. One of Viper's original bragging rights was its place as a true roadster, complete with side curtains, no door handles, and a vestigial soft top design that was so difficult to use, you would swear Chrysler made it that way on purpose so it would never be installed. Rollup windows, wet weather protection, and security? That's all for sissies, right? Well, not anymore. A composite hardtop was now standard (as of the 1996 model), although it could be customer-deleted for a savings of $2,500. It was revised in 1997 for a bit more head

room, and worked in concert with the new sideglass windows that made the cabin quieter, and, for the first time, securable.

Windows? In a real roadster? Yes. And all but the most hard core agreed they were a great improvement. The RT/10 got the power windows and indeed the entire door panel setup from the GTS. Along with windows came (you guessed it) door handles. A neat electronic door-actuator button was integrated into a nicely styled, somewhat retro-looking door pull handle. There were no exterior door keylocks; that chore was left strictly to a remote actuator on the key fob.

Several other GTS interior accouterments showed up in the roadster. For the safety minded, the redesigned dash had dual air bags. Credit Chrysler's interior stylists for a commendable job of integrating the air bag into the steering wheel boss; it's not as slick as the leather covered, three-spoke racing wheel found in the previous roadster, but it's Viper-specific, and as handsome as could be expected.

In the best racing tradition, the new pedal assembly was adjustable; a knob mounted beneath the steering column allowed four inches of adjustment. This, combined with the Viper's tilt wheel and exceptionally comfortable leather sport seats (which themselves had another 5.2 inches of travel), meant just about anyone could get comfortable. Air conditioning came full circle: it was not offered on the earliest cars, then became standard, and was now also offered as a delete option (a savings of $1000).

Those who feared the added creature comforts and revisions to the Viper's suspension would tame its earlier reputation as a somewhat hair-trigger oversteer needn't have worried. The driving experience still delivered undiluted, industrial strength performance.

The GTS-spec motor not only made more beans than the previous generation V-10, but it was a bit smoother in the process. Power could be found anywhere on the tach, and the torque curve was as flat as the deck of an aircraft carrier. Dumping the sidepipes

Chrysler made plans for a first-year run of approximately 1,700 GTS Coupes. More than 2/3 of that total were snapped up by existing RT/10 owners. MSRP for the 1996 GTS Coupe was $66,700, a little less than $10,000 more than a roadster—plus gas-guzzler and luxury taxes. Don't let the power windows and CD player fool you into believing the Viper had gone soft. The GTS featured a substantially revised engine rated at 450 horsepower, only about 75 fewer ponies than the base engine in the GTS-R racer. *DaimlerChrysler*

Striking from any angle, the GTS melds the look of the RT/10 and the early 1960s Cobra Daytona Coupe perfectly NACA hood scoop is functional, and was part of 450-horse V-10's revised intake system. *Bill Delaney, courtesy DaimlerChrysler*

and routing the exhaust out the back was the best thing Chrysler's muffler chefs ever did, and the delicious exhaust note spat out just the right amount of pops and burbles when you backed off the gas. There were others about as fast—the Porsche 911 Turbo comes to mind—but nothing else accelerated with the resolute rightness of the Viper V-10's naturally aspirated cubic inches.

True to form, no automatic transmission was available, with the Borg-Warner T-56 6-speed remaining the only option. Viper's handling improved over the generations, and with the 1997 and later cars, struck a smart balance between rewarding the talented pilot, yet keeping the casual driver from getting in too much trouble. As noted, the earlier cars offered very sharp turn in, and could be provoked into

All Vipers are special, but some, even more so

There have been several "special edition" Vipers offered along the way, but two of the most interesting were based on the GTS Coupe.

The first was the GT2 Championship Edition Viper. It was minted as a 1998 model to commemorate winning the 1997 FIA GT2 Driver's and Manufacturer's Championships. Its color scheme of white with blue stripes acknowledged the look of those factory GTS-R racers and provided a celebratory dichotomy to that of the Shelby Daytona Cobra Coupes, which raced in blue-with-white-striped livery. Though the Championship Edition Viper wore "GTS-R" badges, it is most commonly referred to as the GT2.

This was no mere "paint and stripes" package, however. A revised intake system was good for an extra 10 horsepower, for a total of 460, making it the most powerful Viper sold up to that time. It was also the first Viper to wear factory 18-inch rolling stock, in the form of stunning one-piece BBS alloys and Michelin SX-MXX3 tires. The look was really completed with the addition of a tall rear wing, again resembling that of the real GTS racer, but trimmed "flat" for zero lift or downforce.

The standard black interior was accented with blue trim, including 5-point safety harnesses identical to those of the race car. The obligatory plaque listed the car's VIN and recognized it as one of the limited edition GT2s. MSRP was $85,200, and with only 100 built, they were sold out immediately. Today, the GT2 remains one of the most collectible Vipers ever built, and this author's personal favorite.

Another special, though less limited, edition, is the ACR, for American Club Racer. This lighter-weight, somewhat de-contented Viper is for those who really intend to do some club-level racing—or at least want to give that impression. Introduced in 1999, it picked up some of the hardware first used on the GT2 Championship Edition Coupe; particu-larly its 18-inch BBS wheels, freer-breathing intake system with

This 1999 model was easily distinguishable from a standard GTS, as were all ACRs, by its BBS "lacey spoke" wheels, and the use of plastic vents instead of fog lights in the front fascia. *DaimlerChrysler*

K&N air filter, and 5-point restraint harnesses. Koni racing shocks and Meritor springs replace the stock units. These changes, when combined with the more aggressive rolling stock, gave the ACR a more-firmly controlled suspension, with only a slight penalty in ride quality.

There wasn't a lot of fat that Dodge could trim from the car without major reprogramming of its engine management or electrical systems, but the front fog lights were deleted in favor of vents. The standard air conditioning and audio system bit the dust too, though they remained optional. For the 2000 model year, the ACR was equipped with high performance oil pan, Dynamic Suspensions adjustable shock absorbers, and wore revised ACR badging.

Like the GT2, the ACR boasted a 460-horsepower rating, and was offered from 1999 through the 2001 model years.

trailing throttle oversteer with little difficulty. The retuned suspension took a bit of that edge off but remained top drawer all the way, and the stiffer frame and lighter suspension components made for greater handling consistency. Handling limits were way up there and a good bit of the credit goes to Michelin's Pilot SX MXX3 Z-rated tires, which were specially configured for Viper duty.

Though 1997's $66,900 MSRP was not cheap for any car under any circumstances, Viper still represented a performance bargain. Purchasing the aforementioned Porsche Turbo would have flattened your wallet by nearly twice as much, and while the Acura NSX delivered higher tech and a more polished handling performance, it too was more expensive and just didn't haul the mail like the big bad Dodge. If anything, America's original, the Corvette, gave the Viper its best run for the money.

The Viper's cabin received substantial revisions with the advent of the GTS Coupe, and they were also engineered into the much-revised 1997 RT/10. The main differences were driver and passenger side air bags and higher quality materials, with power side windows replacing the previous removable side curtains. *Wes Allison*

The resemblance is astonishing, by design: Viper GT2 Championship Edition on track with the real thing, a factory GTS-R racer. Note use of similar rear wing. *DaimlerChrysler*

The new-for-1997 Viper looked little different from the 1996, though the addition of solenoid-actuated door handles was one detail change. *Wes Allison*

Though the C5 didn't quite have the Viper's accelerating ability, it's certainly no slouch, and it had a nicer interior, exceptional handling, and maintained a significant price advantage.

Chrysler continued to evolve the Viper throughout that generation's six-year production life. Naturally, colors, trim, and wheel finishes were freshened just about every year. Numerous "special editions" were offered too (see sidebar). The air bag systems were updated for 1998, and a passenger side on/off switch was added. In 1999 came new 18-inch wheels across the board, and an optional Connolly leather-trimmed interior. Big news for Viper owners with families came along in 2000 in the form of child seat tethers. Team Viper finally acknowledged that a well-developed and properly calibrated anti-lock braking system would be a benefit to most drivers and would do nothing to dilute the Viper's no-holds-barred persona, so ABS was made standard beginning with the 2001 model year.

Looking back, it's clear that the 1997 to 2002 model years were the Viper's most successful. Two distinct models and numerous special editions were offered, and the car continued to evolve and improve while it also remained a strong seller, even into its 10th production year. Dodge released the 2002 Viper GTS Final Edition on July 1, 2002, as the team and assembly plant began preparations to produce the new Viper SRT-10 that would bow for 2003.

Right: Who would argue with 50 more horsepower? Nobody, and that's what the GTS and 1997-and-later RT/10s got. Although the engine's architecture remained the same, there were many detail improvements, especially in terms of block rigidity and cooling. It was essentially a new engine.

The end of the road, or at least the end of another chapter in the Viper's book of life. DaimlerChrysler workers marked the last 2002 special Dodge Viper GTS "Final Edition" with a brief ceremony as the vehicle was driven from the assembly line at the Conner Avenue Assembly Plant in July of that year. The Coupe, which represented the last of 360 Viper GTS models built on the 2002 Viper platform, carries the Vehicle Identification Number 102736. *Joe Wilssens, courtesy DaimlerChrysler*

FOUR

Record Breaking: Vipers on Track

I t's the oldest saw in the business: "Win on Sunday, Sell on Monday." One look at the GTS tells you it was meant to be a race car. As discussed, it was clearly cast in the mold of the Cunninghams and Cobra Daytona Coupes of the past, so Chrysler elected to take the obvious step: make a race version. The GTS-R is a limited-production, factory-developed racing Viper that was offered for sale to private teams. Chrysler also fielded its own factory-backed team—to great success as we'll see.

The ultimate triumph: the Beretta/Dupuy/Wendlinger Team ORECA Viper GTS-R on its way to a stunning overall victory in the 2000 Rolex 24 Hours of Daytona, just one of its many important sports car wins and championships. *DaimlerChrysler*

331

The GTS-R was designed to compete in international GT-class competition, homologated for ACO, IMSA/ALMS, and FIA events. According to Bob Lutz, "This is a no-holds-barred competition car care for the world's great events such as the 24 Hours of Daytona and the 24 Hours of Le Mans. It is . . . perhaps the only [production-derived racing car] developed, produced, and sold directly from an American manufacturer through its own organization. Honchoing the development of the GTS-R was Team Viper member (and SCCA national driving champ) Neil Hanneman, and the development partner/supplier Reynard Racing Cars, a highly successful constructor for several racing series such as IndyCar and F3. The GTS-R was introduced to the media in August 1995 at the Pebble Beach Lodge in Monterey, California.

The basic GTS Coupe's steel space frame was retained and strengthened via CAD design enhancements and the integration of a roll-cage structure. Exterior coachwork maintained most of the stock car's dimensions, but the GTS-R body is rendered in carbon fiber. One must wonder how many GTS-R-styled rear wings will end up on street Vipers. The carbon-fiber dash panel carried standard instrumentation, and an otherwise stripped interior also contained an on-board fire-extinguisher system.

For power, special dry-sump versions of the V-10 were constructed in three different states of tune with

The No. 97 Sifton/Robinson/Seibert GTS-R at the GTS-R's second competition outing at the Sebring 12 Hours of Endurance Race in March 1996. *G. Hewitt, DaimlerChrysler*

Wind tunnel testing of the aerodynamics of the GTS-R. A story in *AutoWeek* magazine discussed some of the GTS-R's early teething problems, but this was to be expected with any new racing program. Further development to the GTS-R's shape and cooling made the car more stable and reliable at speed, necessary for both the long straights at Le Mans, and the high banks of Daytona. *DaimlerChrysler*

factory offered ratings of 525, 650, and 700 horsepower; the base version was engineered in-house by Team Viper; the latter two were developed in cooperation with Caldwell Development Inc. A racing version of the production Borg-Warner T-56 six-speed manual helped deliver power through an alloy-cased Dana rear end. A combination of stock and specially built pieces composed the suspension, and Michelin racing slicks, BBS modular wheels, and Brembo disc brakes rounded out the rolling stock. All yours for a mere $200,000. Unfortunately, we don't have the space to delve into the various privateer teams that race GTS-Rs and so have chosen to stick primarily with the factory-sponsored efforts.

The GTS-R got its first taste of competition in the 1996 Rolex 24 Hours of Daytona. Running in the GT-1 class, the Canaska/Southwind Racing Vipers demonstrated class-leading speed in practice qualifying 17th and 30th overall. The No. 97 Sifton/Robinson/Seibert entry was involved in an accident on lap 157 and retired. The Cobb/Dismore/Hendricks No. 98 GTS-R battled with transmission and braking problems throughout the race, but it was running at the end and finished 29th overall. Not exactly a win, but an honest showing for an all-new car, and the lessons learned began to show the GTS-R's development program where they needed to go. Four Vipers were entered at Le Mans in

Here is an important group of men in the Viper's history. From left: Bud Liebler, former Chrysler vice president of marketing and communications; Marty Levine, former Dodge Division general manager; Roy Sjoberg, former executive engineer of Team Viper; Tony George, president, Indianapolis Motor Speedway; Neil Hanneman, project manager, Viper GTS-R; Tom Gale and Francois Castaing, two of the Vipers Fourfathers. This photo was taken at the Viper GTS-R's introduction in August 1995.

1996, two by Canaska and two by the French Team ORECA. That result was also credible, if not all-conquering: 8th, 12th, and 14th in class, plus a DNF. That might be considered what stick-and-ball teams dub "a building year."

Chrysler got more serious with its own factory-backed GTS-R racing program in 1997 but needed to engage a world class partner to compete at the highest levels. In spite of the fact that the genesis of the GTS-R and its early development were very much Chrysler factory programs, it still took a great team

to "teach a car how to race." Team Penske was one of the best examples of an organization that built team infrastructure, attracted top quality drivers, executed a proper testing program, and just "knew the ropes" come race day. Reinhold Joest, whose teams and drivers pulled off Audi's back-to-back-to-back wins at the Le Mans, was another. In NASCAR terms, think Robert Yates Racing, DEI, or Roush Enterprises.

Chrysler found its "Penske" in the form of Hughes de Chaunac and his Team ORECA, which had campaigned two Vipers at Le Mans in 1996. De Chaunac

The Viper GTS-R interior is all business. The dash resembles the shape of the new GTS Coupe unit, but the GTS-R's dash is rendered in carbon fiber. The red handles to the lower right are for the on-board fire-extinguisher system. *DaimlerChrysler*

had already achieved considerable success since winning Team ORECA's first European F2 championship in 1975 and masterminding Mazda's overall Le Mans victory in 1991, to name a few highlights. Team ORECA was experienced in international sports car racing, capable, and available. De Chaunac and company would field Chrysler's expanded factory effort in international sports car racing, running for the FIA GT Championship series, at Le Mans, and, ultimately, in the American Le Mans and Grand Am

This GTS-R engine rendering shows the dry sump and the long tube exhaust headers; it was based on the new GTS Coupe V-10, and was rated at 525 horsepower in base form. As raced during the 2000 season, its output, after considerable development, was more like 750. *DaimlerChrysler*

series. The results rewrote the sports car racing record books.

Though the Team ORECA Vipers did not capture that much sought-after Le Mans class victory in 1997, finishing 5th and 6th in the GT2 class, they did win the FIA GT2 championship, with Justin Bell taking the driver's title. This important European series championship provided the inspiration for the 1998 GT2 Championship Edition Viper.

The year 1998 proved to be the first of three record-breaking, watershed years for the GTS-R. Not only did Team ORECA repeat as the FIA GT2 champions, they bagged that all-important 1-2 class victory at Le Mans. Justin Bell, Luca Drudi, and David Donohue led the effort, with Oliver Beretta, Tommy Archer, and Pedro Lamy completing the 1-2 finish. Two privateer Vipers finished 5th and 7th in class, demonstrating without doubt that the Viper could withstand 24 hours of punishment and had matured into a fast and reliable race car.

This success continued virtually unabated during the 1999 season, in spite of the team adding another dimension to its competition efforts. Don Panoz had taken over the World Sports Car series and rebuilt it around the same rules employed by the ACO at Le Mans. The sports car racing formula that was so

Success at last: the Justin Bell/Donohue/Drudi GTS-R in the pits at Le Mans, 1998, on the way to its first class victory at the all-important French Classic.

The First Viper Road Racer

Strange as it may seem, there was Viper racing before the creation of the GTS-R. An early 1990s reformulation of various GT classes by the ACO opened the door for entries like the Viper. Oddly enough, it was a privateer French team that was first to build one for Le Mans in 1994. LMGT-1 class rules provide for few modifications, and the Rent-A-Car race team's two Vipers were amazingly stock. The cars ran with hardtops and performed well considering the Viper's lack of racing development at the time and the team's limited budget. Intermittent transmission overheating and other niggling problems prevented a class win, but the cars finished 12th and 18th overall. The red No. 40 car's 12th place run, courtesy of Bertrand Balas, Justin Bell, and former F1 ace Rene Arnoux, was also good enough for a 3rd place in class.

Photo finish: Olivier Beretta, Karl Wendlinger, and Dominique Dupuy cross the line to take the class win at Le Mans, 1999, with the Archer/Bell/Duez GTS-R coming home a close second.

successful in Europe had been brought to America; the result was the American Le Mans Series (ALMS). Since the Viper was already a proven winner and America was, of course, its home market, Chrysler elected to not only continue participating in the FIA GT series and at Le Mans, but to add ALMS as well.

The Team ORECA Vipers achieved every goal put in front of them in 1999. They took the FIA GT championship for a third consecutive year and repeated their 1998 Le Mans performance with another impressive 1-2 finish in the renamed GTS category. This time it was Olivier Beretta, Karl Wendlinger, and Dominique Dupuy crossing the line first, with the Archer/Bell/Duez GTS-R coming home second. Even though it entered the 1999 ALMS season late (running only six races) Beretta claimed the GTS class driver's title and ORECA the team

title, and Viper only narrowly missed the constructor's crown for Dodge.

Team ORECA had become such an integral part of the GTS-R's development that Chrysler's Motorsport division appointed Hughes de Chaunac as the car's exclusive constructor and distributor at the end of 1998. This meant that customers could virtually buy the same car as the factory entered.

As if the 1999 season hadn't proven the GTS-R and Team ORECA's worth, the Chrysler/de Chaunac juggernaut added yet another challenge for 2000: the Rolex 24 Hours of Daytona. The Grand Am series had been formed as a competitor to the ALMS, and its crown jewel was the 24-hour enduro in Florida. Further challenge was on the horizon in the form of an increasingly competitive, factory-backed Chevrolet Corvette C5-R effort. Nonetheless, Chrysler, the

Call it a threepeat, hat trick, whatever you like. The 1999 class winners, Olivier Beretta, Karl Wendlinger, and Dominique Dupuy, backed up Team ORECA's previous year's win and made it three in a row for the GTS-R in the GT2/GTS category at Le Mans.

team, the renamed Viper GTS-R/T, and a proven roster of drivers took it all on.

It's rare that a production-based sports car like the Viper stands much of a chance against purpose-built prototypes for an overall victory, especially in a longer event, where the faster, higher-tech machines' lead generally continues to increase as the hours click away. Yet, 24 hours is a long time, and as the saying goes, "anything can happen in racing." Well, anything and everything did at the Rolex 24 Hours on February 5 and 6, 2000. Many of the new Grand Am spec prototypes were yet unproven. Conversely, the GTS-R had benefited from years of development, and tens of thousands of miles of track time and testing.

The GTS-R's freight train–like reliability plus solid driving by Olivier Beretta, Karl Wendlinger, and

Dominique Dupuy—and an inordinate amount of teething problems and accidents suffered by many of the faster prototype class machines—allowed the No. 91 Viper GTS-R to claim a historic overall victory (plus, obviously, the GTO class win) at Daytona. The tables were so turned in Florida that year that the highest finishing prototype came home fourth. The Fellows/Bell/Kneifel Corvette C5-R finished a credible second (losing to Wendlinger in the Viper by just 30 seconds), with Team ORECA's Donohue/Ni Amorim/Belloc/Archer GTS-R finishing third overall. Amazing, and without doubt, the GTS-R's finest hour in competition to date.

Wendlinger, Beretta, and Dupuy kicked off the 2000 ALMS in fine style, notching the Viper's first win at the 12 Hours of Sebring. With the Sebring and

Daytona wins under its belt, the next goal for the now-red Vipers was to make history again with a "threepeat" at Le Mans—and so they did. The same driver threesome finished first in the GTS class at Le Mans, with the Donohue/Ni Amorim/Beltoise GTS-R/T coming in second this time.

Team ORECA went on to win the ALMS championship for 2000, a season that saw the GTS-R/T take sports car racing's "Triple Crown" in the form of class wins at Le Mans, Sebring, and Daytona, plus the overall win at the latter. During its four year, factory-backed stay in international sports car racing, Team ORECA won 44 races in FIA GT, ALMS, ACO, and Grand Am competition, not to mention numerous driver, team, and constructor championships, plus class or overall victories in the world's most significant sports car races. Team patron Hughes de Chaunac summarized his feelings and the team's accomplishments by saying "We have had a lot of success with this car. Now, it will go into the history book as one of the most successful racing cars of its era, and I am quite honored to have been a part of this history."

Thumbs up guys, for a production-based sports car taking an overall win at Daytona in 2000. From left, drivers Karl Wendlinger and Olivier Beretta, Chrysler competition manager Lou Patane, Team ORECA patron Hughes de Chaunac, and third teammate Dominique Dupuy. *DaimlerChrysler*

FIVE

Vipers for a New Millenium: The 2003 SRT-10 and Beyond

Dodge likes to talk about the SRT-10's three 500s— actually, the new Viper's specs are 500 horsepower, 525 ft-lb of torque, and 505 cubic inches. But we're not going to get persnickety with Dodge. These are impressive numbers, any way you make them.

As beloved as the original Viper was—it evolved continuously, but remained architecturally un-changed for the decade it was on the market—it was time for a new one. Enough had been learned about the car's shortcomings, and the wish list was getting long. After the revised 1997 RT-10 and GTS were launched, Chrysler management and Team Viper got to thinking about where they could take the car from there.

There's no mistaking the SRT-10 for anything but a Viper, although the evolution between the two is anything but subtle. All of the proportions have changed, as has the detailing, intake and exhaust vent shapes, and more. Dual HID headlights are seriously bright, and the hood scoop delivers intake air directly into the dual air cleaner system. The author is at the wheel. *Wes Allison*

They spent a good six months conceptualizing, talking, and arguing about what the car ought, and ought *not*, to be. According to comments from several team members and executives, the main challenges were how to update the look, yet have the car still be pure Viper, and how to make the car more sophisticated (and comfortable) without diluting its visceral, raw appeal.

One goal everyone was clear and united on was another horsepower increase. Tom Gale, original Viper Fourfather and Chrysler design director, was quoted in Daniel F. Carney's *Dodge Viper* as saying "We are going to keep our lace in the queue; if that means 500 horsepower and 500 foot-pounds of torque,

then that's what it will be. If it means that we've got to do things that will give it the capability of being the benchmark in terms of slalom, if it means we've got to keep it at the top of the heap in braking, if it means all those things, then that's what we'll do."

"Five hundred has always been a magic number," continued John Fernandez, executive engineer. He was ultimately in charge of the Viper project, and director of DaimlerChrysler's newly created Performance Vehicles Operations (PVO). "It's been a performance target for Viper and the Specialty Vehicles Engineering Team for years." Team Viper member Brian Cojocari was manager of the new program, which was given the internal development

Designer Osamu Shikado's rendering of the GTS-R concept of 2000 (inspired by, but not to be confused with, the race car of the same name) embodies the design cues that would show up on the SRT-10 production roadster a few years later. Is this a long-lead look at a future GTS? We say yes. *DaimlerChrysler*

TV to SVE to PVO

In the early 1990s, Ford elected to gather its various high performance skunkworks entities together under one banner, in order to develop performance-oriented versions of mainstream production models. The group was named the Special Vehicle Team, or SVT. Nobody knows why it took both GM and Chrysler a decade to do the same, but it finally happened: GM now has the General Motors Performance Division (GMPD) and Chrysler has its Performance Vehicle Operations, or PVO. Luckily enough, PVO already had a poster child in house—the Viper, of course—and annexed what was Team Viper (which by then fell under the banner of Special Vehicle Engineering) into the group.

As the SRT-10 was being developed, original Team Viper leader Roy Sjoberg retired and was replaced by John Fernandez. Fernandez, a performance and motorsports enthusiast to the core, was also called upon to lead the new organization; the formalization of PVO was announced to the public in January of 2002.

Fernandez' tenure as PVO boss was short, as he was soon tapped to concentrate fully on the Chrysler Group's motorsports activities, including the NASCAR effort, parts programs, SCCA, and the like. "The same engineers that recently dominated the worldwide GT scene with the Viper GTS-R now have their sights set on the Winston Cup. My job is to get them the resources they need to be successful, and I'm going to do that," Fernandez explained. But he was around long enough to make an indelible mark on PVO, as he oversaw the development of the Viper Competition Coupe.

Dan Knott took over PVO's reigns in the fall of 2002 and remains the group's director as of this writing. It's important to understand the scope of PVO. Unlike the original Team Viper, which was a group of individuals highly focused on a single project, PVO will develop performance variants for not only Dodge, but Chrysler and Jeep branded vehicles. PVO also has responsibility for Mopar Performance Parts, but most importantly for readers of this book, is charged with continuing to develop the Viper SRT-10.

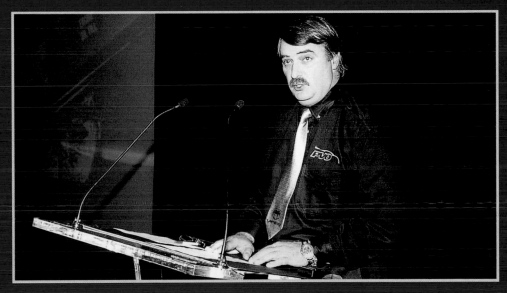

PVO Motorsport Director and all around performance guru, John Fernandez. *DaimlerChrysler*

GTS-R concept's interior was obviously the springboard for what the production SRT-10s cabin would look like. Dodge did a good job of "productionizing" the dream machine's look, retaining the instrument panel layout and similar splashes of aluminum trim. *DaimlerChrysler*

code name VGX.

Enthusiasts got a preview of the 2003 Viper SRT-10 as the Viper GTS-R concept car, not to be confused with the racing Viper of the same name, at the 2000 International Auto Show in Detroit. This was the same venue at which the original Viper concept car had created a production life and legend for itself a little more than a decade earlier. It didn't take a lot of imagination to see that this "concept" was being developed as a show toy to introduce the new production Viper to the public and the media.

There were differences, of course. The GTS-R was presented as a coupe, although the SRT-10 would debut only as a roadster. The concept's interior also foretold the SRT-10's cabin, but most of the expensive materials wouldn't make the mix, although the instrument panel design and some of the aluminum trim ultimately did.

The chassis retained its predecessor's basic architecture, but it had been stretched and updated. The all-new framework on the wish list didn't make the program due to cost restraints, but the SRT-10 was still approximately 35 percent torsionally stiffer and about 40 pounds lighter than before. The wheelbase

This cutaway drawing shows the SRT-10 in final production form, and from the inside out. Sport roof bar gave way to a clean rear deck; the Viper's greater rear track and longer wheelbase are easily noticeable from this angle. *David Kimball, courtesy DaimlerChrysler*

Another important element that separates the SRT-10 from the RT/10 is the use of a conventional convertible top. It does away with the need for a removable hardtop or soft top, and in the case of the early cars, side curtains. Some like the look better, while others prefer the previous design. *Wes Allison*

increased by 2.6 inches, resulting in a more commodious cabin. And the SRT-10 wore bigger tires than ever: 275/35ZR18s on 18x10-inch wheels up front, with steamroller-inspired 345/30ZR19s wrapped around 19x13-inch alloys out back.

Sidepipes returned, an original Viper design cue that had gone away in 1996. Brembo four-wheel disc brakes with ABS were standard and represented an engineering advance on the ABS-equipped system

introduced in 2001. Overall vehicle weight went down by about 80 pounds, though it's still kind of porky by sports-car-purist standards; all the safety, emissions, and convenience stuff demanded by today's government and marketplace conditions add tonnage.

There was a lot of talk among current Viper owners and in the media about the Viper's new design and the work of talented staff designer Osamu

Continued on page 68

2003 Viper Comp Coupe

"Ambitious, yet extremely logical," says John Fernandez, director of Dodge Motorsports operations.

Taking the new Dodge Viper roadster and making a full race coupe out of it was ambitious. While there are plenty of high-performance parts in the SRT-10 street car, there was still loads of work to do to make the Viper a turnkey racer. Logical, Fernandez says, because there's a ready market. After all, dozens of Viper racers were taking a new $80,000 car and throwing away $30,000 worth of safety and comfort equipment—air bags, climate control, seats, stereo, you name it—and spending thousands more to make their cars raceable.

So Fernandez and crew took the platform and basic power-train of the Viper roadster and built their own racer.

We're talking an FIA-legal rollcage, onboard telemetry, a sectioned composite body of Kevlar, carbon fiber, and fiberglass, with front splitters and a rear wing developed in a wind tunnel. And did we mention pneumatic jacks, a fire-suppression system, a Racetech seat with a six-point harness, three-piece BBS wheels with Hoosier racing slicks, Brembo brakes with carbon-fiber cooling ducts, Moton adjustable coil-over dampers, a 25-gallon fuel cell, and electronically adjustable brake bias? For just $100,000 or so.

Two Viper Competition Coupes, flying the PVO banner, at the car's media test program in January 2003. The Coupe won its first Speed Challenge race before the end of that year, and must represent the ultimate club racer. *DaimlerChrysler*

Given the level of sophistication, it's pointed out to Fernandez there's no way he could be making money at that price. He doesn't disagree. What, sell at a loss, and make it up in volume?

No, make it up in parts. Though the Viper Competition Coupe should be exceptionally durable, plans are that each will lead a long and happy life and, as such, will require periodic maintenance, body-panel replacement, that sort of thing. It's something the razor-blade companies learned decades ago: we'll give you a free razor—if you keep buying our blades.

Even so, only the first 32 lucky customers got the $100,000 price. The next 30 or so cars cost $118,000, and the eventual price will settle in at about $125,000. Viper Club of America members, many of whom are avid racers, got first shot. Sales are directly from Dodge—local dealers aren't involved. How hard would it be to make that thing street legal? Unfortunately, the answer is, "very hard." Example: what appears to be headlights are decals. This is a racetrack-only car, folks.

That's the bad news. The good news: it isn't that much faster than the production Viper roadster, which says a lot for the streeter. Of all the work Fernandez and his Performance Vehicle Operations guys did on the Competition Coupe, the one area left comparatively alone is the powertrain. The stock SRT-10 Viper has a 505-cubic-inch V-10, with 500 horsepower, 500 ft-lb of torque, and a Tremec six-speed manual transmission. The Competition Coupe ups horsepower to 520, torque to 540 fr-lb, and has the same Tremec tranny. Though there are a few engine tweaks, most of the modest power boost comes from the lower-restriction intake and exhaust.

It takes a while to warm up the Competition Coupe's fat Hoosier slicks (P305/35ZR18 front, P345/30ZR18 rear), but once you do, they stick quite well. Like all Vipers before it, this one responds to a rather brutal, off/on switch–like driving style. The tires don't offer much warning before they lose traction, but once they do, the result isn't dramatic. Big four-piston Brembo brakes are astoundingly capable and fade-free, lap after hard lap.

The engine's monstrous torque makes the Competition Coupe easy to drive fast. Exit a corner one gear too high, and the massive V-10 shrugs it off and goes. Redline is around 6,100 rpm, with about 5,400 rpm a comfortable shift point. The biggest surprise is that, after driving the stock roadster and the Comp Coupe, you get the feeling that, if it had slick tires, the stock Viper might be only a couple seconds slower than the Coupe on a road course. That a street-legal car could feel so much like a full-on racer again speaks to the extreme nature of the production Viper.

Dodge's Performance Vehicle Operations planned on producing about 60 Competition Coupes for 2003 and at least that many for 2004. Beyond that, they'll build as many as they can sell.

The car is designed to compete in the Skip Thomas Viper Racing League, as well as the Grand American Cup's Grand Sports class (against the Chevrolet Corvette and Porsche Carrera), and in the Speedvision World Challenge.

Gentlemen, your razor is ready.

—Steven Cole Smith, reprinted courtesy *Motor Trend*

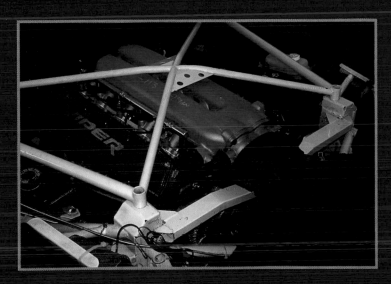

Though the Comp Coupe's engine remains internally stock, it does benefit from improved intake and exhaust systems. This tubular triangulation brace helps stiffen the chassis, sharpening both handling and steering response. *DaimlerChrysler*

PVO's Manager of Vehicle Synthesis Herb Helbig puts the spurs to a late SRT-10 "pilot" prototype. Although it resembles the production version in most details, it's not quite a finished piece. Note missing nose badge. *Wes Allison*

Shikado (see sidebar). Osamu addressed every detail of the car, including a new logo. Some appreciated that the SRT-10 had a more fully-realized and better-proportioned look than before; others said it wasn't "as visceral" as the 1992 to 2002 models. The original RT/10 was an eye-catcher, for sure, but to this author's eyes, it now looks a little cartoonish next to the fresh shape of the 2003.

A lot of the new Viper's shape was driven by wind tunnel testing. While the original car's tapered tail wasn't aerodynamic and occasionally created some high-speed stability issues, the SRT-10's broad shoul-ders and upturned tail created effective downforce, and allowed the air to roll more cleanly off the back of the car. High-speed stability was much improved.

The first-generation roadster's sports bar, removable rear window, and hardtop/soft-top combo all gave way to a conventional folding convertible top. Many felt this was better than the old system, especially that of the 1996 and earlier models, with their Erector Set-inspired side curtains and toupee-like soft top. The manual top folds neatly, and employs a glass rear window complete with defroster. No separate cover was necessary—it creates its own as it folds down behind the seats.

The previous Viper's tapered tail contribution did little to support high–speed stability. The SRT-10s rear styling is more aerodynamically efficient and creates measurable downforce that helps keep the rear end better planted. This new '03 design also represented the often-asked-for return to sidepipes, which had gone away at the end of the '95 model run. *Wes Allison*

The 2003 headlight clusters contain Xenon-gas high-intensity-discharge elements for both high and low beam. A car with this sort of performance should never be short of lighting, and the only brighter eyes than these are found on race cars and jet fighters. There's a somewhat European influence to be found in the new car's muscular shoulders and flipping tail. Yet its square jaw, bodacious stance, and overall aggressiveness are all-American, and all-Viper, all the way.

You can talk 440 Six-Packs, L88s, and Boss 429s until you're blue, but the SRT-10's 505-ci/8.3-liter all-aluminum V-10 (carrying the internal project code DVX) may be the meanest big-block ever put into a series production car. (The NASCAR and NHRA cheater motors dropped into a few factory-supported back-door racing projects during the 1960s don't count.) It's good for 500 real SAE net horsepower on premium unleaded pump gas. It was new, right down to the block, and featured a neater throttle-cable setup than before, as well as an effective cold-air-intake system. This power plant represented a 50-horsepower increase over the previous-generation

Viper By Design

It took Osamu Shikado, design manager, DaimlerChrysler Advance Packaging Studio, about five minutes to sketch for us this rendering of his most recent design project—although he worked on the 2003 SRT-10 for much longer than that. The new Viper represents a considerable departure for this Osaka, Japan–born designer; his previous gig was with Toyota, where he worked on all manner of Camrys and Corollas. The Viper GTS-R concept of 2000 was by no means his first design-study project since coming to the United States; he also designed the stunning Chrysler Chronos concept of 1998, and 1999's Chrysler Citadel. The Viper, however, is his magnum opus to date, and he comments that "it's an honor to redesign an American icon."

Viper SRT-10 lead designer Osamu Shikado.

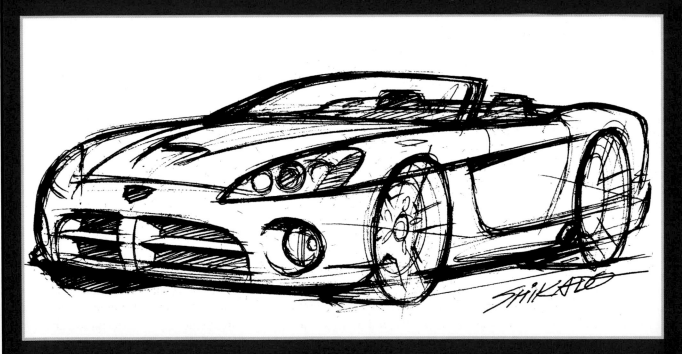

The SRT-10's 8.3-liter (just over 505 cubic inches!) V-10 represents a new high-water mark in terms of domestic production sports car powerplants. It puts out a full 500 horsepower on unleaded fuel, while meeting all emissions and OBD II laws. Although its layout is similar to that of previous Vipers, it's an all-new engine. The most visible features are the dual front snorkel-mounted air filters and neater routing of wiring and throttle linkage. *Wes Allison*

non-ACR-spec V-10. A Tremec T-56 six-speed manual transmission remained your only gear-changing choice. An automatic? Don't even ask.

Hop in, and you'll immediately notice that the pedal box is no longer intruded upon by the front wheelhouse. A large tach now sits front and center, with a smaller speedo just to its right. The rest of the ancillary gauges (oil pressure, oil temp, water temp, and charging system) cascade down the IP just to the right of the steering wheel. There's a new stereo with—you guessed it—500 watts of power; it packs a six-CD changer and even a speed-sensitive volume mode, as if anyone will even listen to it. From there, it's a simple-to-use HVAC system, power window switches, and that's about it.

The quality of the materials used in the interior increased substantially. Splashes of aluminum and aluminum-look trim brightened the interior, and the new leather sport seats are absolutely superb—comfortable, supportive even during aggressive cornering, and handsome. All in all, a much nicer place to be than the previous Viper's cockpit.

Herb Helbig, Keeper of the Viper Flame

The group that conceives, designs, tests, develops, and builds the Viper has changed a lot since the late 1980s. So how does a big company like DaimlerChrysler (which itself was just plain old "Chrysler" when the car first came out) ensure that a Viper remains true to the concepts and tenets of, well, Viperness? It takes a "Grailkeeper." PVO's is Herb Helbig.

By all accounts, Helbig is the right guy for the job. He's educated, with Masters and Graduate degrees in mechanical engineering, plus a Masters in automotive engineering. He's experienced, having been with Chrysler since 1972, and more importantly, with the Viper program since the very beginning. And he's a total and complete gearhead.

His official title is PVO Manager of Vehicle Synthesis. But what does that really mean? "Keeping the Viper, as it evolves through the course of its life, true to the original set of parameters. We've got to keep it simple, we've got to make it fun, its got to be the most outrageous car you've ever touched. When you turn the key on, the hair on the back of your neck has got to stand up. It's got to be a visceral, emotional, almost religious experience. It falls to me to make sure that we don't lose sight of why we started this program. [It's all about] fun, passion, and the desire just to put people back on their heels to say 'I can't believe these guys made such an outrageous, awesome, off-the-scale car,'" explained Helbig. Clear enough.

Helbig was the fourth person hired by Team Viper's original project leader Roy Sjoberg, and has seen a lot of change since the late 1980s. Yet it is this evolution that ended up defining his job. "It's a challenge to mature it, to grow the car up a little, yet not lose its essence, and to allow an expanding customer base to be satisfied. How do you play to a bigger audience without prostituting your-self. Sometimes it keeps me awake at night, " Helbig said. One such example was the development of power side windows for the GTS, a big departure from the original, windowless RT-10 roadster. The team ultimately felt that the move was necessary, both for the flavor and for the design of the new coupe.

Lest you worry that Helbig is about to let the Viper get soft around the middle: "When people come to me and say 'you know it really needs cruise control; I took one to Chicago and my right foot got kinda tired. . . .' that guy gets thrown out of my office. Or a guy comes in and says 'you know, it would be cool if we had power seats' that guy gets thrown out of the building. And the guy who says 'I think we need an automatic transmission' well, they're still looking for his body."

Herb was involved in every step of the SRT-10s development. High and low points? "The thing I'm most pleased with are the brakes. If you look back to the beginning, we tried to build the car with as many off-the-shelf parts as we could because we had a somewhat limited budget. Our original brake system was awesome for the time—for the street. But we didn't realize how many people were going to beat the car on the race track, and how hard they were going to run them. The system evidenced itself as having some shortcomings for that kind of use. On the new car, we said 'by God we are going to make sure you cannot find a weakness on the brake system of the SRT-10.' You can take an SRT-10, go to the Blackhawk Farms road course, run 25 laps with Tommy Archer in the driver's seat, and not diminish the brakes. It won't boil, it won't fade, it'll just stop."

On the downside? "I wished we done a better job of managing the car's thermal load. The car's hot inside. As you know, we went back to sidepipes, because that's what we

and our customers wanted. It spoke to the heritage of the original car. We took the cats that used to be just in the sill, and we split them up. Under your feet, instead of just having pipe, you have a one-cubic-foot cat that's burning at 1,600 degrees. A smaller cat remains in the sill, but its still a 1,600-degree heat source. In order to get good tonal quality, and pass noise restrictions, we had to create a crossover network, so the pipework from each side of the car crosses over to the other side, right under the passenger seats. We've [got] three sides of each passenger surrounded by the exhaust system [under the floor]. We wish we could have figured out a way to do a better job with that."

The future of domestic performance cars like the Viper? "When you think about the guys in Dearborn [Ford], and the guys in Warren [GM], and us guys in Auburn Hills, and there's a lot pride and bragging rights involved, and there's no way that, when the bar gets raised by one of those three groups, the other guys aren't going to be working over their cauldron, boiling something up that's going to put them back on top.

"We're glad that those guys have taken up the challenge. It allows [us] to go to our management and say 'we can't sit on our laurels and rest on our accomplishments. We've got to keep pushing the envelope.' PVO will stop at nothing to continue to be the king of this hill. You can take that one to the bank. I'm really blessed that I get to do this kinda stuff every day, and get paid for it."

PVO Manager of Vehicle Synthesis and original Team Viper member Herb Helbig. *DaimlerChrysler*

Few would argue that the SRT-10's cabin is a major advancement over the 1992 to 2002 Vipers. The longer wheelbase means less wheelhouse intrusion into the foot box, the instrumentation is easier to see and read, and the aluminum trim lends an upscale, racy look. Seating is improved, as is a new 500-watt audio system. The tach also takes its race car-inspired place—front and center—in the instrument panel. *Wes Allison*

Light the V-10, and once again, you'll hear that rumbling, sputtering hum directly to the left and right of your shoulders. We mentioned the return to sidepipes, in part due to customer feedback and request. The exhaust system on 1992 to 1995 models contained no crossover piping, so each side of the car (effectively) emitted the exhaust noise of a 4.0-liter five-cylinder engine. Most feel the Viper pipebenders did a better job this time around; it's a deeper, richer, nastier thrum, replete with some pops and crackle on the overrun.

Fast? Absolutely. *Motor Trend* achieved a 0 to 60 time of 3.9 seconds; a review of most of its test numbers from years past showed RT/10 test times of between 4.0 to 4.2 seconds. *MT* commented: "The word—other than really fast!—that best describes the rest of the driving experience is 'progressivity.' The previous Viper was anything but: twitchy, quick to break away at the limit, a not-so-easy to modulate clutch, ad infinitum. This one is substantially better and more accurately transmits your brain signals and control inputs into appropriate responses. Steering

One of the many detail changes that differentiate the SRT-10 from the previous generation Vipers is the complete redesign of the hood. On the older cars, it's a one-piece clamshell that includes front fenders. This piece was difficult to align properly and expensive to repair. On the SRT-10, it gives way to a more conventional hood, and the previous "speaker grille" vents are replaced by five slats per side, representing the engine's five-cylinder-per-bank layout. *DaimlerChrysler*

turn-in remains fast and sharp, but is more linear, with good feel. Brakes? Plenty, and again, the system is nicely progressive in the way it hauls the car to a stop; pedal feel and modulation have improved, too. Nose dive under braking was never a problem for the old Viper, nor is it with this one. Ride quality feels a bit more supple than before, though that's not to be interpreted as the Viper being in any way watered down."

Road & Track said, "A gentle push of the red button and the 8.3-liter V-10 rumbles to life, each throaty side pipe sounding off from all 10 cylinders, thanks to the way the exhaust is routed and inter-connected . . . the ghosts of the UPS truck exhaust note have been exorcised and now the Viper has the snarl to match the drivetrain's bite." *R & T* continued: "Several quick tours around the 1.7 mile handling track at [Chrysler's] Chelsea [proving ground] reinforced my earlier impressions of the car as being much more civilized in both ride and handling. And yet, when pushed hard, it could deliver the kind of straight-line thrills that have been a Viper benchmark."

It all came at a price, with the 2003 SRT-10's base MSRP increasing to $83,795.

Performance Comparison
Source: *Motor Trend, June, 2003*

Model	0-60 (sec)	0-100-0 (sec)	1/4-Mile (ET@speed)	Top Speed (mph)	Price (as tested)
Viper SRT-10	3.94	12.17	11.77@123.63	182	$83,795
Ferrari 575M	4.16	13.94	12.26@118.58	182	$241,092
Corvette Z06	4.29	13.92	12.44@116.54	174	$51,450
Lamborghini Murcielago	3.51	12.71	11.72@122.52	193	$284,850

Yet when you consider how expensive it is to add horsepower to any car, and that this one comes with 50 more, the increment is a bargain. There's lots of additional content, too—more safety gear, a higher-quality top, high and low beam HID headlights, a more powerful audio system, and better quality materials—so it's easy to see where the money was spent. And still, even at a somewhat higher price point, anything that can outrun it costs a lot more.

The Future

There's little question that the Viper will be a member of the Chrysler's lineup for a long, long time. In just a decade, it has garnered popularity among its owners and fans that matches that of the Mustang and Corvette—cars that have been building a legacy for 40 and 50 years respectively. It's the cornerstone of Chrysler's Performance Vehicle Operations group, and will still draw traffic to Dodge dealers. The previous platform lasted a decade, with one major revision and the introduction of an additional model about mid-way through its production life.

What's next? It's hard to say, and unfortunately, Dodge isn't telling. But there are a few conclusions we can draw. The upcoming Ram SRT-10 (see sidebar) is the first production model to share the Viper's powertrain, making good on the promise of that original 1994 concept, though doing so based on the new-for-2002 Ram platform. It's doubtful there are many other places or products where the big V-10 could be put to use (other than the handful of Tomahawk quadracycles Dodge has announced it will build), so this unique, 500-plus horsepower truck is probably the extent of additional platform sharing the Viper can offer.

Don't expect Viper development to stand still. The next logical step would be a new generation GTS Coupe. And we already know what it looks like; recall that the current Viper design showed up as the GTS-R concept car at the 2000 Detroit auto show. And of course the Viper Competition Coupe, the race version of the SRT-10, wears bodywork that looks like the slightly race-ified variant of the street GTS Coupe that is sure to follow sometime around the 2006 or 2007 model year. The previous generation GTS proved a strong seller its entire career, and the basic design work is complete, so this is all but a done deal as this book goes to print.

It's hard to imagine that the Viper will ever need any more power, but then again, 400 seemed like a world-beating number when the car was introduced. The V-10's power output has gone up a full 20 percent

This "ghosted" image shows the SRT-10s top in both up and down positions. Unlike the old "toupee and side curtains" arrangement, which was a time consuming mess to install or remove, the new convertible top drops in seconds (although the trunk must first be opened), and creates its own cover. *Wes Allison*

in the ensuing decade, yet companies like Mercedes-Benz AMG make luxury sport sedans putting out nearly that much. So perhaps there's room for 550? 600? Where it will end, no one is certain. Dodge may also elect to cook up a special edition Viper now and again, like the previous GT2 and ACR models.

Beyond that, it's possible that, after a long enough hiatus, the Viper will re-enter big bore sports car racing, another arena where the previous GTS-R racer proved literally a world-beater. But more than

one insider has told us that its not likely to happen until Dodge's stock car effort yields a NASCAR championship, so we'll have to wait and see.

No matter, the Dodge Viper enters its second decade with its popularity unabated, and its performance virtually unchallenged by anything that costs less than double its price. It will remain a uniquely American, hairy-chested muscle/sports car. The people who produce it, and the enthusiasts who buy it, wouldn't want it any other way.

SIX

Viper Variations

The amount of enthusiasm generated by the Viper is akin to dropping a very large rock in the middle of a pond: a significant ripple effect was bound to follow. Chrysler gained new understanding of the value of the "team approach" to designing and building cards. It also proved to the world, the car industry, and to *itself* that a large multinational corporation can develop products for niche markets. As discussed, Viper also drew an amazing amount of media reaction; Chrysler PR has probably lost count of how many magazine covers Vipers have appeared on over the years. It's only natural, then, to expect Viper's influence to extend to other Chrysler products,

Jet versus Snake might seem like an obvious win for the fighter plane, but it wasn't that easy. Dodge has staged two such match races at events benefiting the Luke Air Force Base Charity Fund. The first such endeavor in March 2002 pitted a Viper Competition Coupe against an F-16, with the jet narrowly nipping the Viper in the agreed-upon 1/2 mile distance; PVO's John Fernandez was at the wheel. The rematch, a year later, brought an F-16 up against a white, street legal SRT-10 driven by Herb Helbig. Herb was able to get a better launch, and he snaked the F-16 Fighting Falcon Viper for the win, evening the score. *DaimlerChrysler*

the aftermarket, car clubs, TV and movie types, and to the fertile imagination of the buying public. Viper engines have ended up in all sorts of interesting vehicles lately, including those built by Dodge, and others that could only come from the fertile imagination of the hot rodding public.

This is by no means a complete compendium on what people do to and with their Vipers, but it does indicate the sort of enthusiasm and creativity that surrounds and supports this phenomenal car.

Dodge Ram VTS Concept (1994)

Trucks are big business. In fact, the best-selling vehicle in America has been the Ford F-150 for many years running. And modified, personalized, downright *hot-rodded* trucks are a big part of the picture. So in 1994, with Dodge bringing out its first all-new pickup in more than 20 years—with the first-ever production V-10 engine—the Ram VTS concept vehicle is almost no surprise. The Ram's iron V-10 produces 300 horsepower and 450 ft-lb of torque, and it's no secret that it and the Viper's aluminum alloy "Copperhead" V-10 began life on nearby drawing boards. Dodge whipped up the VTS to have a little fun and to gain a little press. "We knew it would only be a matter of time until someone would try to pack a Viper V-10 engine into a Ram truck," said Chrysler designer Mike Castiglione at the Ram VTS's unveiling. "We thought Dodge ought to beat them to the punch."

The VTS carried the Viper V-10 and six-speed transmission, as well as prototype future Viper wheels. The special front air dam included Viper-style fog

The Ram VTS prototype carries as many Viper cues as would translate from roadster to pickup truck, including a special front fascia with fog lights and Viper GTS prototype wheels. The most important part was the V-10 underhood. Fortunately, Dodge didn't forget this idea, and it came back in the form of the Ram SRT-10 for 2003. *DaimlerChrysler*

Dodge turned heads when it fitted a Viper V-10 into a full-sized Ram truck, so why not try to cram one into a smaller pickup? The Dakota Sidewinder concept was one of Dodge's show toys at the November 1996 SEMA aftermarket show in Las Vegas, and it hinted at a few design cues that would appear on the new-for-1997 production Dakota. A 2,700-pound truck with 600 horsepower? Sounds like easy burnouts. *DaimlerChrysler*

lights, and the paint scheme matched the Viper GTS Coupe. It was built from a standard-cab Ram 1500 pickup.

Though the VTS drew both attention and admiration, Chrysler claimed it never intended to put the truck into production. This is understandable, given that others had tried marketing factory high-performance trucks and had experienced only moderate success. GMC's Syclone in 1991, with a turbo V-6, was dropped after two years in production; the Chevrolet SS 454 lived only a bit longer. Ford's Special Vehicle Team fared much better with its fine handling Lightning, but elected to drop it after the 1995 model year, though it returned in supercharged

form in 1999. The original VTS remained but a potent dream . . . for a while, anyway.

Skip Barber Driving School
Slightly modified sedans and detuned Formula Fords are common fare at many racing schools, but the Skip Barber curriculum includes Dodge Dakota V-8 pickups, Neons, open-wheel Dodge-powered Formula cars . . . and Vipers.

Barber opened his first racing school in 1975; as of 1995, all school cars were Dodge or Dodge-powered vehicles. This marketing arrangement is similar to that of the Bob Bondurant School of High Performance Driving, which uses GM products exclusively.

Viper Races Indy

odge was in a bind. It had wanted to promote its new Stealth and swung a deal with the Indianapolis Motor Speedway for the performance coupe to pace the 1991 500-mile race. One rub: the Stealth was built for Dodge by Mitsubishi, along with Mitsu's own quite similar 3000 model. When the word got out that what is essentially a Japanese car was scheduled to pace the Greatest Spectacle in Racing, a rumble of protest issued forth from American enthusiasts. The fix? How about the new-for-1992 Dodge Viper?

Another problem: Team Viper was not yet ready to build production cars, much less one that would be showcased in front of more than 20 million race fans. As usual, they rose to the challenge, hand-building an essentially production-spec Viper prototype capable of exceeding the Speedway's performance criteria—in less than three months' time.

More than 1,800 miles of testing proved the car race-day ready, and two cars were actually prepared for pace-car duty. On May 26, 1991, racing legend and Viper patriarch Carroll Shelby paced Rick Mears' victory in the 75th Anniversary Indianapolis 500. It was Rick's fourth win, and also a big win for Team Viper. What began as a marketing and PR nightmare turned into a dream ride for this most American machine.

Since the Viper's appearance at the 1991 500 proved such a successful part of the car's 1992 model year launch, Chrysler PR and marketing types went back to the same well for 1996. With the GTS Coupe on the way for 1997, it proved a logical move. Fortunately there was no such Stealth-related PR hurdle to climb; the GTS Coupe was clearly the right player from the very beginning.

This time around, Shelby's pal (and then Chrysler President) Bob Lutz was called on for pace car duties. It was a somewhat historic race since 1996 was also the first year of

the new Indy Racing League (IRL). As many of the new series drivers had little or no experience at the Speedway, it was anticipated that the pace car would see a lot of action—which it did. It performed flawlessly, as did Buddy Lazier, earning his first Indy 500 victory that day.

"Follow me, guys!" Bob Lutz at the wheel of the Viper GTS prototype used to pace the 1996 edition of the Memorial Day Classic. As expected, no performance modifications were required. Pacing this race was historic because it marked the first year of the new Indy Racing League. *DaimlerChrysler*

Various Barber courses are offered on several tracks around the country.

The Viper plays an important role at the Dodge/Skip Barber Driving School and is used primarily for autocross portions of the course. It allows the driver a chance to learn in a seriously high-performance vehicle, yet, being a two-seater, an instructor can ride along to observe the student's technique, something not possible in a single seater. According to Rick Roso, the school's PR manager, the Vipers are "*very* popular" with students and teachers alike!

Viper Television Show

You need only look at the specially-equipped Aston Martin DB5 driven by James Bond in *Goldfinger* and *Thunderball* to understand the impact that a starring role in a major movie or TV show can have on a car's reputation . . . and sales. Remember Martin Milner's Corvette in *Route 66?* Sales of black and gold Pontiac Trans Ams skyrocketed after the success of Burt Reynolds' *Smokey and the Bandit*. And so on.

When NBC not only selected the Viper (and several other Chrysler vehicles) to appear in its 1994 action-adventure series, but actually named the show *Viper*, it seemed to be a dream marketing vehicle (pun intended) for Dodge. "In a future where criminals outgun and outrun the law, one man and one machine will change all the rules," according to NBC PR materials. The show starred James McCaffery as Michael Payton, a bad-guy-turned-good who now goes after his old gang, "The Outfit."

The Viper's bag of tricks made most other show-

Viper series star James McCaffery suits up to take a Viper cutaway camera car for a "ride." This rig is towed behind another vehicle for close-up moving shots; a big improvement over the old technique of a movie screen sitting behind the car. *Paramount Television and NBC*

The "Defender" Viper from the TV series *Viper*. Although the show was less than a hit, it was great fun to watch a standard red Viper roadster "morph" into this car. The series' sets and special effects were well done. Metalcrafters, which has built many of Chrysler's modern concept cars, designed the Defender.

time vehicles, such as the "KITT" Firebird from *Knight Rider*, look tame. In off-duty guise, it appeared to be a standard red Viper. When it was time for action the car "morphed" into the armored "Defender" Viper, a gray hardtop complete with "fangs" in the grille. An advanced satellite system, tractor beams, and the like were employed as plot devices intended to render the villains' cars helpless.

Several standard Vipers, plus the Defender show

Left: The Viper has claimed a number of celebrity owners, among them consummate car guy and *The Tonight Show* host Jay Leno and *Frasier* star Kelsey Grammer (who ultimately wrecked his). *David Newhardt*

Below: A Viper kit car? Unfortunately, someone had to try. A British firm named the Fiero Factory (which should tell you something) cobbled together this Viper almost-look-alike. The car could be built on a Corvette C4 chassis and powered by a Chevy engine, or upon its own chassis design employing the powertrain and suspension from a—believe it or not—Ford Granada. The overriding question about the entire project remains: why? *Fiero Factory*

2003 Dodge Viper SRT-10 Venom 650R

With only 500 horsepower and 525 ft-lb of torque on tap, a 2003 Dodge Viper SRT-10 just isn't fast enough for some people. To put added bite in the already ridiculously fast snake, aftermarket venom is available, including from long-time Viper tuners Hennessey Performance. Two years ago, some customers raised concerns about Hennessey's business practices (we heard from a few), and the jury is still out on the validity of those claims. But the distractions haven't stopped Hennessey from developing a cache of new speed parts. We tested two turnkey engine packages, the Venom 600 and Venom 650R, one of which notched the quickest quarter-mile time we've recorded on stock tires.

The Venom 600 package incorporates a host of traditional go-fast upgrades that focus primarily on moving air in and out in quicker fashion. A custom air-inlet tract uses twin free-flowing air filters that mate with a ported throttle body. CNC-ported cylinder heads increase intake port flow from 275 cfm to 325 and also raise the compression ratio from 9.6:1 to 10.2:1, thanks to head decking. A Comp Cams custom ground hydraulic roller camshaft sends opening and closing cues to valves upgraded with extreme-duty valve springs and titanium retainers. Special computer calibration still allows the fortified 8.3-liter V-10 to run on premium unleaded pump gas and comply with 50-state smog certification, according to Hennessey. Venom 1.8-inch-

diameter stainless-steel 5-to-1 headers team with high-flow catalytic converters to quickly vent spent exhaust fumes and deliver a more throaty exhaust note. The $19,500 Venom 600 package includes professional installation, chassis dyno testing, road testing, and a limited two-year warranty, along with the requisite Venom 600 badging to impress your buddies.

Not enough? Consider the Venom 650R package that includes all the above hardware and takes it to the next level by way of a stroker short-block: The 522-cube 650R incorporates JE 10.8:1 forged pistons with heavy-duty pins, moly rings, longer than stock Manley Pro forged-steel connecting rods, and a custom-machined stroker crankshaft. A Comp Cams roller cam is employed along with an upgraded fuel system and specific computer programming to deliver a wider power-band with gobs more torque than stock. Independent chassis dyno testing of the Venom 650R verified 587 horsepower and 584 ft-lb of torque measured at the rear tires. That translates to about 675 horses at the flywheel, assuming an industry-standard 15-percent drivetrain loss.

On the highway, the Venom 650R remains docile during cruising—actually even mellower than a stock SRT-10; but at the track, the package is vicious. Running on stock Michelin run-flat 19-inch radials, we drove the Venom 650R to an amazing 10.76-second quarter mile—making this the quickest stock-tired vehicle we've tested. With cautious throttle modulation, we hustled the 650R to a 3.0-second 0-to-60-mph sprint that beats all-wheel-drive super-exotics like the Lamborghini Murciélago by over half a second. If there's a downside to this performance story, it'll be the hit to your pocketbook, as the 650R package will set you back a solid $34,500. We suggest skipping the Venom 650R badging; let your time slips do the bragging. – John Kiewicz, reprinted courtesy *Motor Trend*

Hazing the skins" is seldom a problem for any Viper, but this 675-horsepower Hennessey-modified SRT-10 makes it even easier, seen here on its way to another sub-11 second quarter-mile pass. *John Kiewicz*

	Viper SRT-10	Venom 650R
0-60 mph	4.0	3.0
1/4 mile	11.77@123.63	10.76@128.67
Braking, 60-0, ft	97	98
0-100-0 mph, sec	12.2	10.4

Collecting Viperabilia *by Maurice Q. Liang*

Whether you own a Viper or not, you can satisfy some of that Viper-lust by collecting Viper memorabilia, or Viperabilia. Viperabilia collecting began as soon as the first Viper concept appeared in 1989. The first Viper toy was Galoob's red Micromachines RT/10 concept car. Since they didn't have a license from Dodge, the toy was quickly pulled off the market, so there aren't a lot of them out there. Other than that, there was a factory issued plastic promotional model from Ertl/AMT, model kits from Ertl and Revell, some shirts and hats, and a couple of posters. That was it, at least at the beginning.

But once the car caught the attention of the public, toy manufacturers jumped on the Viper bandwagon. Soon, Viper models and die-casts were available in all scales, from tiny 1/144 cars that were barely an inch long, to 1/4 scale go-karts. Attesting to the popularity of Viper, Brian Hannah, product manager for Mattel's Hot Wheels Collector Series said, "Viper has been a perennial seller for us. There are also many unlicensed 'Viper-like' models."

Serious collectors not only want the different models, they often collect different colors and variations. The more rare, the better. For example, Matchbox made around 25 samples of the Viper RT/10 concept car for its salespeople to show customers. But when they didn't get the license from Dodge, they modified the mold and sold it as the Sunburner instead. Now those Viper concept models are very desirable. Matchbox also had plans to sell 1/64 and 1/32 models of the *Viper* TV show crime-fighting car, the Defender; it was even listed in their catalog. But when the TV show failed to catch on, they abandoned plans to produce the toys, so only a few prototypes exist.

Viperabilia comes in other forms, too—hats, shirts, underwear, jewelry, dishes —even solid chocolate Vipers. There's also special memorabilia available only at the Viper Owner's Invitationals. Each event generates its own unique set of collectibles, such as engraved wine bottles, coasters, and banners, as well as the highly-coveted table centerpieces. You have to be there to get this stuff, and most people hang on to it.

"Paper" is also collectible. From Viper ads and magazine articles, to Viper brochures, to the more sought after press kits handed out to journalists when each new model is introduced. If you're really extreme, you even collect things like store and dealer displays that feature a Viper on it.

With collecting Viperabilia, you have to be quick. If you see it, buy it, because it may not be around for long. Viper toys are usually the first to fly off the shelves. And if you think a Viper brochure is hard to obtain now, try finding one twenty-five years from now. Unless you have unlimited space and funds, it's a good idea to pick a Viper collecting theme that's more limited than "Anything Viper." Choose your favorite color combination or maybe a certain scale of models. Fortunately, with the Internet and eBay, it's easier than ever to collect now. Happy hunting.

Maurice Liang has been collecting Viperabilia since the concept car first appeared in 1989 and has amassed one of the most comprehensive collections of Viper memorabilia in the world. Liang owns a Viper GTS and an RT/10, and co-founded the Viper Club of America. He is currently authoring the Viper Buyer's Guide.

car (styled by Neil Walling and crew as an official factory project), were employed in production. One had its entire front end removed to create a camera car, and at least two Vipers were fitted with 360-ci V-8 engines and automatic transmissions for stunt work. Though the show featured glossy sets and solid special effects work, the net result was a marginal effort at best. To quote one particular TV critic, it wasn't exactly *Masterpiece Theatre*. NBC canceled *Viper* after just 13 episodes. *Viper* reappeared in 1996 as a first-run syndicated series, this time making it through three full seasons before being permanently parked.

Vipers have also made several other TV and movie appearances. One of the most recent was the use of a yellow SRT-10 in 2003's street racing, car-chasing *2 Fast 2 Furious*. Though only one car appeared in the movie, a total of four were employed in the filming and stunt work. Other than a bit of paintwork to make the "Dodge" and "Viper" logos more visible, the cars were unmodified.

The Aftermarket
Former Chrysler President Bob Lutz said, "Power in the Viper is like your personal bank account.

Continued on page 90

Top and above: Besides factory projects like the original Viper-powered Ram and Sidewinder concepts, Viper V-10s have found themselves under all sorts of hoods. It looks like it absolutely grew under the hood of this 1969 Dodge Charger, and provides an interesting alternative to the period Hemi or 440 Six-Pack. Viper engines have powered numerous street rods, including a 1954 Plymouth custom called the Sniper. *Barrett-Jackson Auctions*

2004 Dodge Ram SRT-10

Now, *that's* a truck

It took Dodge a decade to fulfill the promise set forth by that original Ram VTS of 1994: a full-sized truck packing a Viper engine. But it appears that the Ram SRT-10 will have been worth the wait. The current Ram platform was new for the 2002 model year, and everyone agrees that the 500 horsepower cranked out by today's Viper V-10 is cooler than the "paltry" 400 of the original VTS concept. Why build a monster Ram now? Dodge's own press materials clarify the mission with a clear and succinct proclamation: "Because we can. The Dodge Ram SRT-10 mission is simple: biggest, baddest, and fastest."

The Ram SRT-10 is one of three very different products developed under what is now the PVO banner (the other two being the Viper itself, and the Neon-based Dodge SRT-4).

While, fundamentally, the Ram SRT-10 is a short bed, half-ton Ram with an engine transplant, it's considerably more than that: the PVO group worked hard to ensure that the truck has the suspension, brakes, aero touches, and look to match its 8.3-liter, 500-horse V-10. The rolling stock, for example, is positively huge: 22-inch alloy wheels with low profile, high performance tires. The four wheel disk brake system's rotors are an impressive 15-inches up front, and 14-inches in back. Bilstein provides the shocks, and unlike most trucks, the suspension was calibrated to maximize handling, not tow ratings or payload.

Relatively few tweaks were required to get the V-10/T56 6-speed trans combo ready for super truck duty. There are revised exhaust manifolds, a slightly-modified oil pan, new engine and transmission mounts, a Ram-specific air cleaner

exhaust system (with four Viper catalysts), and a very cool long-handled Hurst shifter. The Dana 60 rear axle runs 4.11 gears and a Hydra Lock limited slip diff. Another important suspension component is the traction bar system, designed to combat the combination of a vehicle that carries relatively little weight over its rear axle, and the tire-melting effects of 500 horsepower. One Dodge truck team member told us that during tests performed with slick tires, the Ram SRT-10 hooks up so well, and launches so hard, it will actually "wrinkle" the tire sidewalls, just like a real dragster.

A Ram is hardly the most aerodynamic device ever built, so considerable attention was paid to aerodynamics. A few lessons were borrowed from Dodge's own NASCAR Craftsman Truck series teams, and the SRT-10 spent time in the company wind tunnel. The front fascia is a unique piece, which incorporates an integrated front splitter to keep the nose stable—important for a truck with genuine 150 miles per hour capabil-ity. There's also a rear wing which is fully functional and reduces lift. Inside, the SRT-10 gets heavily bolstered sport seats, carbon-fiber-look trim on the steering wheel, full instru-mentation—even the Viper's red starter button. The color combinations, as of this writing, are the same as the Viper's too: red, black, and silver.

The Ram SRT-10 was just coming to market as this book was written, so it's difficult to predict how it will be received in the marketplace. But one Dodge dealer told us he's had a lot of interest in the maximum strength Ram from one particular group. You guessed it: current Viper owners.

A large, functional air intake, an aggressive lower fascia with fog lights, and that trademark cross-hairs grille visually tie the 2004 Dodge Ram SRT-10 to the sports car that gave it 500 horsepower. Installation of the DVX-series V-10 into the Ram was generally straightforward but still required considerable re-engineering of many details to make it production ready. The Ram cabin also enjoys several Viper cues. An optional automatic trans? As with the Viper, the answer is "don't even go there." *DaimlerChrysler*

Skip Barber instructor Walter Irvine and course participant Ashley Launey probe the limits of adhesion in one of the school's new SRT-10s. Barber also uses previous generation RT/10s and GTS Coupes at its various schools. *Rick Roso, courtesy Dodge/Skip Barber Driving School*

Dan Fitzgerald attempted to forge the "missing link" between Carroll Shelby's original Cobras and the Viper. Fitzgerald was one of Shelby's top-selling dealers back in the good old days, and he went on to develop a special-edition Shelby-ized Viper. *Visual Graphics*

There's no such thing as too much of it." No matter how much performance and style a manufacturer builds into an automobile, there is an imaginative aftermarket industry waiting to offer parts and accessories intended to increase one or both elements. The Viper is no different. It's natural for enthusiasts to personalize their machines, especially with an automobile that was at first offered in only one body style—and in only one color.

Viper owners' approach toward modification of their cars tends to take two distinctly different forms: (1) those wishing to add on a few goodies to accessorize their toy, or make it different from everyone else's, and (2) serious hot rodders for whom 400 to 500 horsepower still isn't enough. The most common choices for those in the first category are aftermarket wheels, lighting, intake and exhaust systems, interior upgrade trim, and replacement body panels. "Type As" in the second group generally go for more performance-oriented suspensions, brake kits, and big horsepower adders. Several aftermarket companies offer twin turbo kits, nitrous oxide injection, "stroker" blocks for more displacement, hot camshafts, and ported and polished intakes and cylinder heads; the sky, and the budget, are truly the limit. But 600 horsepower Vipers are not uncommon, and a few "hand grenades" have been built (primarily for magazine testing and bragging rights purposes) that crank out more than that.

The answer to a question nobody asked? Automotive sculpture? Ridable engine stand? Everyone has an opinion about the Dodge Tomahawk concept, er, vehicle, which made its debut at the 2003 Detroit auto show. Yes, that's a Viper V-10 sitting between where the driver/rider's knees sit. Amazing as it seems, Dodge announced it would hand-build ten of the "bikes" for its most ardent customers and collectors. The price? $555,000. At least one Tomahawk was to be sold through the Neiman Marcus holiday catalog. *DaimlerChrysler*

Windshield antenna replaced most antennas
Battery relocated to left frame rail
Front and rear bumpers now of composite material

1994 Model Year
Black and tan interior color scheme added
Factory-installed air conditioning available
Passenger-door grab handle added

1995 Model Year
New one-piece cast intake manifold

1996 Model Year
RT/10
Higher output V-10; 415 horsepower
All-aluminum front and rear suspension
Rear-exit exhausts replace sidepipes
New wheel designs
Factory-offered removable fiberglass hardtop replaces
    previous cloth-and-frame top
GTS
GTS coupe model introduced mid-year featuring side
    glass windows
Revised, lighter weight V-10; new block, heads, cool-
    ing tract; 450 horsepower

1997 Model Year
RT/10
Roadster bodystyle received 450-horsepower GTS
    engine
Revised interior incorporates driver/passenger side air
    bags, power side glass windows
Removable fiberglass hardtop replaces previous cloth-
    and-frame top
GTS
Yellow wheel package
Red exterior

1998 Model Year
Both models
Next-generation driver side airbags
Passenger side air bag on/off switch
Revised exterior colors
Limited edition "GT2" model commemorating 1997
    FIA GT2 championship; white with blue trim, 100
    built.

1999 Model Year
Both models
New 18-inch aluminum wheels with Viper-specific
    Michelin Pilot Sport tires
Optional Connolly leather trimmed interior
ACR (American Club Racer) Group model homolo-
    gated for club racing (Spring 1999 intro, available
    on GTS coupe only)

2000 Model Year
Both models
Child seat tether anchorage
GTS
Revised ACR Group model featuring high perfor-
    mance oil pan, Dynamic Suspensions adjustable
    shock absorbers, revised ACR badging

2001 Model Year
Both models
Standard anti-lock brakes

2002 Model Year
Both models carry over unchanged
GTS Final Edition, last 360 Viper GTS coupes built,
    red with white stripes, special badging

Source: *Chrysler*

Index